THE MAKING O1
THE CRETAN LANL

This is the first book to help the visitor to understand Crete's remarkable landscape, which is just as spectacular as the island's rich archaeological heritage.

Crete is a wonderful and dramatic island, a miniature continent with precipitous mountains, a hundred gorges, unique plants, extinct animals and lost civilisations, as well as the characteristic agricultural landscape of olive-groves, vines and goats. Jennifer Moody and Oliver Rackham explain how the island's peculiar and extraordinary features, moulded and modified by centuries of human activity, have come together to create the landscape we see today. They also explain the formation and ecology of Crete's beautiful mountains and coastline, and the contemporary threats to the island's natural beauty. The book draws on a whole range of evidence – field observations, archaeology, ancient and medieval documents, place-names, tree-rings and standing buildings.

To the tectonic forces that shaped the topography; the Pleistocene fauna that shaped the vegetation; the Cretan people who shaped the landscape. Each without the others would have resulted in a dramatically different Crete.

THE MAKING OF
THE CRETAN LANDSCAPE

Oliver Rackham & Jennifer Moody

Manchester University Press
Manchester and New York
Distributed exclusively in the USA by Palgrave

Published by Manchester University Press
Oxford Road, Manchester M13 9NR, UK
and Room 400, 175 Fifth Avenue, New York, NY 10010, USA
www.manchesteruniversitypress.co.uk

Distributed exclusively in the USA by
Palgrave, 175 Fifth Avenue, New York,
NY 10010, USA

Distributed exclusively in Canada by
UBC Press, University of British Columbia, 2029 West Mall,
Vancouver, BC, Canada V6T 1Z2

British Library Cataloguing-in-Publication Data
A catalogue record for this book is available from the British Library

Library of Congress Cataloging-in-Publication Data
Rackham, Oliver.
The making of the Cretan Landscape /
Oliver Rackham and Jennifer Moody.
p. cm.
Includes bibliographical references.
ISBN 0-7190-3646-1. — ISBN 0-7190-3647-X (pbk.)
1. Crete (Greece)—Historical ecology. 2. Ecology
—Greece—Crete—History.
I. Moody, Jennifer Alice. II. Title
DF221.C8R28'9—dc20

ISBN 0 7190 3646 1 *hardback*
0 7190 3647 X *paperback*

10 09 08 07 06 05 04   12 11 10 9 8 7 6 5 4

Printed in Great Britain
by Cromwell Press Ltd, Trowbridge, Wiltshire.

Contents

Illustrations

Plates (*between pages 110 and 111*)

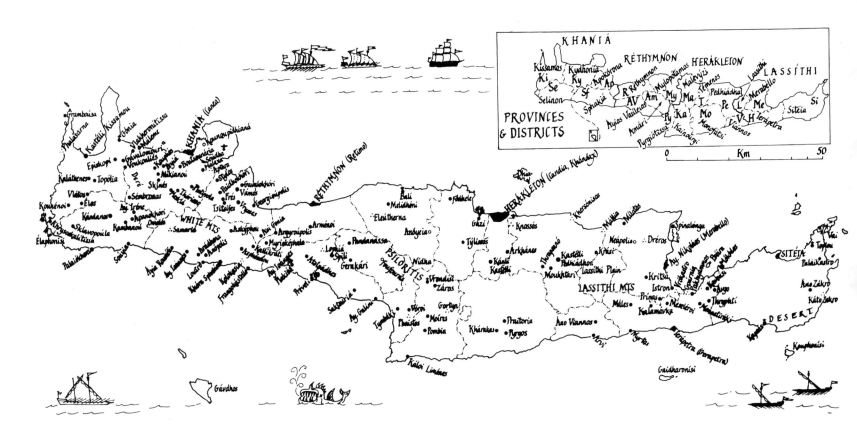

0.1 *Divisions with provinces and districts*

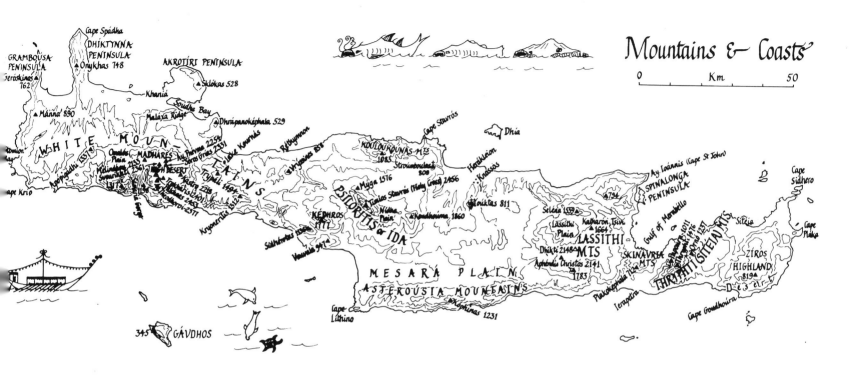

Mountains & Coasts

0   Km   50

Cape Spádha
GRAMBOÚSA PENINSULA
DHIKTÝNNA PENINSULA
Onýkhas 748
AKROTÍRI PENINSULA
Jeráskinos 762
Khaniá
Sklókas 528
Mánna 890
Soúdha Bay
Maláxa Ridge
Dhrapanoképhala 529
WHITE MOUN-TAINS
Apopigádhi 1357
Omalós Plain
MADHARÉS
Ay. Théma 2254
Soros Gries 2331
Theodore Kournás
MÉTH DESERT
Melindáou 2133
Soúrloti 1561
Kástro 2183
Pakhnés 2453
Kédhros 2371
Krýoneritis 1312
Réthymnon
Vrýsines 858
Krýoneritis
KOULOÚROUNAS MTS 1083
Cape Stavrós
Dhía
Stroúmboulas 808
Heráklion
Knossós
Ay. Ioánnis (Cape St John)
SPINALÓNGA PENINSULA
Cape Sídhero
Cape Krió
Sidherótas road
Vouvala 974
Kryonerítis
Mýga 1576
KÉPHROS 1777
PSILORÍTIS or IDA
Timios Stavrós (Holy Cross) 2456
Nídha Plain
Koudhoúma 1860
Kouktas 811
Seléna 1559
LASSÍTHI MTS
Lassíthi Plain
Katháron Tsivi 1664
Gulf of Mirabéllo
SKINÁVRIA MTS
Siteía
THRIPTI SITEIA MTS
Díkti 2148
Aphéndis Christós 2141 1783
Plakoképhala 1120
Ierápetra
ZÍROS HIGHLAND 819
Cape Plaka
MESARÁ PLAIN
ASTEROÚSIA MOUNTAINS
Cape Lithino
Kóphinas 1231
Cape Goudhoúra
345 GÁVDHOS

0.2 *Mountains and coasts*

ix

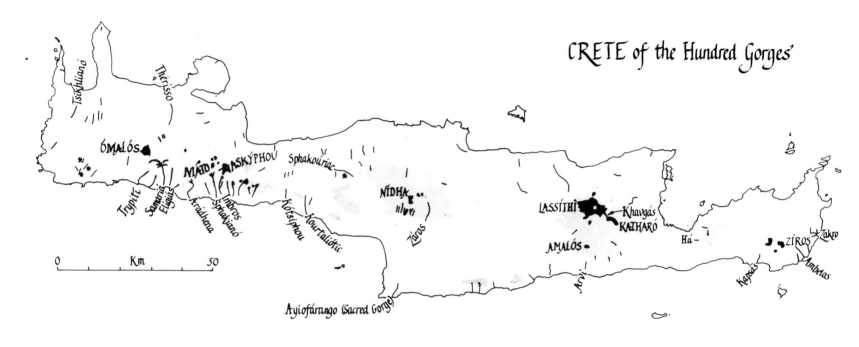

CRETE of the Hundred Gorges

Tsikhliano

Thérisso

ÓMALÓS

MÁTO

ASKÝPHOU

Sphakouriac

NÍDHA

Trypiti

Samariá
Eligiás

Aradhena

Imbros
Sphakianó

Kótsiphou

Kourtaliótic

Záros

LASSÍTHI

Khavgás

KATHARÓ

AMALÓS

Há-

ZÍROS

Zakro

Arvi

Kapsás

Ambelas

0   Km   50

Ayiofárango (Sacred Gorge)

0.3 *Gorges and mountain-plains*

x

Preface

We are unlikely colleagues: a Texan archaeologist, daughter of geologists, and an English botanist, son of a bank-worker. When we first worked together in Crete, in 1981, we had each known the island for several years. We thought Crete the most beautiful island in the world: a miniature continent with its Alps, its deserts and jungles, its arctic and its tropics, its Wales and Morocco and China, crammed into an area hardly bigger than Long Island (New York) or Devon plus Cornwall.

Crete is 245 km long and at most 50 km wide. On it are fifteen mountain ranges, three of them well over 2,000 m high (higher than anything in North America east of the Rockies, and as high as Snowdon on top of Ben Nevis). Its colours are orange and purple and dark green, and the unearthly pink of sunset; it is a land of hollow boulders and hollow cliffs, of mountains cracked across like pebbles, of bizarre plants known nowhere else, of tremendous birds, haunted by the ghosts of surrealist beasts; nothing is quite what it seems. In this glorious theatre were played out a succession of distinctive civilisations, the earliest of which is to some degree the origin of all Western civilisation.

At that time many scholars had studied the peculiar features of Crete, but in isolation. The civilisations were known as a scatter of illustrious sites; what happened in the landscape between those sites, or in the gulfs of time separating them in date, was hardly considered. How the Cretan landscape functions was either not understood, or misrepresented by scholars who thought they knew the answer in advance.

Much of the beauty of Crete is that it is a *cultural landscape*. Its present appearance is the result of millennia of interaction between human activities, human default, and the workings of Nature. It is both natural and artificial. For example, a ruined Venetian wall is artificial, the result of human activity and default. The aeolianite stone of which it is built was produced by natural changes of climate and sea-level. The royal blue *Petromarula* that grows on it is natural (Plate 5): it is a plant found nowhere but on the cliffs (including artificial cliffs) of Crete.

Our book is one of many inspired by that pioneer work, *The Making of the English Landscape,* published by W.G. Hoskins in 1955. Unlike most others with similar titles, ours goes back well before human history to consider the making of the island itself and the doings of its pre-human inhabitants. We are writing for the curious visitor, who wants to know what makes Crete special: why there are so many gorges; what the Minoans made of the high mountains; whether the island was really very wooded in ancient times; why so many hillsides are terraced; how old the great olive trees are; how many legs Cretan wolves had; and how Crete was affected by the discovery of America.

Acknowledgements

Some of the observations in this book were made on our own account, but many come from archaeological and other studies in which we have taken part. Rackham was invited to Crete in 1968 by Peter Warren as the expeditionary botanist for his Myrtos excavation. Moody became fascinated with Cretan archaeology during a course with Jim Wiseman in 1971 and began her work on the island in 1978, directing the Khaniá Archaeological Survey with the help and encouragement of Bill McDonald, Fred Lukermann, Rip Rapp, Peter Warren and Ioannis Tzedhakis. She has since co-directed three other archaeological projects (Vrókastro Survey with Barbara Hayden 1986- ; Sphakiá Survey with Lucia Nixon 1987- ; Atsipádhes Survey with Alan Peatfield and Stavroula Markoulaki 1990-). Rackham has participated in these projects, as well as the Pséira Excavation (directed by P. Betancourt and C. Davaras) and the Kavoúsi Project (directed by G. Gesell, L. Day and W. Coulson).

Both authors have participated in two ecological projects sponsored by the European Community. In 1988-90 we took part in 'Crete and the Aegean Islands: effects of changing climate on the environment', directed by A.T. Grove of Cambridge University and N.S. Margaris of the University of the Aegean. Since 1990 we have taken part in 'Threatened Mediterranean landscapes: West Crete', directed by A.T. Grove and V. Papanastasis of the Aristotelian University, Thessaloníki.

We express our gratitude to all our colleagues on these projects and those who have given us grants and permits. We are indebted for finance to the MacArthur Foundation, the Institute of Aegean Prehistory, the American School at Athens, the British School at Athens, Corpus Christi College, Cambridge, the University of Minnesota, the National Science Foundation and the Gladys Krieble Delmas Foundation.

Among the innumerable Cretans who have helped us we hope it will not be invidious to single out Panayiotis Kalomoirakis, Pavlos and Chryssa Kapageoridhis, the late Eleni Frantzeskaki, Yannis Pappasifis tou Andoniou, Evangelia and Georgos Kalogerakis, Maria Andreadhaki-Vlazaki, Stavroula Markoulaki, Vana Niniou-Kindeli, Elpidha Hadjidhaki, Yanni and Babbis Kopasakis, Chryssa and Theodhoros Athitakis, Yanni and Sophia Pappadhakis, Georgios Trilirakis, Katerina Voreadho, Manoli and Rita Michailoudhakis.

Without the support and encouragement of Wick Dossett and Evelyn Wilie Moody, and the inspiration of John D. Moody, these researches would never have taken place and this book would never have been written. Wick Dossett read an interminable series of proofs and took the cover photo.

Conventions

Quotations from the *Odyssey* are mainly from G. Chapman's translation, 1614. Biblical quotations are from King James's Bible. Tournefort is quoted from the English edition of 1741. Otherwise, most translations are our own.

On Botanical Latin names we follow *Flora Europaea*, first edition, and decline to recognise subsequent name-changes. In a few cases we continue to regard as a separate species a plant which *Flora Europaea* has merged as a subspecies: we refuse to include *Juniperus macrocarpa*, the sand-dune juniper, in the same species with *J. oxycedrus*, the high-mountain juniper.

The grid on maps is derived from the *British Military Map* of 1943, familiar to generations of fieldworkers in Crete. Most distributions are plotted in 2 x 2 km squares. Plant records are mostly from our own observations, but we have incorporated those published by Rechinger and others. Where two maps are printed on a page, we have moved Gávdhos 10 km northwards to save space.

Unless otherwise noted, maps and plans are oriented with north at the top of the page.

Divisions of Crete (Figure 0.1)

Crete has four provinces (*nómoi*), twenty districts (*eparkhíes*) and 580 townships (*koinótites* – the urban ones are called *dhémoi*). Such subdivisions will be familiar to the European but not the American visitor. The lowest unit, the township, corresponds to the English civil parish or French *commune*. Neither 'village' nor 'community' expresses its meaning; it may be a village, or two or three small villages, or an apparently arbitrary cluster of hamlets in areas where settlements are smaller than villages. In the latter case it is an administrative rather than a social unit. This arrangement goes back at least 700 years and has outlived Venetians and Turks.

There are fixed boundaries at all levels. Even by the fourteenth century, every inch of Crete belonged to a *casale*, the predecessor of a *koinótis*, as boundary disputes demonstrate.

Abbreviations

AD, BC   Historic date
ad, bc   Uncalibrated radiocarbon date
AD, BC   Calibrated radiocarbon date
Ay.   Ayios, feminine Ayia, neuter Ayio, plural Ayioi,
        Ayies, 'Saint' (Ancient Greek *hágios*)

Districts (Figure 0.1)

Ak	Akrotíri	Ky	Kydhonía	Py	Pyrgiótissa
Am	Amári	L	Lassíthi	R	Réthymnon
Ap	Apokórona	Ma	Malevyzi	Se	Sélinon
AV	Ayios Vasíleios	Me	Merabéllo	Sf	Sphakiá
H	Ierápetra	Mo	Monofátsi	Si	Sitéia
Ka	Kainoúrgi	My	Mylopótamos	T	Témenos
Ki	Kíssamos	Pe	Pedhiádha	V	Viánnos

Notes and references

ASV   Archivio di Stato, Venice (DC = Duca di Candia; CD = Carte e Disegne; CR = Collegio Relazioni; PTM = Provveditori di Terra e Mare; b = *busta*)
BCH   *Bulletin de Correspondance Hellénique*
BLL   British Library, London
BMV   Biblioteca Marciana, Venice
BNP   Bibliothèque Nationale, Paris
BSA   *Annual of the British School at Athens*
JFA   *Journal of Field Archaeology*
MCV   Museo Correr, Venice
Mn   Σπανάκη Σ. Γ. (S. G. Spanakis) (ed.), *Μνημεία της Κρητικής Ιστορίας*, Herákleion, 6 vols, 1935 and later
NAW   National Archives, Washington (Cartographic Division)

Works referred to by the author's name only, without a note-number, are listed in the bibliography.

Table of dates

Geological history — Crete before human settlement

		Environment	Inhabitants
Cretaceous 135–65 million years ago		Mountains begin to form and emerge from sea	
Neogene 25–5 million years ago	Miocene	Re-submergence 11.5 million years ago	Evolution of endemic plants
5–1.6 million years ago	Pliocene	Mediterranean dries up *c*. 5 million years ago, then partial re-submergence	
Quaternary 1.6–0.7 million years ago	Lower Pleistocene	Crete acquires approximately its present coastline	
700,000–128,000 years ago	Middle Pleistocene	Glacial periods alternating with interglacials	Special fauna established by this time
128,000–12,000 years ago	Upper Pleistocene	Last glaciation 60,000-13,000 years ago; Cretan mountain glaciers 18,000 years ago	Upper Palaeolithic cultures on mainland; discovery of Crete?
11,000–6100 BC	Early Holocene		Mesolithic on mainland; hunters and fishermen visit Crete?; extinction of most large native mammals?

Prehistory

		Environment	Inhabitants
Neolithic			
6100–5000 BC	Early Neolithic		First permanent settlers; cereal cultivation begins; introduction of sheep, goat, cattle, pig
5000–4400 BC	Middle Neolithic		Settlement up to at least 500 m altitude
4400–3500 BC	Late Neolithic		Olive cultivation; higher altitudes settled (including Lassíthi)
3500–2900 BC	Final Neolithic	Tectonic activity resumes	Sites more numerous, reaching highest altitudes
Bronze Age (Minoan)			
2900–2200 BC	Early Minoan I, II, III	Climate begins to get drier?	First bronze-working; settlements get bigger; increase in overseas contacts
2200–*c.*1930 BC	Middle Minoan IA		First peak sanctuaries
c. 1930–1700 BC	First Palace (Middle Minoan IB, II)	Severe earthquakes 1700	Increase in rural settlement; towns; 'palaces'; writing; first datable terrace walls
1700–1450 BC	Second Palace (Middle Minoan III, Late Minoan IA, IB)	Eruption of Santoríni *c.*1630*	Palaces burnt *c.* 1450
1450–1150 BC	Late Minoan II, III	Climate becomes wetter?	Mainland Greeks conquer much of Crete? Knossós sacked *c.* 1350
Dark Ages			
1150–900 BC	Iron Age		Decrease in number of settlements; abandonment of eastern coasts
900–700 BC	Protogeometric and Geometric		

* Dates for the Minoan period are controversial, but are linked archaeologically to the Santoríni eruption. The present majority view places this event at the end of Late Minoan IA and dates it *c.*1630 BC.[1] (P. M. Warren puts it in the middle of that period and favours a date *c.* 1550, adjusting the adjacent periods accordingly.[2])

[1] D. A. Hardy *et al.* (eds) (1990), *Thera and the Aegean World III*, London, Thera Foundation.

[2] P. M. Warren (1991), 'The Minoan civilisation of Crete and the volcano of Thera', *Journal of the Ancient Chronology Forum*, **4**, 29-39.

Ancient history

		Environment	Inhabitants
700–480 BC	Orientalizing and Archaic	Climate not very different from present?	Resettlement of coasts; rise of city-states; writing resumed
480–338 BC	Classical	Colder at high altitudes?	Warring city-states
338–69 BC	Hellenistic		Warring city-states
69 BC–380 AD	Roman		Roman conquest 69 BC; capital at Górtyn; rural settlement increases
380–823 AD	First Byzantine	Huge earthquake ('Early Byzantine Paroxysm')	More rural settlement than at any time since Bronze Age; bishoprics begin

Medieval (Middle Ages, up to 1500) and post-medieval

		Environment	Inhabitants
823–961	Arab		Khandax (Herákleion) set up as capital
961–1210	Second Byzantine		Chapel-building; revolts begin c. 1080
1210–1500	Early Venetian		Black Death 1347; chapel-building; oranges; corsairs; revolts
1500–1650	Late Venetian	Little Ice Age peak in 1590s	Plagues; corsairs; Turkish conquest 1645-69
1650–1770	Early Turkish	Little Ice Age peak in 1690s	Plagues; coming of coffee; Khaniá set up as capital
1770–1898	Late Turkish		Last plague 1821; coming of potato, tomato; revolts; church-building
1898–1913	Independent Crete		First major archaeological activity
1913–present	Crete as part of Greece		Expulsion of Muslims 1923; Battle of Crete 1941; German occupation 1941-45; joined European Community 1982

1
Chronology

*Archaeological data are not historical data, and
consequently archaeology is not history.*

D. L. Clarke, *Analytical Archaeology,* 1978

We begin by summarising the periods which form the framework of conventional Cretan archaeology and history. Periods
before written documents are conventionally identified by technology (e.g. Bronze Age) or styles of artefacts (Middle Minoan II).
Some of the defining characteristics, such as the invention of
metals, may be directly relevant to the evolution of the landscape;
others, such as pottery styles, are probably not.

For the last 2,000 years, the framework is based on the various
empires of which Crete successively formed a province.
Historians, believing Plato, often assume that politics are a
supreme factor, controlling all aspects of human and even natural
activity. In reality, Crete was always an outlying province. The
imperial powers seldom colonised it (by exporting population) to
any great extent, nor did they control it closely; for the most part,
they were content to take over existing institutions. It is easy to
exaggerate the extent to which ordinary Cretans and the landscape were affected by imperialism. Venice influenced the architecture of Crete, but not by making it a replica of Venetian
architecture, which is very different. The apparently even more
momentous conquest of Crete by Turkey is almost invisible either
in archaeology or the landscape.

Crete before human settlement

Crete had no aboriginal human population; its inhabitants were
various extraordinary animals. It was probably discovered by
10,000 BC or earlier: obsidian (volcanic glass) from the island of
Mélos has been found on the Greek mainland, proving that Upper

Palaeolithic people were capable of sailing round the Aegean. But on present evidence Crete, like other large Mediterranean islands, was not settled until much later.

Neolithic (6100–2900 BC)

The first settlers appear to have come to Knossós (T) about 6100 BC, bringing with them a full complement of domesticated plants and animals. Any large native mammals that still existed were probably exterminated, allowing the vegetation to increase until the settlers' sheep, goats and cattle multiplied sufficiently to keep it down.

The vastly long Neolithic period was a time of isolation and internal development. People began civilising the landscape by grubbing out trees and making fields. The extent of this activity is unknown, but by the end of the period even the high mountains were visited if not settled. Olive culture began in the Late Neolithic and has been a fundamental part of Cretan subsistence ever since.

Bronze Age (Minoan) (2900–1150 BC)

The Bronze Age peoples of Crete finished the taming of the landscape. Settlements diversified into a hierarchy of hamlets, villages and towns, culminating in the great 'palaces' and 'villas' of Minoan Crete, which were the focus of the first extensive road system. By the late Middle Minoan period the rural population was probably not much less than it has ever been. The Bronze Age is counted as prehistoric, although the earliest written documents appear after 1800 BC.

Seafaring brought Crete into constant contact with other cultures and overseas markets, and probably encouraged the growing of crops for export, such as olive oil. Great buildings, trade, frescoes and jewellery mark the zenith of Cretan civilization. Bronze itself was introduced from abroad. At first it was soft and little used for working the land.

The famous eruption of Santoríni, once thought to have caused the collapse of Minoan civilization, is now known to have been at least a century too early; it probably had only minor effects on Crete.[1]

Dark Ages (1150–700 BC)

The rapid collapse of Bronze Age civilisation was an important break in Cretan history. Population declined and settlements were abandoned. Fewer people were cultivating and fewer animals browsing than there had been for 3,000 years, which probably allowed woodland to increase. Writing became a lost or rare art (hence the name Dark Ages).

Nevertheless, Crete did not completely lose its cosmopolitan character. Imports from Cyprus and mainland Greece continued; by the eighth century distinctive Cretan metal goods are found abroad.

Archaic, Classical, Hellenistic (700–69 BC)

These are little-studied periods in Cretan archaeology; it is difficult to estimate population or the extent of cultivation and herding. Contemporary writers say that Crete was divided into at least fifty independent, warring city-states. Cretans gained a reputation as pirates, archers, mercenaries and liars, which has been hard to shake off.

Roman and First Byzantine (69 BC–824 AD)

The Roman conquest of Crete was the first time the entire island is known to have been dominated by a foreign power. Crete prospered under Roman rule. Population increased; aqueducts and cisterns were built; villages were spaced a few kilometres apart. Most of the cultivable and browsable land was put to use.

It is hard to claim that Crete became Romanised. Except for officials and a colony of legionaries at Knossós, few Roman citizens moved to the island.[2] Although it is occasionally possible to identify Late Roman field systems, large Roman estates (*latifundia*) were not the norm in Crete as they were in much of the Roman empire. Cretans played a minor part in the Roman empire.[3]

The Roman slides into the Byzantine Empire without any sharp defining date. Some scholars place the division at 324 AD, when Constantinople replaced Rome as the distant imperial capital; but Sanders' book on Roman Crete includes material down to the seventh century. In the landscape a definite change comes in the later fourth century. This began a period of great prosperity with buildings and farms scattered throughout the countryside, and many aqueducts and cisterns. Most of the cultivable and browsable land was again put to use. Architecture was dominated by many massive Christian basilicas. This period we define as First Byzantine, in distinction to Roman.

The bishoprics set up then have been the model for administrative units in all later periods.

Arab and Second Byzantine (824–1204 AD)

Crete at first escaped the invasions and upheavals which convulsed Greece. Then it was captured by Arabs and held for over a century. How momentous the Arab conquest or the Byzantine reconquest were is hard to say. The few written documents are against the theory that there was a complete break in the island's life.[4] The Arabs are remembered as the founders of Khandax, later Candia, now Herákleion (T). Archaeologically, this is a dark age: it is rarely possible to distinguish artefacts of the Arab period from those of several centuries either side.

The Byzantines devised a feudal system which was to endure in Crete until the eighteenth century. In principle, the emperor granted to noblemen the lordship of particular villages or fractions of villages in return for providing men, horses and arms to fight the imperial wars. What was granted was not ownership of the land, which already belonged to the inhabitants, but the right to extract revenues. Northwest European readers will recognise a parallel to the lords and manors of their own feudal system, which was apparently an independent invention. The system was to be found throughout the island, except in Sphakiá where everyone was noble.

In the eleventh century we first hear of the revolts which were to punctuate the history of Crete for over 800 years.

Venetian (1210–1650)

In 1204 the Fourth Crusade turned from its path to sack the Byzantine Empire. After bickering with their fellow Crusaders, the Venetians settled for Crete as the three-eighths share of the plunder to which they were entitled.

3

Venetian nobles were encouraged to take up vacant Cretan lordships, and merchants went to settle in the cities. Some Venetians turned Cretan. There were also colonies of Turks, Armenians and Jews. Cretans played a prominent part in the outside world: there was a Cretan Pope and at least one Cretan Patriarch of Constantinople. Did not a learned Cretan, Nathaniel Conopius, first introduce coffee to England in his Oxford college in 1639?[5]

Venice tended to neglect her distant province and failed to respond to its needs, so that several times she nearly lost it to revolts by Cretans and Creto-Venetians. In 1347-48 the island was very hard hit by the Black Death, the first of the epidemics of bubonic plague which were to keep down its population for the next 470 years. To judge by visible remains, the island had a period of prosperity in the thirteenth century, and again at the end of the Venetian period.

Turkish (1650–1898)

The Ottoman army landed in west Crete in 1645, and by 1651 they had overrun all the island – except the city of Candia (Herákleion) which held out until 1669 in the greatest siege of all history.

This conquest is traditionally thought of as a tragic break in Cretan history. However, contemporary Cretan documents indicate that the Turks took over the island and its institutions almost intact. Their feudal system was more like the Byzantine than the Venetian.[6] The *kavallier* and *sergente* (knight and squire) were replaced by the *zaim*, *timar* and *sipahi*. At least a quarter of the population became Muslim, which hardly suggests that the new regime was unpopular.

Crete, no longer a beleaguered outpost of Christendom, still kept its trading links with Western Europe. Cretans played a prominent part in the Ottoman Empire: two Cretans rose to be Sultana, and the Sultans Ahmed III and Mehmed IV, lovers of tulips, were half-Cretan.[7] Whatever its drawbacks, Turkish rule brought four benefits: the menace of land raids by pirates was greatly diminished, most of the hated labour services imposed by the Venetians disappeared, the Turks restored the Orthodox bishops whom the Venetians had banished for 450 years, and the bureaucratic pressure to grow cereals (which had discouraged Cretans from doing so) was relaxed. Early Turkish-period pottery and buildings, like most other artefacts, are almost indistinguishable from late Venetian ones.

Prosperity rapidly declined in the late eighteenth century, when the authority of the Empire broke down and the aristocracy disappeared. Crete sank into an appalling state of anarchy, crime and feuding between Christians and Muslims, which Cretans today remember as if it were the normal state of the Turkish period. In 1770 there was a great revolt. In 1816 there came the last of the bubonic plagues, followed by the Greek War of Independence, in which Crete suffered terribly but gained nothing. By the 1830s Crete was at a very low ebb of ruin and depopulation. The rest of the nineteenth century was a period of steady recovery which further revolts did little to interrupt.

The twentieth century

Crete left the Ottoman Empire in 1898 and joined Greece in 1913. The intervening years were a high point in the island's history, when it acquired most of the amenities of European life; they are still very visible in buildings and the landscape today.

After 1913 Greece, and Crete with it, was caught up in the woes of the twentieth century. There were ruinous wars, external and internal. In 1923 came the 'Great Catastrophe': the remaining Muslims (about one-sixth of the population) were expelled, and parts of Crete were filled with Christians expelled from Turkey. World War II coincided with a peak of overpopulation. By 1947, as Allbaugh shows, Crete was passing through a period as a Third World country.

From the 1960s onwards the Cretans extricated themselves from this predicament. In the last twenty years the island has made an extraordinary transition. It is now more prosperous, and has a higher population, than ever before; but prosperity and population are unevenly distributed. Most of the remoter areas have become depopulated.

As far as we know, the last seventy years have been a period of more rapid changes than at any time in the historic period, with the abandonment of terraced agriculture, disappearance of cattle, introduction of vehicles, increase of trees, introduction of bull-dozers, disappearance of cereals, rural depopulation, growth of cities, growth of tourism, proliferation of roads, introduction of greenhouses, and growth of piped irrigation.

Notes

1 D. A. Hardy et al. (eds.), (1990), *Thera and the Aegean World III*, London, Thera Foundation.
2 Sanders (see bibliography), chapter 1; confirmed by information from Martha Baldwin-Bowsky.
3 Sanders (see bibliography), p. 179-80.
4 V. Christides (1984),*The Conquest of Crete by the Arabs*, Athens, Akademia Athenon.
5 A. à Wood (1820) (3rd ed.), *Athenae Oxonienses*, **4**, 80 (we are indebted to the Rev. W. Horbury for this allusion).
6 Cf. A. Bryer and H. Lowry (1986), *Continuity and Change in Late Byzantine and Early Ottoman Society*, Birmingham, University of Birmingham Centre for Byzantine Studies.
7 Lord Kinross (1977), *The Ottoman Centuries: the rise and fall of the Turkish Empire*, London, Jonathan Cape.

2
History, pseudo-history, and the use of evidence

Botany is not a sedentary idle science, that can be attained at one's Ease by the Fire-side, like Geometry, History, &c. A Botanist must scour the Mountains and Forests, climb steep Rocks and Precipices, venture down Abysses. The only Books that can thorowly instruct in this Matter, are scattered up and down the whole Face of the Earth, and not to be gathered up without Fatigue and Peril.

M. Fontenelle, *The Elogium of M.Tournefort*, 1715

Kinds of information

Archaeology
The earliest known archaeological observations on Crete were by Cristoforo Buondelmonti in 1415. Knossós was identified by Marin Cavalli, Venetian governor, in 1571–75;[1] the earliest study there was by Onorio Belli in 1583–86;[2] the first major excavation was by Minos Kalokairinos in 1878. Sir Arthur Evans's more celebrated endeavours at Knossós (T) and elsewhere began in 1900.

Excavation and survey have discovered well over 1,000 prehistoric sites on Crete, and almost as many Graeco-Roman and medieval ones. Such investigations discover information on location and size of settlements, building materials, agricultural activity, woodland management and environment. It is our prac-tice in archaeological surveys to record vegetation and geology in parallel with antiquities.

Interpreting archaeological surveys involves questions of preservation and visibility. It is easy to exaggerate the abundance of early settlement on limestone, because sites are less often covered by soil movement or hidden by vegetation than on other rocks. It used to be thought that west Crete was almost uninhabited until the late Bronze Age. This is quite untrue, but dense vegetation and steep mountains often make sites more difficult to find than in the middle and east.

Present vegetation
We have been making field observations for up to twenty-five years. Our first task in a new area is to discover what the present wild vegetation consists of, how it functions and whether it is

changing. We study the parts played by trees, shrubs, under-shrubs, herbaceous plants, mosses and lichens. We inquire how each species responds to browsing, burning or woodcutting, and what the recent history of the site is in relation to these activities. We also consider what happens to areas of abandoned cultivation. In an arid land like Crete it is supremely important to study roots, which is easily done thanks to the Cretan love of bulldozing.

Trees are important as evidence because they can be dated by their annual growth-rings. Ancient trees, especially, are witnesses to a variety of land-forming processes and past human activities.

2.1. *Pollen sites*

Palynology

Crete, having few wetlands, is not a good place for preserving fossil pollen. Four pollen cores are known, and several other sites have been sampled unsuccessfully (Fig.2.1). None of the four is continuous over a long period; the longest record, at Ay. Galíni (AV), goes back (with gaps) to just before the Neolithic.

Documents

The earliest documents from Crete are Linear A tablets (1800–1550 BC). They are written in an undeciphered language, but tell us something about rural activity through ideograms of animals, plants and trees.

The earliest readable records are the Linear B tablets (1400–1200 BC) from Knossós (T) and Khaniá (Ky), written in an early form of Greek. The small fraction of the archive that survives are economic records, dealing largely with the land and its produce. Land holdings are measured in seed-corn. About one-third of the tablets are concerned with sheep and wool.

The surviving writings of the ancient Greeks begin after a gap of some 400 years. They are dominated by Athens. Writings about Crete are fairly copious, but they are of poor quality and have never been properly collected and analysed. Crete was a legendary, little-visited land about which nonsense could be believed: authors could be persuaded that Crete had no snakes and no owls, and that any introduced to the island died.[3]

Ancient Greek and most Roman authors show little interest in landscape and its inhabitants. This lack is supplemented to a small extent by inscriptions. All the writing that survives from the early Byzantine period would go on a single page – and yet, on archaeological evidence, this was the second most active period of Cretan civilisation.

From late Byzantine onwards, Crete is well documented. Much of the island archives are preserved in Venice, in the State Archives and St Mark's and the Correr Libraries; other documents are in Paris and London.

The medieval documents are mostly in Latin. The *Book of Bans* (*Bandi e Proclami*) enrols the decrees proclaimed in Candia

(Herákleion (T)) week by week for most of the fourteenth century.[4] It deals with consumer protection, corsairs, edible plants, murder, pollution of watercourses, rebellions, rubbish disposal, runaway slaves, sheep-bells, state lands, straying animals, unlawful games, weddings and other incidentals of Cretan life. There are at least three registers of feudal estates in various parts of Crete; anyone going to auction and buying seven thirty-seconds of the lordship of a manor was expected to enrol it. They contain hundreds of place-names.[5] Another class of topographical document are *perambulations,* which define boundaries by listing successive features on them: they range in date from Hellenistic inscriptions to Turkish title-deeds.

The task of sorting out the papers of the Venetian Senate and the Council of Ten relating to Crete was begun a century ago by Hippolyte Noiret, but death in Venice overtook him before he had finished; the work has now been resumed by P. Thiriet. This source deals mainly with taxation and commerce, but has something to say about the landscape.

The Venetians later became obsessed with censuses and statistics. In 1536 Marcantonio Bernardo, Rector of Canea (Khaniá (Ky)), made a list of all the adult men in Apokórona.[6] A Cretan 'Domesday Book', by Pietro Castrofilaca in 1583, purports to list all settlements with their populations, together with statistics on taxation, land-use, *angarie* (labour services owed by citizens to the State by way of taxation) and military matters.[7] The Venetian administration was not a model of tyrannous efficiency, for the lists and figures fail to agree; the Venetians never mastered the peculiar settlement pattern of Crete.

In the later Venetian period every *Provveditor* (governor-general) or *Rettore* (provincial governor) sent in a report (*relazione*) on the state of Crete every three or four years. The authors wrote on whatever they felt like, for example crops, attempts to extend the cultivated land, trouble with corsairs or the recalcitrant men of Sphakiá, unusual weather and bad harvests; some dealt with antiquities, especially at Knossós (T) and Górtyn (Ka).[8] *Relazioni* are complemented by letters exchanged between the Cretan authorities and Venice. The Venetians loved maps and pictures. The earliest usable map of Crete may be in the thirteenth-century *Mappa Mundi* in Hereford Cathedral. The Cretan Giorgio Sidheris, *alias* Calapoda, made some magnificent maps of Crete in the 1560s. From the seventeenth century there are many views of places in rural Crete, which can be compared with what is there now: the best are the series by Raffaelle Monanni in his description of Crete in 1631 (Plates 1 and 2).[9]

Another source is foreign travellers.[10] The earliest detailed account, and the best for 400 years, was by Cristoforo Buondelmonti from Florence. He explored Crete in the summer of 1415, first by sea all round the coast with frequent inland excursions and then by land from the eastern to the western tip; he says much about vegetation and local customs.

The Turks, as bureaucratic as the Venetians, kept voluminous records. These are very inaccessible, being written in the official script, language and style of the Ottoman Empire. Few can read the Turkish archives in Herákleion (T), let alone those in Istanbul and Ankara. We have made use of the 2,000 or so items translated into Greek by the late N. S. Stavrinidhes. Censuses, descriptions of lands and properties, and accounts of crops are embedded in a large volume of general administration. Another record is the census of Crete in 1881, also published in Greek, which is a wonderful record of place-names.[11]

The many travellers at this period include Pitton de Tournefort, the French botanist, who toured Crete in 1700. A list of his plants is in the British Library.[12] Robert Pashley, a Cambridge scholar, one of the most thoughtful and precise of travellers, travelled round Crete in 1834. The illustrations in his book can be compared with what can be seen from the same spots today. We have discovered his beautiful original sketches in the British Library.[13] M. V. Raulin studied the geology, botany and land-uses of the island in 1847. Next came Thomas Spratt, a British naval captain, who made good use of his opportunities on a hydrographic survey in 1852-53. Edward Lear, artist and nonsense-writer, left a diary and many sketches from his travels in 1864.[14]

Photography came early to Crete, where Diamantopoulos was a distinguished and prolific photographer in Khaniá (Ky). His country scenes are evidence of the changes in vegetation during the twentieth century. Some of them illustrate the work of A. Trevor-Battye, a traveller in 1909. Photographs and descriptions by early archaeologists, especially Sir Arthur Evans, Giuseppe Gerola, and J. D. S. Pendlebury, the great Cretologist of the 1930s, are also now documents in landscape history.

History or pseudo–history?

A fascinating aspect of landscape history is the rival version.[15] A persistent theory in Mediterranean studies is that of the Ruined Landscape or Lost Eden, which runs like this. Well into historic times, the land was covered with magnificent forests. Men cut down the forests to make houses and ships, or burned them to make farmland; the trees failed to grow again, and multitudes of goats devoured the remains. Trees, unlike other vegetation, have a magic power of retaining soil. The trees gone, the soil washed away into the sea or the plains, the land became 'barren', and some say that the very climate got worse. The 'typical' Mediterranean landscape is pronounced to be the result of 'massive environmental degradation'.[16]

Degradation is supposed to be progressive: damage done in the Turkish period was added to the accumulated damage by Venetians, Byzantines, Arabs and Romans. It can only be reversed by deliberate intervention. It is increased by war and misgovernment, especially under the 'excesses of luxury and disorder' attributed by Europeans to the Turks. Since Greece and Crete were much more wooded in classical times than today and since deforestation is progressive, they must have been more wooded still in prehistory.

This theory is logical and consistent and makes excellent sense. It is set out in many learned books and articles, and was the basis of a television series, *The First Eden*. It flatters the vanity of governments, who like to think they can command the very trees to grow or not to grow. But is it true?

Classically-educated West Europeans assume that what they read of the ancient world took place in an environment not very unlike their own. For example Nahum Tate's vision of Dido and Aeneas in 1695:

> Thanks to these Lovesome, Lovesome Vales,
>   These Desert, Desert Hills and Dales,
> So Fair the Game, so Rich the Sport,
>   *Diana's* self might to these Woods resort;
> Oft she visits this lov'd Mountain,
>   Oft she baths her in this Fountain;
> Here, here *Acteon* met his fate . . .

A century later, the Abbé Barthélémy, in his best-selling reconstructions of Ancient Greece, sets the scene in the landscape of Marie-Antoinette's France.[17] Having had this beaten into him at school, the traveller meeting the tangled prickly-oaks and dribbling springs of the real Greece (and often not knowing the country well enough to discover the noble forests and crystal fountains that still exist) might well suppose that the country had gone to the bad since classical times. The theory of the Ruined Landscape crystallises, in almost its present form, in the writings of Sonnini, the French traveller of 1777–78; the supposed effects on soils and climate are already there. Sonnini wrote about Cyprus and Crete, which thus became type examples of Ruined Landscapes.

As information passes from author to author, it tends to be distorted in favour of Ruined Landscape theory. Scholars play up the landscape of the past and play down the landscape of the present: they write about ancient forests where the original text mentioned only trees; they ignore modern forests or dismiss them as mere 'scrub' or 'maquis'. Even independent-minded Pendlebury declared that 'Crete, which was once one of the most fertile and prosperous islands in the Mediterranean, is now one of the rockiest and most barren' – a surprising statement from one who knew Crete so well.

Since Sonnini, two centuries' evidence has accumulated from excavation, geology, climatology and botany. One might expect the Ruined Landscape theory to have been developed and refined to take account of all this new material. Not so: authors still chew over the same Greek and Latin texts which were all that Sonnini had. The texts are generally taken at face value, without considering the limitations of this kind of evidence or even whether the ancient authors were in a position to know what they were writing about. All ancient allusions to cutting down trees are taken as implying deforestation, not tempered by the thought that ancient authors (like modern) would have been unlikely to notice trees growing up again.[18] In reality, deforestation is felling not balanced by regrowth: to mention the felling but ignore the regrowth is like declaring a firm insolvent without considering its income.

In this book we examine various aspects of Ruined Landscape theory, and see what there is to be said for them. To avoid writing pseudo-history, one must observe certain principles:

1 Don't over-generalise. The Mediterranean is not a unified region. To prove the theory for Cyprus would not prove it for Crete. Within Crete, it would be perfectly possible for Apokórona to be a Ruined Landscape but Kíssamos not.

2 The key to the past lies in the functioning of the present landscape. One should not assert that goats eat everything without having watched goats.

3 Do not rely entirely on written evidence. If you do, you will never learn about periods when nobody was writing.

4 Verify the evidence. Be suspicious of information written down by people living long after the time, or who had not been to the locality.

5 Consult the original texts; do not rely on scholars' interpretations of them.

6 Use all the evidence. An argument based on an allusion in Plato or Homer is weak; it becomes much stronger if corroborated by evidence from archaeology, geology, or the behaviour of the present landscape.

7 Don't be afraid to say you don't know. Pseudo-history is started by scholars clutching at straws.

Notes

1 BMV: Ital. VII. 918 (8392) c. 119.

2 E. Falkener (ed.), (1853), 'A description of … theatres and other remains in Crete … by Onorio Belli in 1586', *Museum of Classical Antiquities*, **2**, **suppl.**, 1-32.

3 E.g. Aelian V.2.

4 Partly published by P. R. Vidulich (see bibliography).

5 BNP: Ital. 2088. ASV: DC buste 21, 78.

6 ASV: CR busta 61.

7 BMV: Ital. VII. 1109 (8880).

8 Of scores of *relazioni* that survive, eight have been published by S. G. Spanakis, *Mn*, **1-6.**

9 BMV: Ital. VII. 889 (7798).

10 See: P. Warren (1972), '16th, 17th and 18th century British travellers in Crete', *Κρήτικα Χρονικά*, KD'[**14**], 65-92; Iliadou D. Hemmerdinger (1967), 'La Crète sous la domination vénitienne … (1322-1684). Renseignements nouveaux … d'après les pélerins et les voyageurs', *Studi Veneziani*, **9**, 535-623.

11 N. Stavrakis (Ν. Σταυράκης) (1890), *Στατιστική τῆς Πληθυσμοῦ τῆς Κρῆτης*, Athens, Παλιγγενεσία (reprinted 1978).

12 BLL: Sloane 4020. For a list of botanical travellers see: E. K. Platakis (Ε. Κ. Πλατάκης) (1955), 'Τό ἱστορικόν τῶν ἐν Κρήτη βοτανικῶν ἐρευνῶν,' *Κρήτικα Χρονικά*, **9**, 119-48.

13 BLL: Add. MSS 31342A,B.

14 R. Fowler (1984), *Edward Lear: the Cretan journal*, Athens, D. Harvey.

15 O. Rackham (1987), 'The countryside: history & pseudo-history', *The Historian*, **14**, 13-7.

16 C. Ponting (1991), *A Green History of the World*, London, Sinclair-Stevenson.

17 J. J. Barthélémy (1788),*Voyage du jeune Anacharsis en Grèce*, Paris, Debure.

18 For example: J. D. Hughes (1983), 'How the ancients viewed deforestation', *JFA*, **10**, 436-45.1 BMV: Ital. VII. 918 (8392) c.119.

3

Making the mountains

What aileth thee, O thou sea, that thou fleddest:
and thou Jordan, that thou wast driven back?
Ye mountains, that ye skipped like rams:
and ye little hills, like young sheep?

Psalm **114**

The mountains have written the history of Crete.

Ioannis Konstandakis of Lákkoi (Ky)

Like Athena bursting fully-armed from the head of Zeus, the mountains of Crete spring from the sea to their full height in less than 10 km. Looking at the White Mountains from off the south coast, one faces a wall of rock 2,200 m high. This is about the same amount of relief one sees from the foot of the Alps, but about 700 m higher than the Rocky Mountains as seen from Denver.

The White Mountains are by far the grandest on the island, with at least 20 peaks over 2,200 m, over 100 sq. km above the tree-limit, seventeen major gorges, and their own unique landscape of the High Desert (Chapter 17). Mount Psilorítis (anciently Mount Ida) is just higher – a single great hog's back rising to the peak of the Holy Cross (Tímios Stavrós) at 2,456 m.

The four great massifs share many features. The White Mountains set a theme repeated with variations around Psilorítis, Dhíkti, and the Thryphtí Mountains. Each has a core of hard limestone, surrounded by lower mountains of phyllites and quartzites. The bold limestone cliffs and bare rock, soaring through woods of cypress, pine or oak, contrast with the rounded, generally well-vegetated outlines of the phyllite-quartzite hills. But the theme is varied by the climatic trend along the island from the wet west to the dry east. There is also a twist in Crete, so that in the west the south slope is more abrupt than the north, which is less marked in the middle and is reversed in the east.

Crete and plate tectonics

Crete rides, as if on the back of a bull, at the point where Africa burrows under Europe. Two of the world's great continental plates are colliding. The pressures generate the Hellenic Island Arc, of which Crete forms the greater part (Figure 3.1). To the north of it lies an arc of volcanoes from Nísyros through Santoríni to Méthana; to the south lies the deep-sea Hellenic Trench.

The enormous mass of rock began to force its way under Crete about the end of the Cretaceous (*c.* 70 million years ago). The pushing and grinding have caused the island to be uplifted in some parts, collapsed in others and cracked by faults. Surface manifestations of the underground movement are jerky: pressures slowly built up give way in the form of frequent tremors and occasional great earthquakes.

Certain periods of history are for some reason more tectonically active than others. On Crete, the Bronze Age seems to have been particularly lively with earthquakes; the last 1,500 years have been relatively quiet.

Tectonic history
During the early and middle Mesozoic (*c.* 225–140 million years ago) most of Greece, including Crete, was under the sea and accumulated immense marine sediments. These sediments were uplifted to form the bulk of the Greek land-mass, the Cyclades, and Crete. This progressive emergence – part of the Alpine mountain-building – began in the east during the late Cretaceous (70 million years ago) and ended in the west during the Miocene (25 to 10 million years ago). One result of this progressive emergence was the sliding from east to west of uplifted massifs on to lower areas that were still submerged.[1] These moving mountains are called *nappes.* In Crete they can range from the size of a large house to a massif 30 km across (the entire western half of the White Mountains). The alternation of nappes explains some of the

3.1 *Tectonic environment of Crete*

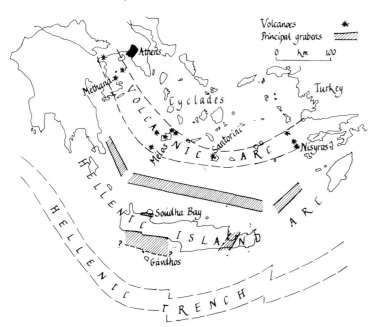

rhythmic repetition of Cretan landscapes.

Once raised from the sea-bed, Crete, the Cyclades and the mainland formed a more or less unified land-mass for several million years. Towards the end of the Miocene, subsidences caused this land-mass to break up and once again sink beneath the waves. On Crete all but the highest mountain peaks were re-submerged. During this period the marly, sandy and clayey *Neogene* formations, characteristic of the north coasts of the island, were deposited. This submergence continued until the middle Pliocene (*c.* 3–4 million years ago). There was a short interval of emergence when the Messenian Salinity Crisis occurred (*c.* 5 million years ago). During this event the Mediterranean almost dried up, leaving Crete at the top of a mountain range of almost Himalayan proportions, surrounded by vast salt flats and brine lakes.[2] The gypsum hills of south-west Crete and elsewhere were probably precipitated during this or similar events.

At the end of the Pliocene or the beginning of the Pleistocene (*c.* 2 million years ago) further movements caused blocks of the earth's crust to subside between faults, forming depressions called *grabens*, or to be uplifted. Three grabens formed deep trenches to the north-west, north and north-east of Crete, permanently separating the island from other land. Block movements in Crete itself, some by as much as 800 m, resulted in the present coastal configuration.[3] For example, the Soúdha Bay graben subsided, creating the deepest harbour in the Mediterranean. Block faulting also isolated the four great mountain massifs, and may have split off Gávdhos. Marine marls, sandstones and clays, accumulated at the base of the mountains when they were submerged, were raised up at this time to form the blindingly white hills of the north coast.

The Middle Pleistocene to the Middle Holocene (*c.* 600,000-5,000 years ago) was a quiet period tectonically.[4] This was the time of the great glaciations. Crete formed only small glaciers on the highest mountains. Moraines, cirques, and *roches moutonnées* have been identified on Mount Psilorítis,[5] uniquely for the south Mediterranean islands. Glacial features have yet to be confirmed in the White Mountains.

Water locked up in ice-caps caused the world's sea-level to rise and fall. The fall in sea-level reduced the gap between Crete

3.2 *Cretan earthquakes, 1946-75, from information by Galanopoulos.*
(a) Locations of epicentres. Small circles: earthquakes of Richter magnitude 5.5–6.0. Big circles: magnitude > 6.0
(b) Dates and magnitudes of earthquakes

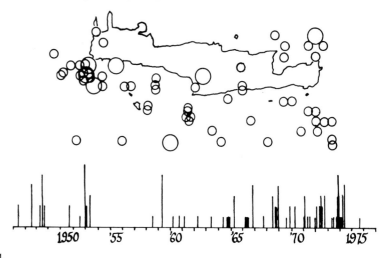

and the mainland, but never closed it. On the coasts of Crete it resulted in alternating deposits of aeolianites (see below) and river gravels.

The Bull of Poseidon woke up again about 3000 BC with a succession of earthquakes, some of which destroyed the first Minoan palaces around 1700 BC.[6] This period reached its climax in the fourth to sixth centuries AD with the 'Early Byzantine Paroxysm', a giant convulsion which uplifted the whole of west Crete by up to 9 m, crumpled central Crete, intermittently submerged the middle and east parts of the north coast, and uplifted the south-east corner.[7]

Big earthquakes have occurred down the centuries, as at Herákleion (T) in 1856. Small shocks occur every year; one of the authors was once nearly shaken out of a museum window. Most of them are associated with the Hellenic Trench south of Crete; they tend to come in groups (Figure 3.2).[8]

The rocks (Figure 3.3)

Phyllite-quartzites

These are metamorphic rocks, apparently the oldest on the island (at least 300 million years). They are mainly composed of silicate minerals, often with a good deal of clay. They can be roughly divided into those with a blocky structure ('quartzite') and those that break into plates ('phyllite'). They vary in colour, commonly brown or greenish, but also black, yellow and red.[9]

Many other rocks are interpolated in various ways: shale and sandstone layers in the upper and middle strata; limestones in the lower strata; sea-water deposits such as gypsum (e.g. at Stómion near Khrysoskalítissa (Ki)); and limonite iron ore (e.g. south of Skinés (Ky)). Most of the iron, copper and other minerals in Crete occur in phyllite. There are small intrusions of igneous rocks (diabase, peridotites, gabbro), for example west of Gourniá (H). Some of the igneous rocks have been serpentinised and are green or yellow-green with a soapy feel, sometimes with veins of asbestos (e.g. near Platyvóla (Ky)).

The Minoans carved stone vases out of serpentine; they may have mined copper ore at Khrysólakkos (Asteroúsia) and Sklavopoúla (Se). Iron ores have been mined at least since Roman times. The asbestos has never been suitable for commerce.

Platey limestones (Plattenkalk)

These hard limestones range in date from Carboniferous to Eocene, 345 to 55 million years ago. Typically they have bands of green, purple and grey limestone alternating with white chert – an unforgettable structure well seen in the walls of the great gorges. In some places (e.g. around Kavoúsi (H)) they pass imperceptibly, via sandstones of similar colour and structure, into the upper layers of phyllite-quartzite.

The chert is rarely good enough for tools, but slabs of it have been used as roof-slates (e.g. in Samariá (Sf)).

Crystalline limestones

Most of these hard limestones are Mesozoic (250 to 65 million years ago). They are uniform in colour (mostly light grey), not banded, and without chert. They may contain fossil rudists (an extinct group of shellfish) and are often brecciated (see below) or chemically changed into dolomite. They range in colour from light grey to bluish to black. A dark variant has a curious holey lava-like texture and a bituminous smell. Crystalline limestones are

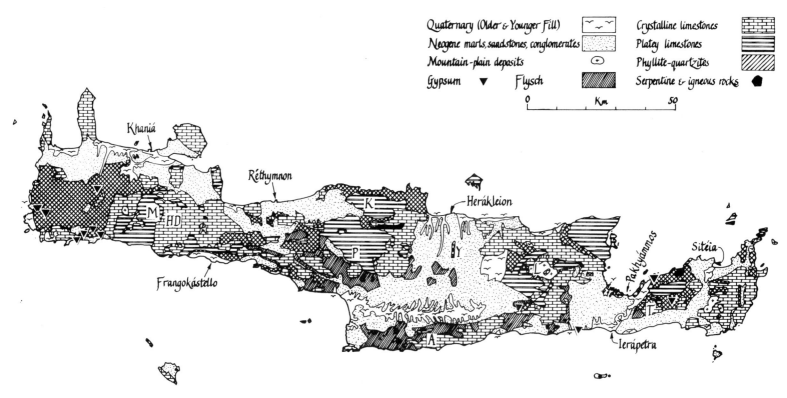

3.3 Geology of Crete, simplified and adapted after Creutzburg, Bornovas, and others
M: Madháres HD: High Desert P: Mount Psilorítis K: Kouloukoúnas
Mountains A: Asteroúsia Mountains Y: Mount Yúktas L: Lassíthi Plain
T: Mount Thryphtí

16

3.4 *Conglomerate boulder, hollowed out by internal decay and used as a field-house. Goúdhoura (Si), September 1986*

dissolved by rainwater to form the razor-edged, boot-eating ridges that all Cretan walkers know. Long-term dissolution creates karst features (see below).

Marls, sandstones and clays

These low-altitude deposits belong to the late Tertiary or Neogene, extending into the Quaternary (25–0.6 million years ago). They are chalky white, yellow or grey; occasionally clayey beds are blue. In East Crete they survive up to 700 m, but in the rest of the island rarely occur above 450 m.

These rocks vary from hardish to very soft. Many kinds will case-harden, forming a very hard crust from which the interior may later erode away (Figure 3.4). An amusing consequence are the hollow boulders of the marly part of the Ayiofárango Gorge (Ka). These dense, soft rocks were favoured for Minoan and Roman rock-cut tombs. Marl makes an excellent building-stone called *koúskouras*.

A very recent sandstone is **aeolianite**, which consists of coastal sand cemented with calcium carbonate. It appears to date from glacial periods, when the lower sea-level exposed a supply of sand. It is preserved here and there up to 18 m above sea-level. From the Bronze Age onwards this soft, golden sandstone has been a favourite building stone, often transported. The Venetians used it for city walls; it absorbs the impact of a cannon-ball.

Breccias and conglomerates

These are natural concretes, composed of rock fragments cemented together. River gravel, composed of pebbles rounded in their passage down the river, cements to form **conglomerate**. Angular fragments, piling up at the base of a cliff, are called *scree*; when cemented they form *breccia*. A gravel beach cements to form *beach-rock*, a Cretan speciality.

Tufa is a thin, hard limestone precipitated out of trickling water. It often coats conglomerate, breccia and marl surfaces, making them difficult to distinguish from hard limestone.

Breccias and conglomerates can be of any date. The youngest and nearly the hardest rocks in Crete are the beach-rocks which form a jagged armour round the Akrotíri Peninsula. Some, with Coca-Cola bottle fragments cemented into them, must be less than fifty years old. Beach-rock deposits are especially common where fresh water seeps out along a beach.

Cretan mountains have been eroding ever since they began to form. Whenever the climate has been wet, huge amounts of material have been carried down. Most has gone into the sea, but north of the mountains there are great beds of gravels in various forms and with various degrees of consolidation. Some are soft, such as the marly conglomerates of the Ierápetra isthmus; but limestone breccio-conglomerates can be extremely hard.

Erosion

[Your theory] seems to me to have only one drawback, Hopkins, and that is that it is intrinsically impossible. Have you ever tried to drive a harpoon through a body? No? Tut, tut, my dear sir, you must really pay attention to these details. My friend Watson could tell you that I spent a whole morning in that exercise. It is no easy matter, and requires a strong and practised arm . . . Do you imagine that this anæmic youth was capable of so frightful an assault?

A. Conan Doyle, *Black Peter*

Most exponents of Ruined Landscape theory assert that human mismanagement has not stopped at the fauna and vegetation, but has ruined the soil too. Erosion is presented, not as the ordinary course of weathering and tectonics (processes that give sedimentary geologists a job) but as an artefact and especially a consequence of deforestation.[10]

This assertion may be true, but we doubt its generality. The most gullied part of Greece that we have seen is the Píndos Mountains; it is also the most wooded. Woods go on continuously for tens of kilometres, and gullies eat into the woods as if they were not there.

This observation alone, which is paralleled in Rhodes, casts doubt on any simple theory that forests universally protect against erosion.

What 'deforestation' means, and its consequences, must vary with each combination of geology, climate and vegetation. Nevertheless, supporters of Ruined Landscape theory in Greece quote observations and experiments from parts of the world, especially the United States, where artificial erosion happens easily.[11] Few have experimented in the Mediterranean, much less in Greece. Other supporters have drawn strength from a misunderstanding of a famous passage of Plato.[12] What Plato said is that Attica was once covered in trees and soil; the soil was washed away in great deluges 9,000 years before; and the trees disappeared in consequence. The passage is in a work of fiction, but if we must read it as history it means that Plato dimly understood the great erosions of the Pleistocene and made a fair guess at dating them. Nevertheless, author after author has stood this passage on its head and made it serve as an example of the evils of deforestation.

Kinds of erosion – gullies

The 'badland' gullies, seeming to eat up whole landscapes in Italy, Epirus, Cyprus, Rhodes and Kárpathos, have no parallels in Crete. Crete is a very eroded land – whole mountain-ranges have disappeared – but the erosion-faces are now consolidated, often tufa-faced, vegetated and provided with old trees and archaeological sites; they appear to be tens of thousands of years old. Raw gullies occur only in little patches here and there.

Most gullied patches in Crete involve beds of blue clay, mainly in Pliocene marls. Where the clay is exposed in a clay-pit or by the downcutting of a stream, it erodes and causes the overlying, less erodible beds to collapse; a system of gullies develops which branches out over a few hectares; then it gradually ceases and bushes grow over it. The Pliocene deposits of Gávdhos (Se) and the Ierápetra isthmus are (for Crete) especially prone to this type of erosion. The testimony of old men and of early air photographs is that each badland is active for only a few decades; only on Gávdhos are there huge gullies which go on for centuries.

The main determinant of gullying is geology. Certain types of clay, clayey marl and loose sands or gravels are much more erodible than other rocks, especially where tectonic action has tilted them to unaccustomed angles. These happen to be rare in Crete. The red gravels south of Khaniá (Ky) have eroded in the past into spectacular ridges and peaks, but are now just too strongly cemented to erode further.

The 'goating' of abandoned terraces is a form of miniature gully-erosion (p. 163). It is common in Crete, but we have never seen it lead to major erosion.

Slumping

This form of erosion, too, depends on geology. Where rocks are weak and lubricated by springs or beds of clay, slopes collapse under their own weight: the rock fractures and slips, often rotating as it does so. Where the geological conditions are met, anything that steepens a slope promotes slumping. The commonest natural process is when streams enlarge their beds by side-cutting. The commonest artificial process is the excavation of unwalled road- and terrace-scarps. Earth-tremors also contribute. Slumping is prevalent in Ayios Vasíleios district and western Amári; occasionally it threatens whole villages.

Sheet and wind erosion

Sheet erosion is the gradual, even creeping or washing of soil down a slope: it is promoted by ploughing, and to a lesser degree by the treading of animals. Soil accumulates at the bottom of a field to form a **lynchet** against a cross-slope obstruction like a hedge, road, or chapel. The size of the lynchet is a guide to the amount of sheet erosion.

Wind can pick up silty or fine sandy soils when dry, but is usually blocked by even the thinnest plant cover. It can erode patches of bare ground between plants, leaving behind previously buried pebbles and sherds. We have found ancient fields (for example on the plateau of Ayios Ioánnes (Sf)) which have lost their soil down to the bare limestone, apparently by this process, since Roman times. Such **deflation** reaches an extreme on Gávdhos (Se), where areas of countryside are now armour-plated with potsherds.

On hard limestone slopes, a sign of erosion is in the patination of the teeth of limestone that project from the soil. Exposed limestone is covered with microscopically thin lichens of distinctive colours, that take many years to form; where the soil has receded, each tooth has an un-lichenised zone round its base.

3.5 *Root-buttresses of a tree such as an olive, showing the effects of erosion*

soil gain   neutral   soil loss

Soil loss or gain is also manifested in the extent to which old trees have their roots exposed (*empedestalled*) or buried (Figure 3.5). Typically a 500-year-old olive-tree would be empedestalled, or buried, by no more than 50 cm. On a shorter time-scale, phrygana bushes may be empedestalled by the removal of soil around them.

Effects of deluges

Writers on how forests are supposed to prevent erosion emphasise ways in which trees delay the rate at which water reaches the ground or runs off from it. These qualities, shared to varying degrees by other vegetation, are real up to a limit. Their effectiveness depends on the theory that erosion is gradual (the accumulation of thousands of ordinary rains) rather than catastrophic (the effect of the greatest rain in a thousand years). For a few minutes a tree may retain a few millimetres of rainfall as a film of water on its leaves and twigs; if it retains more than 10 mm or so (as in an ice-storm) it collapses under the load. It may retain up to 20 mm in leaf-mould underneath. If there is a deluge, a fall of (let us say) 100 mm in two hours – the kind of rain that most Cretans experience three or four times in their lives – the tree can have little effect; if the deluge comes when the ground is already soaked by previous rains the tree might as well not be there.

We were privileged to be at Pakhyámmos (H) on 23 September 1986. For some days black clouds had been building up portentously on the Siteía Mountains; and then, as Noah would have said, 'the fountains of the great deep were broken up, and the windows of heaven were opened'. It rained a day and a half with the sort of rain which goes through an umbrella, or the canopy of a tree, as if it were not there. The dusty street became a river of blood. The dusty little river, down which no water had come for years, tore away the main road bridge, and great tamarisk trees sailed majestically down it and out to sea. Rifts in the cloud revealed curtains of water, far higher than Niagara, pouring straight over the cliffs around the gorge Há (H). Over 300 mm – half a year's average rain – fell within thirty-six hours. As with flash floods in Texas, the effects were localized, affecting an area 40 by 25 km.

This deluge produced its greatest effects at low altitudes. In gorges, juniper-woods, grown up since the previous deluge, were torn away. Well-rooted oleanders clung on, their bark and wood sandblasted away by sand- and rock-laden water tearing past. In

3.6 *Plough-marks around olive-trees, buried by a previous deluge and uncovered by a new one. Istron delta (Me), 28 September 1986*

cultivated basins, tree-trunks and debris were piled high against olive-trees. In the delta of the Istron river, flooded a metre deep, silt and gravel were deposited in some places; elsewhere, previous sediments were removed (exposing, in one spot, the marks of the plough which had been at work just before the last deluge had covered them (Figure 3.6)).

Most of the mayhem in the valleys was the recycling of deposits already in them. There was not much input of new sediment, apart from pine-trees, branches and the occasional vehicle. Rivers enlarged their beds sideways rather than downwards, causing slumps. Gravel washed down the rivers formed small bars at their mouths, which lasted a few days until a storm at sea removed them.

At intermediate elevations, all the mountain roads were destroyed. Tractors were immobile, but those farmers who had not thrown away their mules and donkeys went about their business almost as usual. Fields showed considerable sheet erosion, but only where newly ploughed. Old-fashioned terraces with dry-stone walls were knocked about, but only to a degree which a winter's work would repair. Even neglected terrace walls withstood the deluge surprisingly well.

The most potent agent of erosion turned out to be the bulldozer. Not only roads but newly-bulldozed fields were torn into gullies. The blood-red rivers came from a freshly-bulldozed area of red soil. Whole flights of new terraces, dug out in the all-too-prevalent fashion without retaining walls, melted away like glaciers in Hell (Figure 3.7).

Higher on the mountains, the degree of damage lessened. Sheets of water poured over roughland without disturbing the soil. Only much-trampled goat-paths were somewhat gullied.

A small pre-existing clayey badland, some forty years old, was not appreciably extended. Although the slopes are not vegetated, it is clearly approaching stability.

It is often claimed that heavy rain after fire is a particularly potent agent of erosion. It happened that a marl slope of about 30°, covered in undershrubs and shrubs, was burnt nine days before the deluge. We found afterwards that the ash and charcoal had been washed away, and there was some very slight gullying, but that was all. Neither then nor since has any appreciable sediment been caught by a roadside ditch which runs across the slope.

Such a deluge interrupted D. G. Hogarth's studies at Káto Zákro

3.7 *Bulldozed terraces, melted away by a deluge two days before. Gourniá (H), 28 September 1986*

(Si) on 14 May 1910. A wall of water emerged from the gorge, bearing 'gnarled planes and centenarian holm-oaks' and sweeping away terraces and olive-groves. On the next day 'all the ancient tangle of forest had vanished to the last shrub', the cattle and mills were no more, and the very bay had been filled with gravel.[13]

Deluges are rare but normal features of the Cretan environment. The sedimentation sequences in plains and deltas suggest that they have shifted more soil and bedrock than any other agency. Ours, though the biggest in that spot for at least seventy-five years, was not abnormal. It shifted table- or occasionally car-sized boulders; previous ones have shifted boulders as big as houses. The visitor should look for sandblasting scars on trees and bushes in gorges, and should work out, from the amount of regrowth since the damage, when the last deluge occurred. Debris caught in trees on cliffs will show how high the waters raged.

The only plants to confer any significant protection turned out to be the smallest, no more than 5 mm high: the lichens, mosses, liverworts, *Selaginella* and blue-green algae that encrust bare ground. (Sometimes, as on burnt ground, chemical crusts are effective.) These crusts were surprisingly strong, withstanding flowing water and even trundling boulders.

Conclusions

The variety of erosion in the Mediterranean defies generalisation. Erosion in Crete is not the same as in Epirus or North Carolina. On a historical time-scale, Crete is not very erodible. Observable erosion is determined by local peculiarities of geology and tectonics.

Most erosion in Crete is catastrophic rather than gradual; it depends on rare events. We have mentioned some types of catastrophe; there may be others which no living eye has seen. We cannot imagine what a thousand-year-maximum rain does, nor what happens if, for an hour, a Cretan gorge contains a river equal to the Mississippi, nor when a mud-flow bursts out over a plain.

Vegetation plays a relatively minor part in preventing erosion (except for wind erosion). The most important kind is not trees but moss and lichen crusts.[14] The absence of crusts makes ploughed land erodible; goats cause erosion chiefly by their hooves breaking up the crusts. Most surfaces in Crete crust easily; in erodible Rhodes and north-west Greece they do not.

Erosion is often thought of as destructive of soils and therefore of agriculture. However, most of the flatter, more easily cultivable soils on Crete were created by past erosion washing sediments off hillsides. Erosion control is not the only reason for making terraces (Chapter 12), and crops can be made to grow in broken-up bedrock as well as in soil.

Crete can be persuaded to erode by the vigorous application of the bulldozer. Roads are liable to gully themselves, and also to create other gullies by collecting water as it runs down a hillside, channelling it into places where Nature did not mean it to go. This effect is multiplied on hairpin bends. Roads cut into landslip-prone slopes encourage slumping; for example, the highway from Spíli (AV) to Tymbáki (Py), built in the 1970s, has ever since been under repair for one slump after another. Gullying is encouraged by bulldozing new fields, and especially by digging out new terraces and leaving them to stand up as best they may. Terrace walls were not built for fun, nor just to use up the stones.

Erosion in antiquity

Erosion was very active in Crete during the Pleistocene, long before there were human inhabitants. The great screes on the mountains, and most of the gravel and silt deposits in the plains, were formed then (Figure 3.8). We now see them much as they appeared to the Minoans.[15]

Deposits from within the period of human settlement are on an altogether smaller scale, more complex and more difficult to interpret. Claudio Vita-Finzi put forward the theory of the Younger Fill. He claimed (mainly on evidence from Africa) that erosion and

3.8 *The immense fault-scarp which forms the edge of the Ierápetra plain, bisected by the gorge Há. The screes below the cliffs are of Pleistocene date, and are mostly as hard as concrete. In front of the gorge are the hedged fields of Monastiráki (H). The grid of roads in the foreground is recent. September 1986*

deposition were not continuous throughout human history. There was a period, roughly AD 500 to 1500, in which rivers were bringing down material and laying down deposits in valleys and plains around much of the Mediterranean. He considered that this was a period when human activity was in recession; he decided (though not very strongly) that there had been a period of more erosion-promoting climate.[16]

More recent work challenges both the observation and the interpretation. Younger Fill (that is, deposits that contain potsherds) has been found elsewhere to be of a wider range of dates. In any one site it is strongly episodic, and sometimes seems to coincide with an expansion of human activity: for example Bronze Age activity has been proposed as a cause of the great sheet of alluvium which covered the plain of Tiryns in the Peloponnese.[17] As far as we know, however, it has nowhere (at least in Greece) been possible to connect a particular episode of past erosion with the expansion of a specific kind of human activity that is definitely known to promote erosion in a similar locality today.[18]

In Crete, Younger Fill is not everywhere present. The ruined Palace of Knossós was not covered by much more than its own debris. Buondelmonti visited many Roman sites where, in 1415, 'busts of idols and marble columns' still lay where they fell. But some plains have been covered over by deposits, which can be dated from buildings on them. The magnificent church of Aikyrgiánnis, between Alikianoú and Kouphós (Ky), is of three phases: one attributed to the eleventh century; an extension, also Byzantine; and an inserted Gothic doorway. The church, originally at ground level, is now three steps below ground. The original and the extension have been buried, but the Gothic threshold is at the present ground level. The extra material, which extends all over the surrounding plain, was therefore deposited between, roughly, AD 1200 and 1400.

Our observations on the plains of Khaniá, of Frangokástello (Sf), and around Vrókastro (Me) indicate deposits of great local variety. They agree in date neither with each other nor with the coming of agriculture. The known peak of human activity in the early twentieth century failed to produce such a deposit. They greatly exceed the deposition of the Pakhyámmos Deluge, even though that was assisted by mechanical de-stabilisation which ancient peoples would not have had. What is there that would produce such a colossal but sporadic effect? The answer may well be deluges even greater than that of 1986.

The question of human influence *versus* climate as the agency of Younger Fill is still open. The answer may be complex, varying from site to site, and not always demonstrable in terms of processes still going on. Cretan evidence is, on the whole, against the human theory. The climatic argument is usually presented in a gradualist form, as if a generally moister climate were capable of reviving erosion. Our own studies indicate that single, unrepeatable freak storms may be much more effective. What really matters is weather, not climate.

Special features

Karst: sinkholes, caves and underground rivers
Among the few hazards of Cretan travel are the crevasses and holes that riddle the limestone. They are made by the process of **karstification.** Normal rainwater is slightly acid; when it trickles over limestone it dissolves it. Any crack or depression, once started, collects water and tends to enlarge. On the surface this

3.9 *Karst hollows in the high limestone of the Madháres. July 1992*

produces, over millennia, a funnel-shaped sinkhole. Underground fissures enlarge into systems of channels and caverns on many levels, like a petrified Spaghetti Junction. These underground roadways direct the flow of groundwater.

The ceilings of some of these caverns gradually get thinner until they collapse, adding to the solution sinkholes that pock the Cretan landscape. A sinkhole can appear by this process overnight, perhaps swallowing a field.

In Crete, karst readily develops in crystalline limestones. The grandest examples are in the high White Mountains (Figure 3.9); the less energetic traveller will find beautiful sinkholes in the conglomerates around Khrysoskalítissa (Ki). Platey limestones, in which the original cracks run horizontally, less easily form karst (except at high elevations). Sinkholes can even form in phyllite as a result of collapses in underlying limestone (examples at Límni in Elos (Ki)).

Many karst caves are wonderful, labyrinthine chambers bristling with stalactites and curtained with calcite drapery. Some caves were sacred (Chapter 16). Some were hiding-holes in wartime; in 1823-24 there were dire massacres in the caves of Mílatos (Me) and Melidhóni (My).

Gorges

Crete is the land of a hundred gorges (Figures 0.3, 3.10 and Plate 4). They are part of the island's personality: the orange and grey of their walls, the wonderful plants which are found only in Cretan gorges, their great trees, the part which they play in legend and song, and the deeds of valour and blood enacted in them. Our favourite is the lush, winding, shadowy gorge of Thérisso (Ky), an afternoon's excursion from Khaniá, with endemic plants growing all over its walls as in a botanic garden. At the opposite extreme is the stern arid gorge behind the Kapsás Monastery (Si) in the south-eastern desert, a fit home for hermits. The Cretan word for gorge is *farángi*, carefully distinguished from *roúma*, *révma*, or *riáki*, 'ravine'.

Most gorges are in platey limestone or conglomerate. A typical gorge has sheer walls, with rock-screes (often cemented as hard as concrete) beneath them. Its floor is covered with nearly level

3.10 *Trypití Gorge (Sf). July 1992*

3.11 *Cave in the Ayiofárango ('Sacred Gorge', Ka), bisected by the formation of the gorge. The stalactites were presumably formed deep in the bowels of the cave. April 1982*

reaches of gravel, alternating with abrupt dams of boulders. The gravel-reaches and boulder-dams are rearranged whenever there is a deluge great enough. Gorges are old features, of at least Pleistocene age, as the cemented screes bear witness; the Minoans would have seen them almost exactly as we do. But they do not – or not all – go back to the geological beginnings of Crete. A narrow gorge, like Há, cuts through the rock-beds and their folds, which match exactly on the two sides. Some, like the Ayiofárango ('Sacred Gorge'), slice through caves, filled with stalactites like

teeth in sharks' mouths (Figure 3.11). The caves, folded rocks and stalactites are evidently older than the gorge. The average age of Cretan gorges is perhaps 2 million years.

How were the gorges made, and why has Crete so many? Earlier travellers thought such mighty chasms were created overnight by 'convulsions of nature'. Later science would have us believe that they are an erosion phenomenon, the result of rivers wearing away the rocks – they are merely ravines writ large. If gorges were cut by erosion, this happened long ago and is not continuing. Most gorges are partly choked with boulders, scree and gravel, and the rock bottom is hidden. Even deluges never reach the floor of the gorge, let alone cut into it, and so erosion must have happened in times of greater rainfall than now.

Erosion undoubtedly formed the gorges of rivers such as the Colorado and the Danube. But it fails to account for the multiple gorges in Crete, of all places – a narrow island which can never have had big rivers. Where are the catchments to collect the necessary water? Granted that when the gorges were formed the topography was different, how can each one – in Sphakiá there are fifteen parallel gorges in a distance of 35 km – ever have collected enough water?

The key to Cretan gorges is tectonics. In the uneven upheaving of the island, some rocks were put under tension and cracked as masonry does when stretched. The cracks have been enlarged sideways by erosion: by rivers, and by changes of temperature splitting off stones from the cliffs. We interpret the stupendously narrow gorge Há (H) (a thousand feet deep, and surely the world's biggest crack), at right angles to a huge fault-scarp, as an early stage in this process. At the other extreme, the gorge Khavgás, connecting the Katharó and Lassíthi Plains, has been so worn

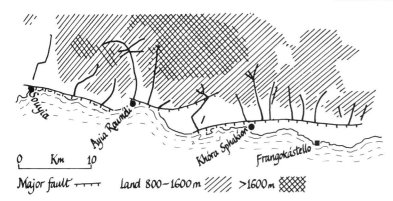

3.12 *Multiple gorges of Sphakiá, at right angles to the great fault-system which defines the very steep south coast. Simplified after Hempel*

down by later erosion as to have lost almost all title to being a gorge. The multiple gorges of Crete (Figure 3.12) have indeed originated in convulsions of nature, masked to a greater or lesser degree by later processes.

On this interpretation, gorges can form in any rock, but persist best in platey limestone and conglomerate, which are hard and sustain vertical cliffs. In crystalline limestone they widen through karstification and seldom last. In other rocks, gorges are quickly worn down by erosion, except for the hardest quartzites and for those soft limestones which have case-hardened.

Mountain-plains

These are another part of the personality of Crete. The biggest flat area in the island is the Lassíthi Plain (Figure 12.8), situated 850 m

up in the mountains; it is about 5 by 5 km, and is surrounded on all sides by higher mountains; it is very fertile and tilled with wheat and potatoes. This is the largest of about twenty-five such plains (Figures 0.3, 10.6), each of which plays its own part in the island's history and culture. Many have peculiar plants, such as *Polygonum idaeum* on the Nídha Plain (p. 57).

There seems to be no distinctive Cretan word for mountain-plain. Learned Greeks call them *oropédhi*, which also means 'plateau', which the mountain-plains certainly are not. Another technical term is **polje**, Croat for 'field', used for supposedly similar features in the Balkans. The Venetians called them *campagna*, which (like the Greek *kámpos*) is used for any flattish cultivable area. The Cretan word *lákkos* is used for smaller depressions up to about 0.5 km across.

Mountain-plains are all in limestone country, except that a few have phyllite on one side. They are floored, and partly filled, with various materials (Figure 3.13): some, like the Távri, are choked with scree; others, like the Omalós, have gravel deposits. The typical mountain-plain soil is a deep yellow-brown silt overlying red earth or limestone gravel; it is partly composed of impurities dissolved out of limestone, and partly of dust blown from outside Crete. All mountain-plains are filled almost to the brim: one never has to ascend more than 130 m from the floor of the plain to the lowest point on the rim.

Mountain-plains collect water from rain and snow-melt; the bigger ones have regular, seasonal rivers. The river of the Lassíthi disappears into a great cave, the *Khónos*, in the hillside at the north-west corner. With the other plains the water disappears into one or more swallow-holes in the floor. The Omalós has a formidable swallow-hole, a fearsome chasm among limestone boulders at the

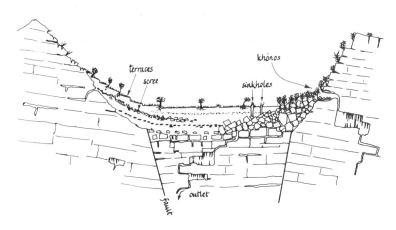

3.13 *Typical features of a mountain-plain, in section*

island's peculiar tectonic history. Like the gorges, they originated as tension features: as blocks of the earth's crust which subsided between faults, not unlike the Soúdha Bay graben.

Once initiated, a mountain-plain would collect rain water and snow-melt, which would enlarge it by dissolving the limestone, and would smooth its angular outline. The Omalós, for example, is now nearly circular but retains traces of its original triangular outline between three faults. Vegetation encouraged dissolution: dead leaves would rot, releasing organic acids which percolated down to attack the limestone.

The history of mountain-plains is a contest between enlarging processes and the tendency of basins to fill with scree, gravel, limestone residues and Saharan dust. The nature of the outlet will have varied, especially according to whether or not there was a suitable cave for a *khónos*. As recently as Venetian times, the *Khónos* of the Lassíthi was inadequate to drain off the water, and the Omalós was mapped as a lake. In recent decades, the swallow-hole of the Omalós has become more active; its gully extends and branches out into the plain, presumably because of changes which have reduced some blockage in the caverns beneath.

Fault-scarps
A **fault** is a line where one part of the earth's crust is, or has been, sliding past another. Most of the abrupt, straight edges of mountain massifs – the north side of the Frangokástello Plain, or the south-east side of the Ierápetra Plain (Figure 3.8) – are major faults. Lesser faults can appear fresh and newly-formed, with rock-faces that display details of the crushing and jamming which happen when an irresistible force meets an immovable object. Good examples are the faults which snake across the mountains west of

bottom of a gully cut through some 10 m of silt. There is also a big *khónos* cave at the north corner of the Omalós, but it is several metres above the floor of the plain and no longer functions. The sacred cave of Mount Ida (Psilorítis) may represent a former *khónos* of the Nídha Plain, and the sacred cave of Psykhró may be an earlier *khónos* of the Lassíthi. An unfortunate pussy-cat, we are told, was once cast into the main swallow-hole of the Askyphou Plain, and emerged in the great spring of Vrysses (Ap), 9 km away.

Mountain-plains are a speciality of Crete: the mainland does not have them in such profusion. They are a different phenomenon from the smaller sinkholes, even though we cannot draw a sharp line between the two; they are probably another aspect of the

Lastrós (Si), the cliffs across the bay from Plakiás (AV), or the smooth rock-faces around Mount Yúktas (T).

Geology and landscape

Hard limestones

The hard limestone cores of the four great massifs are often exposed right down to sea-level. Lest Cretan topography should be boring, lesser massifs of hard limestone protrude through the foothills of other rocks; most of these we interpret as small nappes. The most famous is the sacred mountain Yúktas (T). Others form the cores of the Kouloukoúnas and Asteroúsia Mountains, all the peninsulas and about half the islets. The most remarkable are the twenty or more isolated spikes of limestone which give a Chinese aspect to the landscape around Kalamávka (H).

Platey limestone is rugged with sharp, well-preserved gorges. It tends to be relatively well vegetated, because trees such as cypress can get their roots between the plates; plants such as pine, which depend on soil, are more limited to screes and lower slopes. On crystalline limestone, which is more karstified, soil gets washed into pockets and basins, where most of the vegetation, and nowadays most of the cultivation, occur.

Both kinds of limestone have a long history of settlement with major ancient sites (e.g. Káto Zákro (Si) on crystalline, Dréros (Me) on platey). Their lower slopes, where there is more soil, display great extents of former cultivation terraces.

Phyllite-quartzite

In west Crete, metamorphic rocks stretch from the limestone to the west coast, ending dramatically in two mountains of gypsum.

They often form a shallow, clayey, water-retaining soil, covered with maquis or low woodland of arbutus and tree-heather. This smooth dark green blanket, diversified by the triangular scars of pattern-burning (p. 118), covers the hills of far-west Crete except where the bulldozer has been at it in the hope of growing olives. Solid phyllite-quartzite, despite this verdure, is a difficult rock to cultivate: in most places cultivation is limited to lower slopes, where the rock has been broken up and redeposited.

There is a beautiful, regular pattern in the valleys. Rocky slopes are wooded, sometimes with a jungle of towering deciduous and evergreen oaks and occasional cypress above an understorey of arbutus and phillyrea, impenetrable with brambles and greenbrier. Where soil has accumulated there are flights of terraces with giant chestnuts, venerable olives and irrigated terrace-gardens. In dim, headlong, tangled ravines live strange, water-loving plants including primrose and royal fern. The bottom of every ravine has a ribbon of plane-trees, often extending far up into the hills. Here we see the ancient hamlet settlement pattern at its best (p. 89-92).

Phyllites and quartzites of lesser extent go with the other great massifs. The hills are not rugged, but the valleys are intricate and breakneck, occasionally turning into real quartzite gorges. The luxuriant vegetation of phyllite extends locally even to the otherwise arid Thryphtí Mountains.

But metamorphic rocks are not simple, and they have some of the most arid as well as some of the lushest vegetation in west Crete. There are few greater contrasts than between the heather-arbutus of Ay. Iréne (Se), on phyllite, and the arid quartzite, with only the occasional pear-tree, 2 km down the road at Apanokhóri (Se). In places the tall tree-heather maquis is reduced to a kind of heathland. The cause must lie in the environments which different metamorphics create for plant roots. Similar contrasts are repeated within the phyllite-quartzites all over Crete.

Phyllite-quartzite is not as easy a terrain in which to make a living as it looks. From the middle ages onwards it has supported many small settlements but not a dense population. Its archaeology is almost unknown. The apparent absence of sites does not mean that there are none: the dense leaf-litter and the brambles around every spring – and there are countless springs – make this the most difficult terrain to survey in all Crete.

In middle Crete much of what looks like phyllite-quartzite in the landscape (though without the lush green maquis) is *flysch*, a miscellaneous series of deposits that eroded from the mountains in the earlier stages of mountain-building and then were uplifted and folded in later stages.

Neogenes

Marls and marly sandstones of the Miocene or Pliocene are the most extensive rocks in lowland Crete. The harder forms stand out from the generally rounded landscape. A hard layer, overlying softer marl, may act as a cap-rock, forming a plateau with over-hanging edges – a characteristic land-form of Gávdhos (Se). Soft, clayey marls can erode locally into gullies, as around Knossós (T). Occasionally there are marl gorges, for example on the south side of the Akrotíri Peninsula.

Marl is not usually a good substrate for vegetation. Even the softer kinds are very compact, and plant roots cannot penetrate to get at the moisture which they hold. The natural vegetation of the marls in Monofátsi looks arid, with hardly any trees or shrubs except where a fissure or a boulder affords a little root-room. These desolate hills are clothed with undershrubs, whose shallow roots are adapted to making do with very little moisture. Occasionally, where not browsed, the hills are brought to life by the beautiful undershrub *Ebenus cretica*. In west Crete, marls are usually better vegetated and often have deciduous oak.

However, marl which has been reworked or shattered is less exacting, and is often colonised by pine in east Crete. Marl broken up by terracing is very good for vines and olives. (This is doubtless the reason for much ancient terracing, as well as for the modern Cretan fondness for bulldozing.) Most of the time, from Knossós onward, marls have supported the greatest density of population in Crete.

Conglomerates

Some conglomerates and breccias behave as hard limestone. A ridge of Miocene conglomerate contains an amazing series of gorges in the hills behind Kastélli Kissámou (Ki); another forms the outer part of the Thérisso Gorge (Ky). When the cliffs are coated with tufa, which hides the individual pebbles, these gorges look like hard limestone. However, breaches in the tufa crust allow pebbles to drop out from within, creating sharp-edged caverns. *Cavernous decay* – which happens in any rock which case-hardens – creates wonderful and surrealistic landscapes of ragged cliffs, especially in south-west Crete.

Less strongly cemented gravels, probably of Pleistocene date, comprise the 'red-beds' in the hills above Khaniá (Ky), with pebbles of phyllite and quartzite in a red matrix. Around Alikianoú (Ky) they form bizarre, steep little hills, thickly vegetated and eroded into peaks and spires.

Conglomerates can be among the least vegetated and most inhospitable rocks in Crete (as around Herákleion airport).

Red-beds are well wooded and have deciduous oak.

Alluvial basins

Much of the best land in Crete is in lowland plains such as the Mesará and at Alikianoú (Ky), Stylos (Ap), Mállia (Pe), and Kavoúsi (H). These are filled with silts and clays brought down by rivers, probably in the Pleistocene. Pits dug by builders into the Alikianoú basin reveal at least 8 m of clayey silts with occasional lenses of gravel. Similar deposits at Mállia are dated to the late Pleistocene.[19] Much of the material in both places seems to have been reworked during the Holocene.

Very little natural vegetation remains. A patch of meadow persists in the wettest part of the Alikianoú basin. The middle of the Mesará is still called *Livádha*, 'Meadow'. Remnants near Stylos (Ap) suggest that elmwood may have been prominent in the past.

Conclusion

The processes in this chapter have very different time-scales. Most of them are still going on. Mountain-building will certainly continue into the future, and erosion may or may not keep pace with it. The functioning of the landscape is now more complex than ever before, because in the last few decades human activities have been added to the other geologically significant processes.

Notes

1 J. Angelier (1979), 'Neotectonique de l'arc égéen', *Publications de la Société Géologique du Nord*, **3**, 418.

2 J. E. Meulenkamp (1977), 'The Aegean and the Messenian salinity crises', *VI Colloquium on the Geology of the Aegean Region III*, Athens, 1253-63.

3 N. Fytrolakis (1980), *Der Geologische Bau von Kreta*, Athens.

4 J. L. Mercier (1977), 'Principal results of a neotectonic study of the Aegean Arc and its localisation within the eastern Mediterranean', *VI Colloquium on the Geology of the Aegean Region III*, Athens, 1281-91.

5 G. Fabre and R. Maire (1982), 'Découverte de relief glaciaire dans l'île de Crète', *Comptes rendus de l'Académie des Sciences*, Paris, **sér. II 294**, 1135-7.

6 Y. and J. Thommeret et al. (1981), 'Late Holocene shoreline changes and seismo-tectonic displacements in western Crete', *Zeitschrift für Geomorphologie*, **NF suppl. 40**, 127-149; J. A. Moody and F. Lukermann (1985), 'Protohistory: the reconstructions of probable worlds', in N. C. Wilkie & W. D. E. Coulson (eds), *Contributions to Aegean Archaeology: studies in honor of William A. McDonald*, Minneapolis, University of Minnesota, pp. 61-89.

7 P. A. Pirazzoli (1986), 'The Early Byzantine Tectonic Paroxysm', *Zeitschrift für Geomorphologie*, **NF suppl. 62**, 32-49.

8 A. G. Galanopoulos (1977), *On the Difference in the Seismic Risk for Normal and Tall Structures at the Same Site*, Athens, University of Athens Seismological Laboratory.

9 N. Creutzburg et al. (1977), *General Geological Map of Greece; Crete Island*, Athens, Institute of Geology and Mineral Research; J. Bornovas and Th. Rondogianni-Tsimbaou (1983), *Geological map of Greece* (2nd ed.), Athens, Institute of Geology and Mineral Research.

10 The theory is eloquently if uncritically followed by J. R. McNeill (1992), *The Mountains of the Mediterranean World*, Cambridge, Cambridge University Press.

11 A famous example is C. V. Jacks and R. O. Whyte (1939), *The Rape of the Earth*, London, Faber.

12 *Critias*, 111.

13 D. G. Hogarth (1910), *Accidents of an Antiquary's Life*, London, Macmillan.

14 For a parallel in Spain see R. Alexander (1991), *Bulletin of the British Lichen Society*, **68**, 8.

15 L. Hempel (1991), *Forschungen zur Physischen Geographie der Insel Kreta im*

Quartär, Göttingen, Vandenhoeck & Ruprecht.

16 C. Vita-Finzi (1969), *The Mediterranean Valleys*, Cambridge, Cambridge University Press.

17 T. H. van Andel, E. Zangger and A. Demitrack (1990), 'Land use and erosion in prehistoric and historic Greece', *JFA*, **17**, 379-96.

18 The best attempt so far (though there are still missing links in the chain of argument) is perhaps that of E. Zangger (1992), 'Neolithic to present soil erosion in Greece', in J. Boardman and Martin Bell (eds.), *Past and Present Soil Erosion*, Oxford, Oxbow, pp. 133-47.

19 Hempel (1991, note 15).

4

Weather and water

[On Crete] Twelue daies the Greeks staid, ere they got them freed,
A gale so bitter blew out of the North,
That none could stand on earth . . .

Homer, *Odyssey,* XIX, 199-201

Since first I left the snowy hills of Crete . . .

Homer, *Odyssey,* XIX, 338

The present climate of Crete

Crete is thought of as a typical 'Mediterranean' land where the year is sharply divided. The rainy season of winter, warm and seldom frosty, is the time of activity and growth, while the dry season of summer is hot, arid, relentlessly sunny, and is the dead season.[1]

The new year opens with the hot and windless month of September. The rainy season begins abruptly in October, often with a small deluge – a joyous time that heralds the return of vegetation. After a lull in November, rainfall (and snow on the mountains) builds up to a peak in January. It declines gradually in spring and peters out in April or May, after which most plants wither away to their long summer sleep, but the vines keep growing.

So much for a typical season; but few seasons are typical. Crete is a miniature continent, and there are huge variations from place to place (Figure 4.1). In Venetian and Classical times the climate was not quite what it is now; the farther back we go, the less 'Mediterranean' it becomes.

Crete lies at the junction of four great weather systems. In summer it comes between the Azores High and the Indo-Persian Low. The interaction of these creates steady north-westerly winds, now called *meltémi,* anciently Etesian – which bring dry, sunny, often hazy weather. These winds are tempered and complicated by mountain winds, or by a daily alternation of land and sea breezes.

In winter, Crete lies between the North Atlantic Low and the high-pressure belt over south-west Asia and north Africa. Depressions arise around the low-pressure area and move

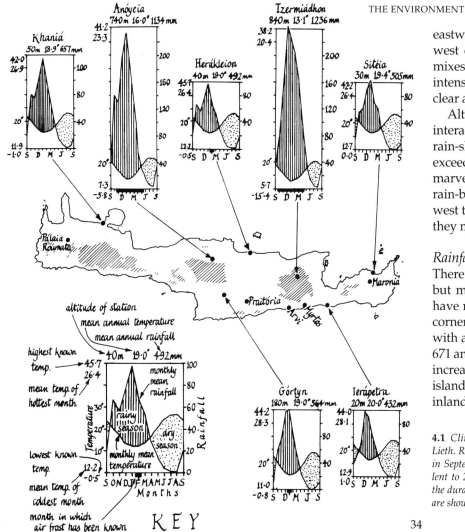

4.1 *Climatic diagrams for Crete, plotted according to the convention of Walter & Lieth. Rainfall and temperature are plotted round the year, month by month (beginning in September), on a common graph on which 10 degrees C of temperature are equivalent to 20 mm of rainfall. The excess of rainfall over temperature or vice versa marks the duration and intensity of the rainy and dry seasons. Other sites of climatic interest are shown.*

eastward over Crete; many of them originate over the stormy sea west of Crete, where cool, dry air off the European land-mass mixes with warm, moist air over the open sea.[2] Cloudy days and intense rain alternate with spells of brilliant sunshine and crystal-clear atmosphere.

Although the seasonal winds come from fixed directions, their interactions with the complicated mountains of Crete produce rain-shadows and rain-excesses throughout the island. This exceedingly diverse microclimate contributes to the island's marvellous variety in plant communities. In general, however, the rain-bearing west winds progressively drop their moisture from west to east – especially on the north slopes of the mountains – as they move across the island.

Rainfall

There have been at least eighty-five raingauge stations in Crete, but most of them have operated for less than twenty years; we have no records for mountains above 900 m, nor for the outlying corners of the island. The records range from Pálaia Roúmata (Ki), with an average of 1,429 mm per year, through Khaniá (Ky) with 671 and Herákleion (T) with 501, to Ierápetra (H) with 432. Rainfall increases regularly with altitude, decreases from west to east of the island, decreases from north to south, and increases from the coast inland (Figure 4.2). We estimate that rainfall (and snowfall) should

34

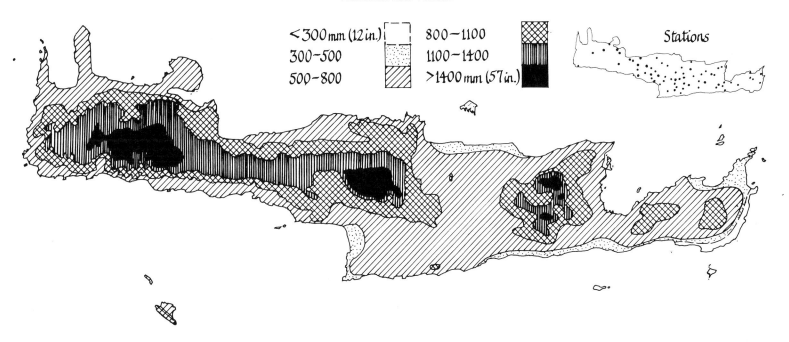

4.2 *Mean annual rainfall (including snow) for the period 1970 to 1982, estimated from the records of 65 stations*

reach nearly 2,000 mm at the top of the White Mountains; it should be about 240 mm in the south-east corner of Crete. (Both of these areas are deserts.) Crete has nearly as wide a range of rainfall as the United States. [3]

In wet places the rainy season begins earlier and ends later than in dry, although most of the difference is in the intensity of rainfall.

Showers have been known in July and August (disastrous for the raisins and currants), but the amount of out-of-season rainfall is negligible even at Pálaia Roúmata (Ky).

Rain varies from year to year. The season may begin as early as August or as late as December, and may end in January or run on into July. At Herákleion (T), where there are seventy years of records, the wettest year (September-August) was 1962-63, with 946 mm; the driest was 1950-51, with 229 mm. The rainfall in any one place can vary from well under half the long-term average to nearly twice the average. The year 1950-51 was disastrously dry all over Crete, and 1937-38 was very wet in most places; but there is a tendency for wet and dry years not to be the same everywhere. Even Siteía and Maroniá (Si), 7 km apart, have very different patterns. Places where crops have failed can sometimes be helped out by others that have fared better.

In dry areas, moisture may come from fog. The south-facing side of the Asteroúsia Mountains, which ought to be in a double rain-shadow, is wooded and has moisture-demanding vegetation. We suppose that these crags, plunging 1,000 m into the sea, intercept damp air and produce something like the cloud-forest on similar peaks in the Caribbean. A similar effect may explain why the island of Gávdhos (Se) is less arid-looking than the coast opposite.

Temperature

At Khaniá (Ky) the mean temperature ranges from 11.9°C (53.4°F) in January to 26.9°C (80.4°F) in July (roughly the difference between summer in north Scotland and in the middle United States). Inland places have hotter summers and cooler winters. The south coast tends to be a little warmer in winter and summer. Its winter warmth made it the refuge of a very impoverished species of visitor known as 'winter-hippies' (khimoniátichi khíppis).

Temperature in mountains normally falls by 6°C (11°F) for every 1,000 m ascended. In Crete the fall may be a little more rapid – Tzermiádhon, at 820 m on the Lassíthi Plain, has a mean of 5.7°C (42.2°F) in January and 20.4°C (68.7°F) in July. This may account in part for the compression of the vegetation zones on the mountains of Crete (p. 190).

Frost can occur everywhere, but in most lowland places even ground frost is rare (about one year in four at Khaniá (Ky)). Air frost does not occur every year even on the Lassíthi Plain. Frost is the chief constraint on olive-growing (p. 80). Some gorge plants, such as Origanum dictamnus and Hypericum amblycalyx, are quite frost-sensitive; these presumably have been preserved through frosty periods in prehistory by lurking in crevices where the rocks store heat.

Athens in summer can be a hell of humidity and smog in which, when the temperature goes above 40°C (104°F), people die in hundreds. We have known people to die of heat in southern Crete, but without pollution the danger is much less. Temperatures above 40°C have been recorded at most lowland stations, but not every year.

Local topography counts for much. High south-facing cliffs, like those behind the outdoor banana-groves of Arvi (V), radiate heat in summer and winter, while frost-hollows on still, starry nights form lakes of cold air. The highest and lowest temperatures regularly recorded in Crete are both from Praitória (Mo) in the Mesará: air frost occurs every year, and temperatures of 40°C occur roughly once in two years. This place is evidently a frost-hollow, and escapes the tempering influence of the sea.

The extreme temperatures that we have ourselves encountered were both in July: 42°C (108°F) at Myrtos (H) on 9 July 1968, and ground frost at Katsivéli (Sf) (at 1,950 m in the White Mountains) on 6 July 1992. The highest temperature ever recorded was 45.7°C (114.3°F) at Herákleion (T) in 1914; the lowest was -15.4°C (4.2°F) at Tzermiádhon (L) in 1966.

Wind

Crete is a windy island. We, like other travellers, have seen stones blown away; and we, like Homeric warriors, have been blown over by gusts.

Wind makes the Cretan summer tolerable for northern visitors, especially near the coast. At other times, wind limits the growth of trees by the coast and in the high mountains, pruning them into characteristic shapes. Cypresses in mountain passes grow into a flag-like shape pointing away from the north. On the exposed north side the foliage and even bark are scoured away, probably by flying ice-spicules in some unimaginably terrible storm. (Because they have so much root, Cretan trees rarely blow down.)

North to north-west winds prevail all the year, but are most constant in summer. The Venetians referred to the windward and leeward sides of the island. Local topography makes the details complex. For example, at Myrtos (H) there is often a south day-wind during the summer, which gives way soon after midnight to a strong, gusty land-breeze roaring down from the mountains. Measurements confirm this complexity. North-west winds prevail at Siteía (Si) throughout the year, whereas Khaniá (Ky) has no predominant wind direction.[4]

The *sirócco* or south-easter, blowing off the Sahara mainly in spring and autumn, can bring intense heat. We have known its gusts to fling open a locked iron door. In 1992 an autumn *sirócco*, like the blast of a furnace, drove a fire which consumed several townships in upper Apokórona; the fire, though in only moderately combustible vegetation, leapt across gorges.

Snow

In winter the mountains above 1,400 m glitter with snow. On the High Desert several metres must fall each year, but rain is probably rare. The snow usually melts in May; the melt-water immediately disappears into the porous limestone, which is why this is a desert. Occasional flecks remain until August in sunless places, for example opposite the Xylóskala at the top of the Samariá Gorge (Sf). At sea-level snow falls only about once in ten years, and seldom lies.

In the very snowy winter of 1992, a metre of snow fell at quite low altitudes; the weight broke boughs off olives and deciduous oaks, and occasionally pushed olive-trees off cliffs. In July, our expedition through the High Desert was hindered by snow, which our pack-animal refused to cross, and it was clear that some snow would remain at least until August. Very unexpectedly, most snow-patches were not in the shade but on south-facing slopes.

Humidity

Crete is very evaporative. In summer the heat, dry atmosphere, strong wind and cloudless skies make life difficult for any plant that is not irrigated, or provided with ground water (like a plane-tree), or very deep-rooted. Some plants like prickly-oak conserve water efficiently, but most shut down and await the rains.[5] Near the coast, humidity can be stifling on windless days; it is noticeably less only a kilometre or two inland.

In the south-east fringe of Crete the relative humidity can go as low as 20 per cent. Should the temperature be in the forties (over 100°F), the sirocco blowing, and the cisterns empty, the traveller is in trouble – as has happened to us more than once.

Dust

Late in the rainy season, the atmosphere becomes unusually murky during a sirocco, and it then rains mud. This *kokkinovrokhí* (red rain) leaves a red deposit on newly-whitewashed houses and turns mountain snow pink.

The red material is dust, picked up in the Algerian Sahara, and blown by weather systems to Crete. Over thousands of years, Cretan soils have gained dust at the rate of at least 1 mm a century. This may in part explain why Crete is so unexpectedly fertile – the minerals in the ground being topped up from an outside source.[6]

Changes within this century
For the five places for which there are long-term records (Herákleion (T), Khaniá (Ky), Anóyeia (My), Ierápetra (H), Siteía (Si)), changes are not very great nor very consistent. The 1920s were about 1°C warmer than the 1980s and about 10 per cent wetter. There has been a gradual cooling, most marked in autumn. Rainfall was low in the 1930s, rising to a peak in the 1960s and again in the 1970s, and falling in the 1980s. All these changes are small compared with the fluctuations from one year to the next.

There is, as yet, no sign that global warming has had any effect on Crete. If it occurs it is believed to operate mainly at night,[7] and so will escape detection in Crete, where it is not the custom to record night temperatures.

Greece and Crete have a reputation for unusually clear atmospheres and brilliant light: writers venture to suggest that this is why Ancient Greek philosophers were so clear-headed. In our experience this is now true only sometimes in winter and spring; in summer the sky is usually hazy. This is unlikely to be due (as in Athens) to pollution, as pollution-sensitive lichens still flourish. We cannot say whether there has been a real change, or whether the reputation was a factoid, repeated from author to author without being verified.

Climate history

There is a belief that the climate of a region can be altered by activities such as deforestation or agriculture. Whether there is any truth in this (recent research has failed to confirm it) it is most unlikely to operate in a narrow, windy, mountainous island. The Cretan climate is part of the global scene, imposed from outside, and nothing Cretans can do will affect it.

Late Pleistocene
Crete has not always had a 'Mediterranean' climate. In the Pleistocene, although the ice-sheets of the glaciations never came near Crete, climatic changes had their effects. Their consequences can be seen in the huge screes and gravel deposits on and around the mountains, which cover about one-third of the island. During the glacial periods erosion took place on a far larger scale than now; this implies the action of frost and of great deluges.

Ludwig Hempel has dated some of these deposits. In the lowlands, it appears that the most active erosion was during the latest (Weichsel) glaciation, whereas at higher altitudes the previous (Saale) glaciation is most conspicuous. For example, the big gravel-fan on the south side of the Omalós Plain has a most probable age of 180,000 years, with numerous stages of reworking. This is somewhat paradoxical. In the mountains the Saale was undoubtedly severe, with small glaciers on Psilorítis; at low elevations its effects may have been masked by the deposits being reworked in Weichselian times.[8]

A limit is set to the possible severity of the glacial climate by frost-sensitive endemic plants, such as the Cretan palm. The glaciations cannot have been so severe as to exterminate them altogether.

Early Holocene (12,000–6000 BC)
The climatic history of this period is inferred mainly from the vegetation record in pollen deposits on mainland Greece. There is (so far) very little of a pollen record on Crete before human settlement, but what exists confirms this story.

As we shall see (Chapter 11), Crete and Greece were distinctly less arid than they are now: not wet enough for continuous forest, but with more extensive trees, including less drought-resistant species. Although some of the differences are due to the effects of civilisation, others (such as the complete disappearance of alder and lime) can only be explained by a change of climate. The climate then was wetter and probably less strongly seasonal than today. In Crete lime (basswood) and olive grew side by side; to see them growing together now we have had to go 500 km north to the Acheron gorge in Epirus.

The change to a 'Mediterranean' climate seems to have developed gradually during the Bronze Age, being completed by the middle of the first millennium BC.

Greek and Roman
Ancient authors could not measure climate and rarely tell us about it. Crete was known as a stormy area: such storms were experienced by Odysseus[9] and St Paul as they were by Raulin, the nineteenth-century traveller (and by President Reagan and Mr Gorbachev at a shipboard meeting not far away in 1989). We ourselves have been storm-bound on Gávdhos.

One of the few definite impressions given by ancient mainland authors is that winter snow was less rare in inhabited places than it is today. Xenophon, in his book on hunting, expected to go out after hare or boar in snow.

Crete is one of the very few places where an ancient author mentions a change of climate within the Graeco-Roman period. Theophrastus states:

> The Cretans among others say that nowadays the winters are more severe and more snow falls, adducing as evidence that the mountains were settled in olden times and bore grain and [tree-]fruit as the land was planted and tilled. For there are extensive plains among the mountains of Ida and in the other mountains, none of which are worked now because they do not bear. Whereas in those days . . . they were settled . . . because then the rains were generous, and wintry weather did not often occur.
>
> *On Winds* [10]

This implies that winters had become more severe in the fourth century than previously. The remarks seem to apply to the Nídha Plain (My), well above the present limit of settlement, and probably also to the Lassíthi and Omalós Plains. In Lassíthi (the only one fully investigated archaeologically) there is indeed a decline in the number of settlements at this time, although other explanations are possible (p. 95).

Venetian and Turkish – the Little Ice Age
Dr Jean Grove has collected much information about the impact on Crete of the Little Ice Age. In north and middle Europe this was a cold period of some 300 years, the coldest decades being the 1590s and 1690s. Here it was a time of violent weather fluctuations, which appear in Venetian and Turkish records:

... in November it was hotter than August and now [January 1586] it is still hotter than March and there was no rain until [1 November]. There was therefore great fear about because until that time they had not yet begun to sow, an extraordinary thing in this climate ... everyone will die of hunger ... Wheat costs 6 *lire* the *mouzouri*, an extraordinary thing; in other years it cost 3. There is no meat to be found because from the past drought the animals died of starvation; usually they are always kept in the country where all winter they eat the grass that grows with the October rains. But until now everything has been parched; there is no grass to be seen except when it sprouts through the earth now and then.

Letter by Onorio Belli [11]

There were also frequent deluges, which destroyed buildings. The years 1569-96 and 1683-96 stand out for combinations of heat, cold, drought and excessive rain.[12]

The Little Ice Age was probably a time of greater average rainfall. There was a trade in snow from the White Mountains for cooling drinks, which suggests that a snowy winter like that of 1992

4.3 *Perennial rivers reaching the sea in 1625, 1847 and 1990*

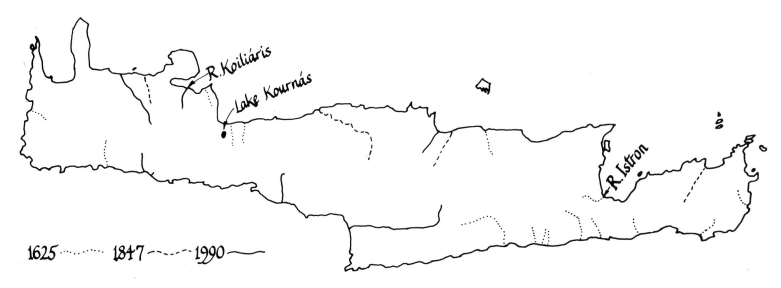

was then normal, and there were many more permanent rivers than today (see below). The Lassíthi Plain was difficult to cultivate because of flooding, which is no longer a problem (p. 150).

The Little Ice Age may be the only well-established climatic fluctuation in the historic period, but it came at a time of very good documentation. It is a fallacy to assume (as most scholars do) that the climate remained constant at other periods when little was being written down.

Water

> Where Alph, the sacred river, ran
> Through caverns measureless to man
> Down to a sunless sea.
>
> Samuel Coleridge, *Kubla Khan* (1816)

Of the moisture (rain, snow-melt, fog) that falls on Crete, some evaporates from soil or is transpired back into the atmosphere by vegetation; some runs off in rivers and streams. The greater part percolates into the rocks, especially into the fissures which riddle the hard limestone. Here it may come back to the surface as springs, or go right down to mingle with the sea.

Cretans are particular about their water. They use springs wherever possible; countless settlement sites are determined by a spring. Rivers are unimportant except to fish and passing ships. Where there are no springs, rainwater from house roofs is stored in *cisterns*, underground tanks lined with waterproof plaster. Many Roman buildings relied on cisterns, as do most houses today in the springless district of Sphakiá. Wells are a poor third choice.

Rivers

The visitor to Crete soon learns that *pótamos*, 'river', does not imply a permanent or even seasonal stream. There are only about ten rivers which reach the sea year-round; most of these arise from a great spring not far inland, for example the Koiliáris river (Ap) from the springs of Stylos. The countless other streams which dissect the Cretan mountains flow in winter, and often not even then: we have never seen water in any river on the Akrotíri Peninsula. When water does flow the consequences can be tremendous.

Crete has not always been so. In Venice there is a list, dating from 1625, of rivers 'abounding in good water'.[13] The Venetians were interested because galleys carried huge crews and needed to fill up their drinking-water every few days; they operated mainly in late summer, when rivers were at their lowest. Nevertheless, the list names twenty-eight rivers (including six in the arid east of the island), only four of which abound in good water today (Figure 4.3).

Why do these rivers no longer flow? Partly because modern irrigation works have drunk them dry; this is not the whole explanation, since Raulin, who visited Crete in 1847, included only five of the twenty-eight in his list of rivers which reached the sea all the year. Europeans like to think that forests and wild vegetation (although they themselves evaporate water) promote the year-round flow of watercourses.[14] Texans claim that an increase of woodland (especially juniper) reduces the flow of springs. Pliny, the Roman naturalist, believed that cutting down trees increased the flow, and illustrated it with a Cretan example.[15] In Crete, forests and wild vegetation, though they diminished down to Raulin's time, are now better developed than they were in 1625. However, the greater flow of rivers in the seventeenth century was probably dominated by the effect of the Little Ice Age on rainfall.

Springs

To form a spring requires an **aquifer** – a porous, water-bearing rock fed by percolating rainwater – and a **barrier** which prevents the water from percolating further. In Crete, the best aquifers are hard limestone, conglomerate and gravels. Barriers can be formed by impermeable marls and shales, or by geological faults, or by the sea. Most of the great springs of Crete, such as the three at Ayiá (Ky) which supply the drinking water of Khaniá, are formed where underground rivers are interrupted by fault-planes.[16]

These words are written at Boutsounária (Ky), where water bursts out of a mountainside dripping with sedges and maidenhair fern beneath enormous plane-trees around a ruined Venetian palace. In the sixteenth century this was the source of the Khaniá aqueduct. The seventeenth-century writer Boschini describes the palace and its marvellous water-gardens, 'of truly royal and imperial grandeur'.[17] Another beautiful perennial spring is at Argyroúpolis (R), a place thought to be the ancient city of Láppa, which flows out of a conglomerate cliff inside a small chapel. Ruins of a Roman aqueduct and more recent mills can be seen below, and lush vegetation with taro and many aquatic plants. Except for the plane-trees, it reminds us of Homer's spring:

> . . . a Fount they reacht,
> From whence the Towne their choisest water fetcht,
> That euer ouer-flow'd; and curious Art
> Was shewne about it . . .

> . . . It had a Sphere*
> Of poplar, that ranne round about the wall;
> And into it, a lofty Rocke let fall,
> Continuall supply of coole clear streame . . .
>
> *Odyssey*, XVII, 204-10

* border

Another famous source, *Evlogía Kyriou* ('Praise the Lord'), bursts out sideways from the cemented screes in the otherwise arid Kourtaliótic Gorge (AV). St Nicholas the Kourtaliote smote the rock with his staff like Moses, and seven springs gushed out, and there they are.

Large limestone massifs, lacking barriers, have few, weak springs which, nevertheless, are very important to shepherds. These tend to occur where two kinds of limestone join: for example, the spring Linoséli above the Samariá Gorge (Sf).

Phyllite-quartzite hills are full of small, perennial springs and seeps. Phyllites and shales are clayey and porous, but not necessarily very permeable; if fractured, they can become moderate aquifers.[18] Phyllites are interbedded with quartzites, which form good aquifers. This structure results in constantly dripping but seldom gushing springs.

Crete is famous for its *almyroí*, brackish springs arising inland. The biggest are the Almyrós at Georgioúpolis (Ap) and the one at Gázi (T). Sea-water evidently diffuses into the caves which supply the springs. Small freshwater springs occur all round the coasts, wherever an aquifer meets the sea.

Another Cretan curiosity are undersea springs, especially along the south coast from Khrysoskalítissa (Ki) to Khóra Sphakíon (Sf). Fresh water rises to the surface and is drunk by passing fishermen.

Swimmers notice them as patches of icy, slightly oily-looking water in an otherwise warm, clear sea.

Lakes and wetlands

The only sizeable lake in Crete is Lake Kournás (Ap) – set dramatically at the north foot of the White Mountains, in a landscape which Edward Lear called 'Cumberlandish'.

Variations on *límni*, 'lake', are fairly common place-names. They usually refer to karst depressions that seasonally hold water, or were thought to have held water once. Only a few contain water year-round. The most notable are two near the hamlet of Límni in Elos (Ki), and one (with a pollen deposit) at Límnes near Tersaná (Ak). The seasonally-wet sinkhole, Límni Kephála in Stylos (Ap), has good semi-aquatic vegetation.

Fens are more common than visitors might think. Cretans, like most Europeans, fail to appreciate wetlands and try to destroy them. The survivors are small (a hectare or two), fed by springs, tucked away in seldom-visited ravines (even on the islet of Gávdhos (Se)) or perched on a dry hillslope (e.g. near Pyrgos (Mo)). Some of the best are around coastal springs, for example the fens below the cliffs at Frangokástello, a colourful oasis in an otherwise arid landscape. A more extensive survival is in the northwest corner of the Alikianoú basin, near Kouphós (Ky); although damaged by drainage, it still has some beautiful fen vegetation. Words for fen – *élos, váltos, vlátos* – rarely enter into place-names.

There is one good peat-bog known in Crete, high in the eastern White Mountains above Así Goniá (Ap). Samples taken from the bottom of the peat show that the bog was formed in the Early Byzantine, possibly as the result of a landslip (maybe set off by the Early Byzantine Paroxysm (p. 131)). Until recently it contained the only sphagnum moss known in Europe south of Albania.

Salt-marshes are scattered round Cretan coasts – even at the southernmost point in Europe on the tip of Gávdhos (Se). One of the best, the Aposelémi river-delta, survives miraculously among the hotels east of Herákleion.

Wells

Wells – shafts sunk down to a water-table in an aquifer which does not reach the surface – are commonest in coastal districts and mountain-plains. On the Lassíthi Plain are thousands of wells each of which, until recently, had a cloth-sailed windmill raising water for irrigation from some 3 m down. Similar pumps still operate near Ierápetra. These wind-pumps were introduced in the 1920s, a hybrid of Greek and American technology.[19] Previously there had been dipping-wells, once widespread in Europe, where a pole is pivoted unequally on a forked post, with a bucket on the long arm and a counterweight on the short arm. Dipping-wells are still used on the Katharó Plain (Me). Their name *geráni*, 'crane', is that of at least two villages.

Most shores, even on waterless islets, have wells. Their contents are often brackish or contaminated by gypsum, but may serve for watering gardens. Many wells (and springs) have dried up; Mrs Rachel Hood says that none of the ancient wells excavated around Knossós (T) now contains water. There are two, possibly three, main causes. Recent irrigation schemes have drawn water from the aquifers, caring little for the effects on local hydrology. The hydrology itself may have changed due to tectonic movements in the bedrock. The wells may have been dug at a time of higher rainfall.

Disused wells and cisterns are often hard to see: shepherds block the mouths with spiny but flimsy branches in the hope of keeping animals from falling in. The bones of sheep, goats and donkeys fill many such pitfalls.

Town water supplies

The Romans built many aqueducts, but they were difficult to maintain against earthquakes and flash floods, and later fell into disrepair. Those of Eléutherna (My), Khersónisos (Pe), Górtyn (Ka), and Soúyia (Se) can still be seen.

Khaniá and Herákleion again acquired aqueducts in the sixteenth century. The Herákleion aqueduct, the plans for which are preserved in Venice, went about 18 km into the hills. It was taken over by the Turks (who as Muslims were required to wash) and maintained until the liberation of Crete. The most conspicuous part is a great Gothic arch at Knossós (T), probably an Egyptian work of the 1830s.[20]

Herákleion (T) is the most difficult place for water in Crete. Its aqueducts were supplemented by cisterns and by thousands of wells, often mentioned in seventeenth-century property conveyances. Their contents, easily contaminated by sewage and salt, were probably used for watering gardens; drinking water was normally fetched from the public well called Katsambás, 1 km outside the walls. Water supplies are still difficult: in the 1980s the Knossós road was thronged with tanker trucks going to and from the great spring at Arkhánes (T).

Notes

1 This chapter is a summary of our analysis in *Crete and the South Ægean Islands*, forthcoming in Petromarula, **2**. For many of the data we are indebted to the Agricultural Service in Herákleion. See also: P. I. Pennas (Π. Ι. Πέννα) (1977), *To Κλήμα τής Κρήτης*, Ph.D. dissertation, Thessaloníki; D. A. Metaxas (1992), 'Climatic fluctuations in Crete during the twentieth century', *Petromarula*, **1**, 21-4.

2 T. M. L. Wigley and G. Farmer (1982), 'Climate in the eastern Mediterranean and Near East', in J. L. Bintliff & W. van Zeist (eds.), *Palaeoclimate, Palaeoenvironment and Human Communities in the Eastern Mediterranean Region in Late Prehistory*, British Archaeological Reports International Series, **133**, pp. 3-37.

3 H. Walter and H. Lieth (1960), *Klimadiagramm-Weltatlas*, Jena, Fischer.

4 Pennas (1977, note 1), chapter 6.

5 Rackham (1972, see bibliography).

6 Z. Antonojiannakis (1992), 'Dust deposition around Crete', *Petromarula*, **1**, 70-3; K. Pye (1993), 'Aeolian dust transport over Crete and adjacent parts of the Mediterranean sea', *Petromarula*, **2**, forthcoming.

7 C. Tickell (1993), 'The human species: a suicidal success', *Geographical Journal*, **159**, 219-26.

8 Hempel (1991, Chapter 3, note 15).

9 *Odyssey*, XIV, 298-315.

10 Translation revised after V. Coutant and V. L. Eichenlaub.

11 Biblioteca Ambrosiana, Milan: MS 122 c. 391-2.

12 J. M. Grove (1992), 'Climatic reconstruction in the eastern Mediterranean with particular reference to Crete', *Petromarula*, **1**, 16-20.

13 BMV: Ital. 340/5750.

14 The complexity and lack of knowledge of the true situation are pointed out by M. D. Newson and I. R. Calder (1989), 'Forests and water resources: problems of prediction on a regional scale', *Philosophical Transactions of the Royal Society*, **B324**, 283-98.

15 *Natural History*, XXXI, xxx, 53.

16 E. D'Assiras (1992), 'Aquifers and irrigation water in the Khaniá area', *Petromarula*, **1**, 68-9.

17 BNP: Ital. 383.

18 H. L. Levin (1981), *Contemporary Physical Geology*, Philadelphia, Saunders College, pp.460-2.

19 Allbaugh (see bibliography).

20 S. G. Spanakis (Σ. Γ. Σπανάκη) (1981), *Ὑδρεύση τοῦ Ἡράκλειου 828-1939*, Herákleion.

5

Wild animals

The high hills are a refuge for the wild goats: and so are the stony rocks for the conies.
Psalm 104,18

Who hath sent out the wild ass free? or who hath loosed the bands of the wild ass?
Whose house I [the Lord] have made the wilderness, and the salt places his dwellings . . .
The range of the mountains is his pasture, and he searcheth after every green thing.
Job 39, 5-8

Extant mammals

Distant islands, like Crete, have odd zoological histories, with peculiar animals and missing animals. Crete has never had wild cattle, wild pig, or any beast fiercer than a badger or cat.

The agrími
One of the symbols of Crete is the wild goat, *agrími* or *kri-kri* (*Capra aegagrus creticus*). The *agrími*, bigger than a domestic goat, is admired for its magnificent horns, its nimbleness on cliffs and its ability to vanish into the mountain vastness. Travellers often confused it with the Alpine ibex. Within the last century it was found in all the high mountains, but hunting with rifles then restricted it to the White Mountains. It was the first objective of modern conservation on Crete. In the 1920s this took the form of moving some of the animals to three islets. Conservation of *agrími* was one of the reasons for setting up the Samariá National Park in 1962.

Apart from one early and vague report which may be due to confusion with dwarf deer,[1] there are no Pleistocene goat remains on Crete. This indicates that the animal was not indigenous. The first secure find is in the Bronze Age,[2] which suggests that the *agrími* was introduced to Crete by the Minoans. Marvellously-horned goats leap all over Minoan art, and there is little doubt that they were a Cretan speciality. Although the Minoans could have introduced it to Crete for hunting, it is more likely that the *agrími* is a *feral* animal descended from herded livestock. Since their introduction in the Neolithic, goats have had many opportunities to escape and set up independent populations, which would diverge from the original stock in the gradual course of evolution.

The *agrímia* of the Samariá Gorge (Sf) seem to prosper; they are spreading in the White Mountains, and we have reports from other parts of Crete. It is feared that their genes may become diluted through breeding with modern domestic goats, but if this were a real threat it would surely already have happened centuries ago. The island exiles survive but do not prosper: a small, low, waterless islet is not a good habitat for a mountain animal. They are disastrous for the islets' vegetation, devouring *Centaurea diae,* one of the world's rarest plants.[3]

Other mammals

Mammals native to Crete, as demonstrated from Pleistocene finds, include badger, marten, fat-dormouse and several species of bat. The Cretan badger is gregarious, like the European, but is smaller and is often regarded as a peculiar subspecies; so is the Cretan fat-dormouse. The marten is the commonest carnivore, doing duty for the absent fox and stoat.

The Cretan wildcat is an elusive and mysterious animal, sometimes regarded as a separate species, *Felis agrius*.[4] We have never seen it, but shepherds and hunters speak of it; our nights in the depths of the Samariá Gorge were enlivened by the squalling of cats. The wildcat (not the ancestor of domestic cats) is native all over mainland Europe, and is found in Upper Palaeolithic deposits in the Franchthí Cave in Greece.[5] The earliest known cat remains on Crete are probably domestic cat, from a mixed Bronze Age and Roman level at Knossós (T).[6] Cats appear in Minoan frescoes and on sealstones, along with blue monkeys, lions, griffins, and other exotic beasts. The Cretan wildcat seems to be a feral derivative of the domestic cat.

The same process of naturalisation can be seen beginning in the wild asses well established on the Gramboúsa Peninsula (Ki).

Beasts with no fossil record include hare, hedgehog and weasel; these may have been introduced. The hedgehog is sometimes regarded as a Cretan subspecies. The rabbit, undoubtedly an introduction, is peculiar to offshore islets (Chapter 19). Crete, like the rest of Europe, probably acquired the mouse in early historic times and the rat in the Roman period. A small rat, perhaps a variant of the plague-bearing 'black' rat, is a frequent visitor to village houses.

As in ancient times, hunters in Crete pursue mainly hare, but also occasionally badger, marten and hedgehog.

The monk seal (*Monachus monachus*), now nearly extinct, still frequents rocky coasts.[7]

Lost mammals

The original mammals of Crete were quite different from these. In the Pleistocene there have been at least seven species of deer, ranging from the size of a small dog to one taller than any known mainland deer.[8] More bizarre beasts included an elephant the size of a bullock (*Elephas creticus*), a pig-sized hippopotamus (*Hippopotamus* creutzburgi), giant rodents (Kritimys species) and giant insecti-vores.[9] These coexisted with marten, badger, a sort of otter and various mice and shrews, but no large carnivores.[10]

The ancestors of these animals (all of them present in Europe) presumably reached Crete unwillingly by swimming or on drifting logs. This happened very rarely, otherwise they would not have given rise to new, diverging species. It was, however, a repeatable process, since other large Mediterranean islands had similar bizarre faunas. (The alternative theory, that the animals walked across a land connection, fails to explain why none of the islands ever had large carnivores or wild pigs.[11]) The majority of the fauna had arrived by the Middle Pleistocene.

Most Mediterranean island mammals were dwarfed (deer, elephant, hippo), but occasionally they were larger than usual (rodents, insectivores). Unusual sizes were evidently adaptations to island environments.[12] Lack of predators seems to have been the major factor: the small size of the big mammals would be an adap-tation to eking out the food supply in a world without enemies. On the other hand, larger rodents and insectivores, which no longer needed to escape into holes and cracks, might be favoured over smaller individuals because they could compete more successfully.

Cretan animals adapted in other respects to life in a mountain-ous land where there was nothing to run away from. The dwarf deer exhibit shortening and broadening of their forelegs and fusion of metacarpals, comparable to what happens in the Alpine ibex and in the most mountain-living of deer. It is claimed that such adaptations would have improved the animal's jumping but reduced its ability to run.[13] The hippopotamus was a non-aquatic, long-legged, mountaineering little hippo, with a life-style like a leaf-eating pig.[14]

The detailed history of these animals is difficult to work out because most of the remains are from cave deposits, which are notoriously difficult to date. Finds are chiefly single bones rather than complete skeletons, and do not span a long period in any one cave. The 'Simonelli Cave', on the coast west of Rethymnon, has been dated stratigraphically to within the last glaciation, 19-22,000 years ago. It contains dwarf deer, dwarf elephant, marten, badger, White-fronted Goose, gannet, a gigantic little-owl, and a tortoise and a lizard. The classic hippopotamus site in the Katharó Plain, 1,100 m above sea-level, has been radiocarbon dated to c. 10,000 bc. Dwarf deer were the most abundant towards the end of the Pleistocene, the larger ones having died out.

Bones of fallow and red deer have been recognised in several Minoan deposits; fallow deer occur up to Late Roman, and Pliny says there were deer in west Crete in the first century BC.[15] Assuming that all these are correct records (not confused with surviving or fossil native Cretan deer), this implies that red and fallow deer were introduced to Crete in the Late Neolithic or Early Minoan (as fallow deer were later brought to other European countries[16]) and persisted until Late Roman times.

What happened to the peculiar mammals?

Successive glaciations and interglacials would have resulted in substantial, but not overwhelming, changes in the environment of these animals.[17] At least the deer and hippopotamus can be shown to have survived up to the last glaciation, but only a shrew (Crocidura caneae) and the spiny-mouse (Acomys minous) survive today. What happened to the others?

On Cyprus and Sardinia the bones of peculiar mammals are found together with the earliest human artefacts, but this cannot be proved in Crete: no deer or hippopotamus bones have yet been identified in any Neolithic deposit on the island. But people were capable of getting to Crete from at least the tenth century BC, little later than the last datable record of the endemic mammals. The most plausible cause of their extermination is explorers or settlers; but which?

Lax and Strasser argue in favour of spreading cultivation and habitat destruction as the agency, but we are not convinced. Cretan mammals were certainly very vulnerable to hunting (or to people walking up to them and wringing their necks), but they seem not to have been specialised nor particularly vulnerable to habitat destruction. Even in the Early Bronze Age there would have been plenty of habitat remaining; and if their demise had been so late their bones ought to be found with human artefacts. But if Mesolithic obsidian trips to Melos were combined with hunting trips to Crete, the large beasts could have gone before there was any settlement that left an archaeological record. The irruption of man and man's henchmen (especially the dog) into a world of edible animals that could not even run away would have been as catastrophic in Crete as it was later in New Zealand and Mauritius.

Birds

The birds of Crete are grander than the surviving beasts. Many a time our only companion in some waterless gorge has been a monstrous vulture, bigger than ourselves, floating effortlessly past ('Aren't you dead yet?'). The high mountains are one of the last strongholds in Europe of the Lämmergeyer or Bearded Vulture and the Griffon Vulture, and other great birds of prey such as Golden and Bonelli's Eagles.

Crete is within flying range of the mainland; it is on a major migration route, and receives winter visitors. Modern birds include a variety of warblers and shrikes. Crested Lark, finches and serins dart among olive-trees, and swifts and martins soar from high walls and cliffs. Along the beaches are numerous gulls and terns; in salt-marshes the Little Egret, Glossy Ibis, and flamingo can be seen. Among many lesser birds of prey, the rare Eleanora's Falcon nests on remote coastal cliffs; quail and Rock Partridge live in the maquis of the foothills and mountains, as do the brightly plumed bee-eater and hoopoe.[18]

Almost any bird is considered huntable, especially partridge, quail and dove. These birds (along with swallows) were favourite subjects of Minoan artists. Pleistocene records have been proved only for White-fronted Goose, which is still a winter visitor to the island, and gannet, which now visits only the western Mediterranean. A giant 'walking' owl appears in Pleistocene deposits.[19]

Carnivorous birds have been the only major predators on the island since the Middle Pleistocene. (Could they carry off a baby hippo?)

The modern fashion for draining fens threatens the habitats of migrating birds. Although Crete's coastal wetlands have moved many times because of tectonic activity, it is unlikely that there has ever been a time with as little wetland as there is now. Tourist hotels are now added to all the other encroachments.

Worms, insects and creeping things

There are at least three snakes, various lizards and frogs, and a terrapin on Crete.[20] The fossil record is poor, but includes a tortoise, which Crete now lacks.

The skink, *liakóni*, is a beautiful pinkish-green lizard, some 15 cm long, which moves like a snake, making little use of its tiny legs. Cretans are terrified of it: 'If the *liakóni* bites you with its mouth call the doctor, but if it stings you with its tail call the priest.'[21] In summer 1992, we saw workmen, removing a tile roof, discover two large *liakónia*, which they slew with whoops and yells and heroically displayed to the neighbourhood. (They are harmless.)

The most impressive reptiles are the great loggerhead sea-turtles that frequent the beaches near Réthymnon (R) and west of Khaniá (Ky). These long-lived creatures return after many years to the beach of their birth at dead of night to lay their eggs. They clash with hotels, with bright lights at night, and with the things that hoteliers place on beaches. However, providing for the needs of turtles is one of the few successes of Cretan conservation in recent years (Chapter 20).

Among insects, mosquitoes abound in many wind-sheltered places; they can make do with surprisingly little water. The dacus fly attacks olive fruits, which fall prematurely and rot. Scarabs (dung-beetles) busily roll their balls through the phrygana. Ant-lions continually dig out funnel-shaped pits to catch passing ants. Cicadas chorus throughout the olive groves during the heat of the summer, and various grasshoppers and crickets populate the phrygana and steppe. Butterflies abound in spring and autumn. Fleas and bed-bugs, the F-sharps and B-flats of travellers, are not the hazard that they were.

The hornet, a gentle creature, is the biggest and commonest wasp. Yellow-jacket wasps swarm around wet places, and can eat the very meat off a *souvláki*. Another wasp (*Blastophaga psenes*) does a useful job in fertilising the wild fig. (Some cultivated figs retain this symbiotic relationship, but others develop their fruit without fertilisation.)

Large, colourful spiders weave their webs from bush to bush and across goat-paths. Scorpions lurk under stones, tiles and potsherds, and sting archaeologists. Another venomous creature of Crete, celebrated since antiquity,[22] is the *rogalídha*, which looks like a black-widow spider:

> The two legs in front on each side are for walking forwards, and the two others behind are for going in reverse . . . Their body is ash-grey above, and in front there are two reddish spots on the back; and if one overturns them, one finds a black spot . . . Their belly is yellow; and anyone who wishes to know with what they can hurt, looks at their mouth, and one will see two little black fangs, resembling those of the Centipede; with which they bite.
>
> Belon, 1555

Alas, we have never seen it, although one of us may have been bitten. Spiders and scorpions are motifs on Minoan sealstones.

Snails leave trails across rocks and plants; after rain they can completely cover bushes, especially spiny-broom. In summer they hide under rocks and in walls, or cluster in masses at the tops of plants and telegraph-poles away from the hot ground. For some they are a staple food: cooking them is a great art, and ordinary Cretan snails can be better than French *escargots*.

Earthworms are most common under deciduous trees at moderate altitudes, where there is some soil development. After rain one occasionally sees a worm frying on a rock in the coastal plain.

Freshwater fish

In Venetian times Cretan freshwater fish were not to be despised. Tench 'as good as those of the river at Verona' and pike were especially popular: Raulin (1868) mentions four species in the river of Stylos (Ap). Eels were fished for 'with naked swords' at Georgioúpolis (Ap), and were a delicacy of Lake Kournás (Ap).[23]

Trout still lurk in mountain streams at Kakodhíki (Se), Mesklá (Ky), and Spíli (AV). Signs saying 'Please Do Not Poison the Water' admonish the fishermen, much as in Venetian times:

[Ordered that] no person dare to poison any river, lake, spring or water, or put *flomum* there, for the purpose of fishing or any other purpose, on pain of 25 *hyperpera** for each offence.[24]

* A deterrent fine, the price of an average slave.

Book of Bans, Municipality of Candia, 18 September 1344

We have seen great bream in the spring of Vrysses (Ap). Landcrabs are frequent in damp places.

Freshwater fish fare badly through irrigation drying up the rivers, and olive-processing residues polluting them. The latter, though not a new problem on Crete, has much increased.

Effects of native fauna on the landscape

We do not know what the extinct beasts liked to eat, or what there was for them to eat. (What would we give to observe the likes and dislikes of the Cretan hippo!) Food rather than predation probably limited the numbers of deer, elephants, and hippopotamuses. Unpredated island faunas tend to suffer boom-and-bust cycles depending on fluctuations in the environment. *There can be no doubt that in Crete, 'excessive' browsing is not an artefact, but is the natural state to which the flora, and especially the endemics, are adapted.* This is no mere supposition: several of the deer were rather goatlike in habit and (when the population was high) would have browsed the vegetation within an inch of its life, were it not for the extraordinary ways in which Cretan plants, more than any others in Europe, have adapted against browsing (pp. 54, 57). On Crete, the now typical 'Mediterranean' vegetation mosaic of maquis, phrygana and steppe may not have originated with man and goat, as is often claimed, but may date back to the Pleistocene.

The wild fauna that greeted settlers in the Neolithic may have differed only slightly from that of today, with surviving dwarf deer, badger, marten and various lesser beasts. The *agrími* has replaced the deer, but to the best of our knowledge all the others survive. Besides *agrími* the only other notable additions to the modern wild fauna are hare and wildcat, both of which may yet have Pleistocene records. A few introduced wild animals, such as fallow deer, have come and gone.

Apart from the shrew and spiny-mouse, Crete has no surviving mammals, peculiar to the island, that compare with the endemic plants. However, there is a tendency for distinct island subspecies to evolve not only among the native mammals (e.g. badger) but among the ancient introductions.

Notes

1 D. M. A. Bate (1913), 'The caves of Crete', in Trevor-Battye (see bibliography), p. 246.

2 A. J. Evans (1897), 'Further Discoveries of Cretan and Aegean Script', *Journal of Hellenic Studies*, **17**, 327-95.

3 G. Lucas et al. (1978), *IUCN Plant Red Data Book*, Morges, International Union for the Conservation of Nature, p. 139.

4 D. M. A. Bate (1905), 'On the mammals of Crete', *Proceedings of the Zoological Society*, London, **1905(2)**, 315-23; D. M. A. Bate (1913), 'The mammals of Crete', in Trevor-Battye (see bibliography), pp. 254-6.

5 S. Payne (1982), 'Faunal evidence for environmental/climatic change at Franchthi Cave … from 25,000 BP to 5,000 BP … ', in Bintliff and van Zeist (Chapter 4, note 2), pp. 133-6.

6 M. R. Jarman (*c.* 1982), *Human Influence in the Development of the Cretan Mammalian Fauna*, privately circulated MS.

7 T. R. Goedicke (1981), 'Life expectancy of monk seal colonies in Greece', *Biological Conservation*, **20**, 173-81.

8 Lax and Strasser (see bibliography) give an excellent summary of what is known about Cretan native mammals. For a general discussion of island mammals see P. Y. Sondaar (1986), 'The island sweepstakes', *Natural History*, **95(9)**, 50-7; S. Davis (1985), 'Tiny elephants and giant mice', *New Scientist*, 3 January, 25-7.

9 P. Y. Sondaar and G. J. Boekschoten (1967), 'Quaternary mammals in the south Aegean island arc; with notes on other fossil mammals from the coastal regions of the Mediterranean, I & II', *Akademie van Wetenschappen Proceedings*, **B70**, 556-76; S. E. Kuss and X. Misonne (1968), 'Pleistozäne Muriden der Insel Kreta', *Neues Jahrbuch für Geologie und Paläontologie, Abhandlungen, Stuttgart*, **132**, 55-69; A. Malatesta (1980), 'Dwarf deer and other Late Pleistocene fauna of the Simonelli Cave in Crete', *Problemi attuali di scienza di cultura*, **249**, 2-128, Accademia Nazionale dei Lincei, Rome.

10 K. Zimmermann et al. (1953), 'Die Wildsäuger von Kreta', *Zeitschrift für Säugetierkunde*, **17**, 1-72.

11 P. Y. Sondaar (1971), 'Palaeozoogeography of the Pleistocene mammals from the Aegean', in A. Strid (ed.) *Evolution in the Aegean*, *Opera Botanica*, **30**, 65-70.

12 S. E. Kuss (1965), 'Eine pleistozäne Säugetierfauna der Insel Kreta', *Berichte der Naturforschenden Gesellschaft zu Freiburg in Breisgau*, **55**, 271-348; P. Y. Sondaar (1977), 'Insularity and its effects on mammal evolution', in M. K. Hetch et al. (eds.), *Major patterns in vertebrate evolution*, New York, Plenum, pp. 671-707.

13 Malatesta (1980, note 9), Sondaar and Boekschoten (1967, note 9).

14 G. J. Boekschoten and P. Y. Sondaar (1966), 'The Pleistocene of the Katharo basin (Crete) and its Hippopotamus', *Bijdragen tot de Dierkunde*, **36**, 17-44; D. S. Reese (1989), 'Tracking the extinct pygmy hippopotamus of Cyprus', *Field Museum of Natural History Bulletin*, **60(2)**, 22-9.

15 *Natural History*, VIII, 228.

16 O. Rackham (1990), *The Last Forest*, London, Dent.

17 B. Messerli (1967), 'Die eiszeitliche und die gegenwärtige Vergletscherung im Mittelmeerraum', *Geographica Helvetica*, **22**, 105-228; W. R. Farrand (1971), 'Late Quaternary paleoclimates of the Eastern Mediterranean', in K. K. Turekian (ed.), *The Late Cenozoic Glacial Ages*, New Haven, Yale University Press, pp. 529-64.

18 S. Coghlan (1990), *Birdwatching in Crete*, no publisher given.

19 F. Suriano (1980), 'Fossil Birds of Simonelli', *Problemi attuali di scienza di cultura*, **249**, 123-6; Sondaar (1986, note 8).

20 H. Peiper (1971), 'Über die Bedeutung rezenter Verbreitungsmuster von Tieren für die Paläogeographie', in Strid (note 11), pp. 13-19.

21 E. K. Platakis (Ε. Κ. Πλατάκη) (1979), 'Το Λιακόνι της Κρήτης στην Λαογραφία', *Κρητολογία* **9**, 99-118.

22 Pliny, Natural History, VIII, 228.

23 For example BNP Ital 383 f. 25v (Boschini); CMV: Cicogna 2856 c. 179-96 (anonymous travels 1560).

24 ASV: Duca di Candia, Bandi 14, c. 179.

6

Wild trees and plants

*[The Lord] bringeth forth grass for the cattle: and green herb for the
service of men;*
*That he may bring food out of the earth, and wine that maketh glad
the heart of man:*
*and oil to make him a cheerful countenance, and bread to strengthen
man's heart.*
*The trees of the Lord also are full of sap: even the cedars of Libanus
which he hath planted;*
*Wherein the birds make their nests: and the fir-trees are a dwelling
for the stork.*

*Psalm **104**, 14-17*

Compared with northern Europe or America, Crete has a very different but not wholly unrelated flora. The first-time visitor from Britain or the United States will recognise many of the genera – heather (*Erica*), oak (*Quercus*), greenbrier (*Smilax*) – but most of the species will be unfamiliar and will not have English names, although they have Cretan names. (Some of these vernacular names may be appearing in print for the first time; we prefer them to those in Greek botanical books.)

Origins of the Cretan flora

Crete lies between Europe, Asia and Africa, but most of its plants – where a distinction is possible – have European connections.

There is, however, a large Asian minority. The Cretan cypress is an Asian tree, scattered in mountain-ranges from Rhodes to Persia; it extends into Crete but (as a native tree) no farther into Europe. Cretan pine also has its homeland in Asia, extending into Crete and the toe of Italy.

The African connection is smaller. Outliers of African plants include the yellow violet *Viola scorpiuroides*, which straggles through spiny bushes at the south-west corner of Crete. *Aristidia ascensionis*, a Saharan representative of the three-awn grasses of the United States, grows in hot dry places in east Crete: one of us found it at Myrtos (H) in 1968, and it has since done well on road-works. Even more remarkable is the lush tropical fern *Woodwardia radicans*, to be found in very damp shady places in the far west.

Endemic plants

A special delight of Crete are the **endemic** plants which grow nowhere else, some of which are both common and arrestingly beautiful. In Khaniá the wonderful blue spikes of *Petromarula pinnata* (*petromároula, petrokarés*) come out in May and June from the masonry of Venetian buildings (Plate 5); it is common on cliffs except in the driest parts (Figure 6.1a). For a brief period in May the dusty hillsides around Knossós are cherry-red with blooms of *Ebenus cretica* (*katsouliés*), a leguminous undershrub. This plant is very sensitive to browsing: once confined to dry, south-facing crags, it is now abundant all over east Crete wherever there are few sheep and goats (Figure 6.1b). Millions of white cyclamen, *Cyclamen creticum*, carpet west Cretan groves in spring; this cyclamen is peculiar to Crete and Kárpathos.

Crete has many more endemic plants than any other European island; something like 180 species, or one-tenth of the total flora, are wholly or mainly confined to Crete.

Some endemics are confined to part of Crete. *Verbascum spinosum* (*galatoatsivídha*), spiny mullein, is common in Sphakiá, where its grey spiny cushions, with yellow flowers, are familiar from the coast up to the highest mountains. But it is rigidly confined to west Crete – or so we thought until we discovered it, equally abundant, in one gorge in the south-east (Figure 6.2a). Some are among the world's rarest plants. *Bupleurum kakiskalae* appears to grow only on one particular cliff of the White Mountains;[1] we have had the unusual privilege of finding it blooming, which it does only at long intervals.

Endemics are of three main kinds. Cretan cyclamen is one of many kinds of cyclamen in and around the Aegean; evolution has been active in this genus, producing a host of local species within the last million years or so. *Petromarula*, however, is the only one of its genus and is not closely related to anything else; if it evolved on the island, it took a much longer period to do so. The Cretan palm (p. 65) is the shrunken remnant of what was once a much wider distribution.[2]

Two habitats are particularly rich in endemic plants. Many are to be found on cliffs, out of the reach of goats. Each of the hundred gorges of Crete has its own combination of endemics, according to the rocks and the way the cliffs face. The other concentration of endemics is in the high mountains. A spring walk above the Omalós Plain reveals the extraordinary, elm-like tree *Zelkova cretica*, and under it carpets of the delicate pale-blue *Chionodoxa cretica* (Plate 7). At higher altitudes the number of endemics increases, until in the High Desert they form a whole landscape.

Few Cretan endemics are plants of woodland, wetland or the coast. Endemics particularly do not like shade (with a few exceptions such as *Cyclamen creticum*).

Endemics are adapted to browsing in various ways. Many, such as *Petromarula*, are palatable, but are adapted to an inaccessible life on cliffs. Others are spiny or distasteful. All elms are highly edible, but *Zelkova* resists browsing in a unique way. Its tough little leaves are borne on short-shoots with a woody core. The first time an animal nibbles the shoots, it pulls off the bark with the leaves, exposing the sharp-pointed woody core; the tangle of spines thus created protects the inner leaves from further attack.

Other endemics protect theselves by developing into **hedgehog-plants** (p. 112) or **flat-plants**. *Polygonum idaeum* is a knotgrass which – unlike all the world's other knotgrasses – forms a massive woody underground stock from which the shoots and leaves arise so close to the ground that animals cannot pick them up (Figure

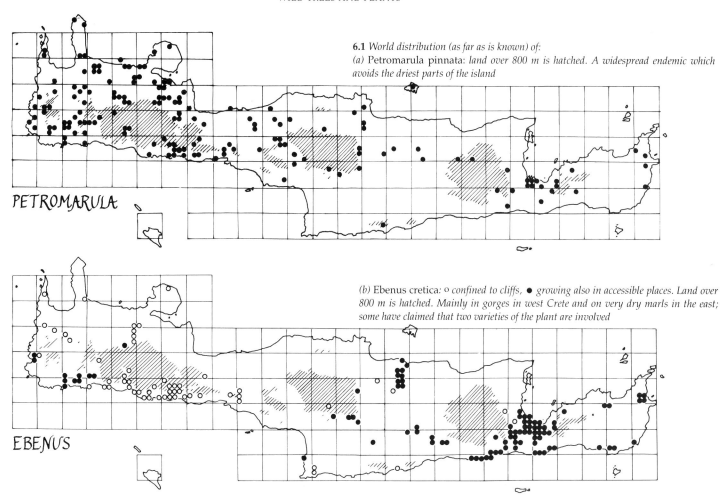

6.1 *World distribution (as far as is known) of:*
(a) Petromarula pinnata: *land over 800 m is hatched. A widespread endemic which avoids the driest parts of the island*

PETROMARULA

(b) Ebenus cretica: o *confined to cliffs,* ● *growing also in accessible places. Land over 800 m is hatched. Mainly in gorges in west Crete and on very dry marls in the east; some have claimed that two varieties of the plant are involved*

EBENUS

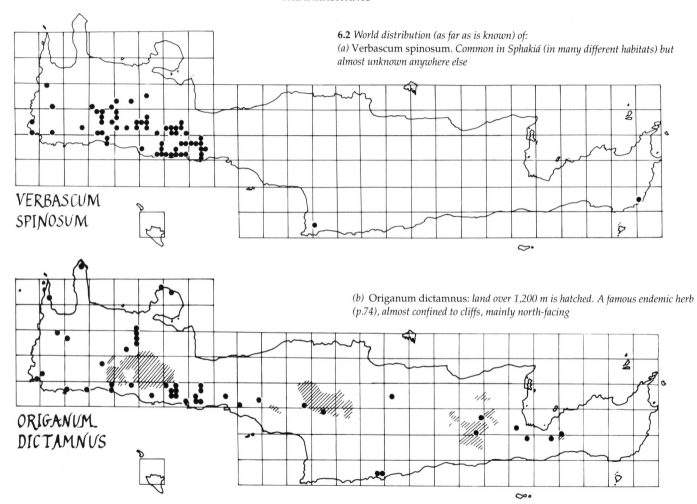

6.2 *World distribution (as far as is known) of:*

(a) Verbascum spinosum. *Common in Sphakiá (in many different habitats) but almost unknown anywhere else*

VERBASCUM SPINOSUM

(b) Origanum dictamnus: *land over 1,200 m is hatched. A famous endemic herb (p.74), almost confined to cliffs, mainly north-facing*

ORIGANUM DICTAMNUS

6.3). It is the commonest plant on the Nídha Plain (My) and its satellite plains, but is found nowhere else in the world.

A speciality of Crete are plants protected in more than one way. The world's species of *Anchusa* are clothed with nasty sharp bristles which ordinarily are a sufficient deterrent. *Anchusa cespitosa* (*bláves*), peculiar to the High Desert, is additionally protected by being a flat-plant; its deep-blue, stemless flowers make it one of the most beautiful Cretan plants (Plate 10). *Verbascum spinosum* is not only protected, like other *Verbascums*, by poison and distasteful fluff, but is a hedgehog-plant as well. This profusion of defences, unique in Europe, cannot have evolved in the few

6.3 *The endemic* Polygonum idaeum, *flattest of flat-plants. Note the massive woody taproot. Nídha Plain (My), July 1989*

millennia since sheep and goats arrived. It supports the argument in the last chapter that 'excessive' browsing is not due only to human intervention but has been the natural state of the island for two million years.

Introduced plants

The ***native*** plants of Crete are those which arrived spontaneously in prehistory or evolved on the island, in contrast to ***introduced*** species which have come, intentionally or accidentally, by boat. Some introduced species are ***naturalised*** – once here, they propagate themselves without further human intervention. Others do not and remain exotics. These distinctions do not depend on the lapse of time; mulberry has been in Crete for thousands of years but remains exclusively a cultivated plant.

The commonest naturalised plant in Crete is *Oxalis pes-caprae* (*mártolouloudhi*), whose bright green foliage – with yellow flowers, usually double – so completely carpets the olive-groves in spring that it is prominent in pictures from space. It is said to come from South Africa, and reached Crete about 1880. It spreads by bulbils, and is perfectly adapted to the seasonal ploughing of the groves. The plains of Crete are full of generalised tropical weeds, such as Johnson-grass (*Sorghum halepense*), which can live with ploughing and weedkillers. However, Crete is not overrun with wild American plants to the extent that California is overrun with Mediterranean plants.

The most enduring legacy of Sir Arthur Evans to the Cretan countryside may be the tree-of-heaven (*Ailanthus altissima*). This Chinese tree, with huge compound leaves, was apparently introduced to the Villa Ariadne, his home at Knossós (T), about 1910, and was widely planted elsewhere. It spreads by suckers and is uncontrollable: at Knossós it has pushed out into a busy road and has begun to occupy the excavations.

Except for plants from another hemisphere and endemics, it is not easy to determine which are the naturalised and native plants of Crete. Much has been written by Greuter[3] and others, but there are few objective criteria. Some plant geographers dismiss as an introduction any species that does not fit a theory about how plants should be distributed. The spread of cultivation through Europe brought weeds as well as crops; the distinction between crops and weeds was not well defined at first. Plants such as shepherd's needle (*Scandix pecten-veneris*) and annual dog's-mercury (*Mercurialis annua*) occur in England always in cultivated ground, and were presumably introduced along with crops. But in Crete, closer to the origin of cultivation, they also grow in limestone rock-pockets and other natural habitats. They could have come with crops; but these localities could be the original habitat from which they emerged to take on a new life as weeds.

It is even possible that some plants, now more widespread, originated as Cretan endemics. A parallel would be the legume *Medicago arborea*, now widespread in Greece and Crete. Pliny claimed that it had originally been endemic to the island of Kythnos.[4]

Native Cretan trees

Trees are wildlife, with their own patterns of behaviour. Table 6.1 summarises their essential properties. In Greece, trees and shrubs are poorly distinguished; individuals can pass from one state to the other. We shall often use the term 'tree-or-shrub'.

Trees respond to woodcutting in various ways. A few species

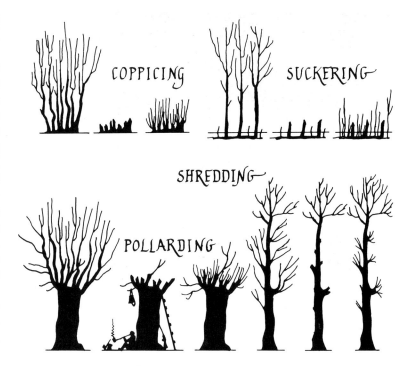

6.4 *Woodcutting, and trees' responses to it. For each of the four methods, the tree (or group of trees) is shown before cutting, immediately after cutting, and one year after cutting.*

die and will grow again only from seed. Others respond by *suckering*, sprouting from the roots (Figure 6.4). Others sprout from the stump, a response known as *coppicing*. Most European

6.5 *A coppice stool of holm-oak, 3.7 m in diameter. This tree is several centuries old, and has been cut down and has grown again many times. Angathé massif (Sf), August 1989*

6.6 *Ancient goat-pollard prickly-oak. Originally it stood in open savanna; the surrounding woodland has grown up subsequently. Skinávria Mountains, September 1986*

woodcutting traditionally depends on this response for a continued wood supply. Coppicing turns the tree into a multi-stemmed *stool* which may live indefinitely (Figure 6.5). An alternative to coppicing is *pollarding*, cutting the tree 3-4 m above ground. The decision whether to die, sucker, or coppice is the tree's. The decision whether to coppice or pollard is the woodman's. Pollarding is the custom in places and for species where coppice shoots would be destroyed by browsing animals. Repeated pollarding and coppicing prolong a tree's life, and have much to do with the

ancient trees which are a special feature of Crete (Figures 6.5, 6.6).

The response of trees to browsing depends partly on their palatability – whether goats prefer them – and partly on their capacity to survive in a bitten-down state (see prickly-oak below). Another factor, to be explored in Chapter 10, is how fast new shoots grow and get away above the reach of goats.

Burning depends on how easily a tree burns and on whether it is killed by fire. Most Cretan trees, if they will burn, are killed to the ground by fires but sprout.

Cypress

This most famous of distinctively Cretan trees is the chief wood-land tree of the White Mountains, with smaller populations in other mountains (Figure 6.8a). It is ordinarily a gregarious tree: either there are whole woods of it, or nothing. But wild cypress also grows scattered in field and hedgerow, as a sacred tree at chapels, and even in the middle of the road, like the great cypress of Bábali Kháni in Païdhókhori (Ap). Sir Arthur Evans thought the field cypresses of Knossós (T) were the remains of a forest, but they are far too young and too uniform in age. These non-woodland cypresses may be the tree's natural response to opportunities in the cultural landscape, rather like oaks in English hedges or junipers in Texas.

This wonderful tree embodies the fierce diversity of its island. It can grow into almost any shape that trees assume. Some cypresses, scorning soils, root into fissured rocks on almost the hottest south-facing crags. If sheltered from wind cypresses can grow into tall stately trees. In north-exposed passes they grow into ice-scoured flag-shapes. Most cypresses tend to grow out sideways, but for some reason those of the White Mountains have recently taken to upright growth, resulting in a curved or L-shaped trunk. The biggest cypresses in Europe are a dozen around the chapel of St Nicholas in the Samariá Gorge (Sf). In 1989 one was 35.0 m (115 feet) high, and another was 7.11 m in girth (7.5 feet in diameter). They are sacred trees, but many years ago someone impiously cut one down; its annual rings show that they are at least 500 years old. The highest cypresses at the tree-line are among the oldest and most distinctive trees in Europe.

Cypresses, though conifers, will coppice, and at Anópolis (Sf) are still coppiced for firewood (Figure 6.7). (The new shoots are not much eaten by animals). Another regular use is the cutting-out of rectangles of bark, about 45 by 30 cm, for making beehive-roofs. This curious practice does not much hurt the tree; all the older, non-sacred, easily-accessible cypresses in the Samariá Gorge bear these scars, sometimes embedded in at least 300 annual rings.

All this applies to the *wild* cypress, *Cupressus sempervirens* variety *horizontalis*; not to the 'vertical' cypress, the narrow, stiffly-erect, formal tree, familiar in gardens in Italy and the Peloponnese. This is one of Europe's oldest ornamental tree varieties, originating probably in ancient Greece and propagated by Roman, Byzantine, Venetian and Turkish gardeners. It is not now common in Crete.

6.7 *Coppice stools of cypress*

	Cretan Greek name	Suckering	Pollarding	Coppicing	Palatability	Survival of browsing	Combustibility	Survival after fire	Occurrence on cliffs	Rooting depth	Ancient trees	Recent expansion
Table 6.1. *Properties of Cretan trees*												
Conifers												
Cypress	kyparíssos	—	++	++	+	++	++	+	++	+++	++++	++++
Pine	pévkos	—	+	—	—	++	++++	++	—	++	—	+++
Land-juniper	kédhros	—	0	++	—	?	++	—	+	+	0	+
Sea-juniper	kédhros	—	+	+	—	?	?	?	—	—	+	+
Wild evergreen broadleaves												
Prickly-oak	prinári	+	+++	+++	+++	++++	+++	++++	++	++++	++++	++
Holm-oak	azyláki	—	+++	++++	++++	(+)	+++	++++	++++	++++	+++	0
Phillyrea	elaióprina	—	+	++	+++	+++	+++?	+++?	++	+++	+	+
Wild-olive	agrielaiá	—	+	++	+++	++++	+++	++++	+++	+++	0	++
Lentisk	skhinós	+	0	+++	—	?	++	++++	++	++++	0	+
Arbutus	koúmara	—	+	++++	++	+++	+++	++++	+	++	0	+
Andrachne	andhrákhli	—	0	+++	+++	+++	++	++++	+	?	0	0
Laurel	dháphne	+	+	+++	++	+++	?	?	+++	?	0	+
Wild deciduous broadleaves												
Oak	dhrys	—	++	++	+++	++	++	+++	—	+	+	+++
Valonia oak	velanídhi	—	0	+++	++	?	++	+++	—	+	0	++
Maple	asphéndamos	—	+++	+++	+++	++++	?	+++?	++++	?	0	++
Terebinth	terevínthos	—	(+)	++	+++	+++	?	++++	+++	?	0	0
Plane	plátanos	—	+++	+++	++	++	+	++	0	?	++++	+++
Wild pear	agriakhládhi, agriapídhi	—	+++	0	++++	++	—	+++	+	+	++	+++
Hawthorn	mourtsiá, trikoukiá	—	0	0	++++	+++	+	+	+	?	0	+++
Elm	fteliá	++++	0	—	++++	—	—	+++	—	?	0	+
Willow	itéa	—	+++	0	++++	—	—	0	—	?	—	0
Zelkova	ambelitsiá	++++	+++	—	++	++++	—	0	—	?	++	++
Other Wild Trees												
Palm	phoenix, vaï	++++	—	—	++	+++	++++	++++	—	?	—	(+)
Cultivated Trees												
Olive	eliá	+	++++	+++	++++	++++	+++	+++	0	+	+++	++++
Carob*	kharoúpi	—	++++	++	+++	++++	+++	+++	++	?	+++	0
White mulberry	mourniá	—	++++	0	++++	0	—	0	—	+	—	0
Chestnut	kastaniá	—	+++	+++	++	0	+	++	—	+	++++	+
Walnut	karydhi	—	—	0	+++	0	—	++	—	?	—	++
Ailanthus		+++++	?	—	++?	+++	—	++++	0	?	—	++++
Eucalyptus	evkályptos	—	0	++++	—	0	++++	++++	0	?	0	0

Trees that exhibit a particular property abundantly are marked ++++; those that have it sparingly are +; those that have it very sparingly are (+); those that lack it are marked —.
The symbol 0 means that the property exists but is seldom used.
The * means also wild.

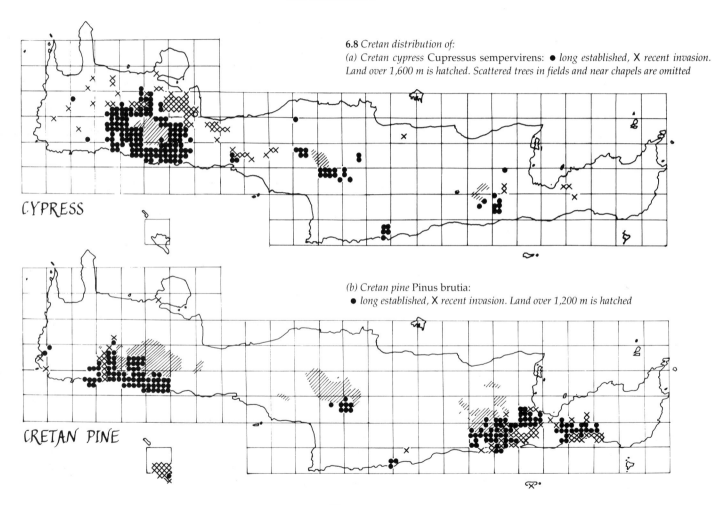

6.8 *Cretan distribution of:*

(a) Cretan cypress Cupressus sempervirens: ● *long established,* X *recent invasion. Land over 1,600 m is hatched. Scattered trees in fields and near chapels are omitted*

CYPRESS

(b) Cretan pine Pinus brutia:
● *long established,* X *recent invasion. Land over 1,200 m is hatched*

CRETAN PINE

Pine

Another distinctively Cretan, non-Greek tree is *Pinus brutia*, a massive tree with a distinctive flat top. Its thick, rugged bark proclaims it as a fire-resistant pine. It refuses to coppice but can be pollarded. It is even less palatable than cypress.

Crete lacks the pines of mainland Greece: Aleppo pine, *P. halepensis* (the thin-barked, lowland pine common around Athens), and the *P. nigra* group (thick-barked mountain pines). The Cretan pine does the ecological job of both: it grows at almost every elevation where there are trees. Most planted pines in Crete are Aleppo (for instance at Knossós (T) and Khóra Sphakíon (Sf)); they do not spread.

Cretan pine, rather like cypress, is gregarious: the common tree of some areas but totally absent from others. It is a southern tree in the White, Lassíthi and Siteía Mountains, and several outliers (Figure 6.8b). It grows on various rocks and soils; unlike cypress, it favours talus slopes and places with some soil. It is the chief tree on gypsum. It is evidently drought-resistant, but has its limits: a 1940 air photograph of Myrtos (H) shows that pinewoods were then limited to the north, less thirsty, sides of the marly hills of that parched area.

Pine grows fast except in very dry places. A pine 30 cm in diameter, with rugged bark, is often no more than twenty-five years old; even the biggest pines, over a metre thick, are seldom much over 200 years.

Pine in Crete is used as a building timber, but also provides resin, which is tapped from the living tree in two ways. The ridges of the bark may be cut off and shallow axe-cuts made into the cambium, from which resin exudes and may be scraped up. Trevor-Battye in 1909 wrote that all the pines between Arádhena and Ayios Ioánnes (Sf) 'had been cruelly hacked about for resin'. In fact the tapping does little damage, and most of these pines are still alive but bear faint scars. A more businesslike method, of which traces are visible for instance in the Samariá Gorge (Sf), involves a single deep incision to which a little galvanised-iron cup is attached to collect the resin. One of the main uses of resin is for making retsina, but resin-gathering died out in Crete in the 1950s and has not revived, despite a recent fashion for making retsina in Crete.

Junipers

'Land-juniper' (*Juniperus phoenicea*) is the common tree between Ierápetra (H) and Ayios Nikólaos (Me), growing from the tips of the peninsulas to the tops of the mountains. It also occurs in south-west Crete and on Gávdhos (Se).

The tree is gregarious, forming extensive woods. It rarely grows more than 5 m high, typically with a weak central stem and strong low branches, giving a coppice-like appearance. It is also capable of real coppicing, and was extensively cut until about fifty years ago.

'Sea-juniper' (*J. macrocarpa*) forms woods in sand-dunes; it is rare in Crete itself, but abundant on the islets of Gávdhos (Se) and Gaidharonísi (H). It is bigger than land-juniper, with a single trunk, often fantastically gnarled. If its roots are exposed by the sand blowing away, the branches recede to sharp, hard, bleached points – a surrealistic skeleton of a tree, but still very much alive. The queen of the sea-junipers, a giant 12 m high and 2.6 m in girth, is at the south tip of Gávdhos – the southernmost big tree in Europe (Figure 6.9).

Sea-juniper is coppiceable. Its fruits were exported; we find them marginally edible; they are said to induce fertility in women and concupiscence in men.

6.9 *The queen of the sea-junipers* (Juniperus macrocarpa), *the southernmost big tree in Europe. South tip of Gávdhos (Se), May 1989*

Prickly-oak

This evergreen oak (*Quercus coccifera*) is perhaps the most adaptable plant in the European flora. It can be bitten down to a few cm high and live indefinitely; it can also be a giant oak with a trunk 3 m in diameter (Figure 10.4). If it grows more than 60 cm high, it does the duties of an oak-tree, producing pollen and acorns. It burns quite readily; if cut down or burnt it sprouts from the base. It roots deep into limestone fissures.

Prickly-oak is widespread in the Mediterranean. In Crete, it is perhaps the commonest tree-or-shrub on hard limestone, less common on other substrates (Figure 6.10a). It seldom grows nearer than 1 km to the sea, perhaps because it dislikes salt. In the White Mountains it goes up to 1,780 m – the fourth highest tree in Crete, much higher (as far as we know) than anywhere else in its range. We suspect that there may be different genetic variants at different altitudes. At any one altitude, the tree and bush forms appear to be identical, one freely turning into the other.

The tree seems indestructible, but replaces itself very slowly. We have rarely seen either a dead or a young one, and infer that most individuals are centuries old. It may be that virtually every fissure capable of holding a prickly-oak already has one.

This oak is a major source of firewood, a minor source of timber, and a major food for goats. It is often pollarded or coppiced. A minor product used to be scarlet-grain, the dried carcasses of the semi-parasitic insect *Kermococcus vermilio*, used as a scarlet dye; for some reason it is now very rare.

Holm-oak

Quercus ilex is the evergreen oak common in Italy and introduced into England; it looks very like the American live-oak. In Crete it is much less common than prickly-oak and is ecologically very different; it grows mainly on cliffs in high-rainfall areas (Figure 6.10b). With one curious exception in east Crete, it does not have prickly-oak's ability to survive in a bitten-down state. When it grows in accessible places, it is mainly on phyllite with plenty of moisture.

Holm-oak grows to a big tree. The pale undersides of its leaves are easy to spot, shimmering in the breeze on high cliffs. Most specimens are pollards or coppice stools, even where woodcutters must have let themselves down on ropes to get at them.

The word 'ilex' or 'holm-oak' in travellers' accounts should be viewed with extreme suspicion. By a misunderstanding which goes back to the sixteenth century, Ancient Greek *prínos* and Modern Greek *prinári* are translated 'holm-oak'. It is perfectly clear from Theophrastus that prickly-oak was meant.[5] In every place where travellers mention holm-oak, we find abundant prickly-oak and little or no holm-oak. None of the travellers noticed the real holm-oak on cliffs.

Deciduous oaks

The common deciduous oak in Crete (*Quercus brachyphylla*) is a big tree looking like an English oak or American post-oak. (Many authors mistake it for *Q. pubescens,* a north Mediterranean oak which does not occur here.) Like most deciduous oaks, it is shallow-rooted; it grows on marl and gravelly soils (and sometimes metamorphics) that hold plenty of water, and therefore competes with cultivation. Deciduous oak had at least a proverbial association with Crete among ancient authors.[6] In the recent past it held a precarious position as a hedgerow and field tree, often pollarded. Whole woods of deciduous oak are now springing up on abandoned farmland, especially in Ayios Vasíleios district and the western Amári (Figure 6.11a).

A second deciduous oak is *Quercus macrolepis.* It is also a big tree, remarkable for its huge acorns and acorn-cups. It is the common oak around Arménoi (R), where *brachyphylla* is mysteriously absent, but is rare elsewhere (Figure 6.11b). It grows on the same terrain as *brachyphylla* and is shallow-rooting; visitors to the Minoan underground tombs at Arménoi can observe how seldom,

and only along cracks, its roots penetrate the marl. The acorn-cups, known as valonia, used to be a source of tannin, exported by the shipload from Greece to English tanneries. The use of valonia in Crete itself seems to have begun in the 1570s[7] but was never very important, nor were oaks deliberately cultivated for valonia in Crete. This oak too is increasing.

We have recently found a third deciduous oak, *Quercus frainetto.*

Cretan palm, Phoenix theophrasti

Tourists visit the famous palm-grove of Vaï (Si) on the east coast; they are told that this is the only palm-grove in Crete and is a relic of Arab introduction. In fact the tree is widely scattered around the coasts (Figure 6.13), often only as single, dwarfed tufts. Far from being an introduction, it is almost peculiar to Crete, though we have recently found it on Rhodes and other islands and it is known from south-west Turkey.[8] It propagates by suckers and is extremely persistent. It is well adapted to burning. Some tufts are male, others female; its dates are doubtfully edible.

This is a most important historic tree. Its remains are found in the Pleistocene volcanic ash of Santorini, where the tree still grows wild. On Crete it would only just have escaped being pushed off the island during glaciations. Palms are common motifs in Bronze Age art and on various ancient coins.

Werner Greuter recognized the Cretan palm as a distinct species[9] and named it after Theophrastus, the first to describe it in the fourth century BC:

They say that the palms in Crete more often than not are double, and that some of them have three stems; and that in Lapaia [location unknown] one with five heads has been

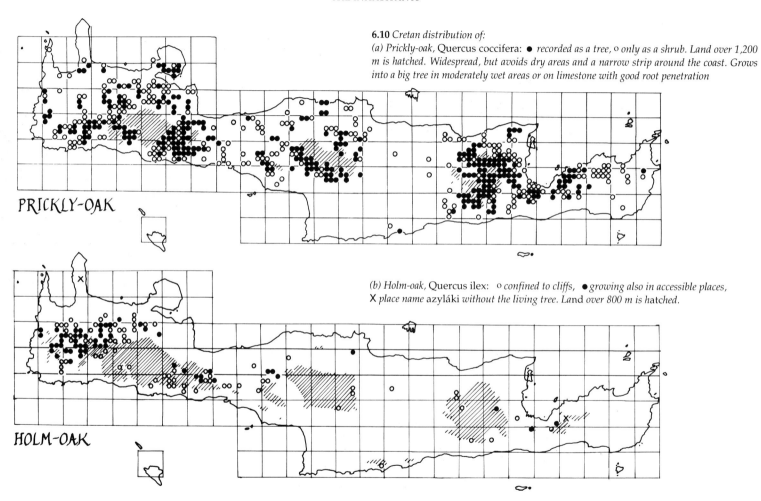

6.10 *Cretan distribution of:*

(a) Prickly-oak, Quercus coccifera: ● *recorded as a tree,* ○ *only as a shrub. Land over 1,200 m is hatched. Widespread, but avoids dry areas and a narrow strip around the coast. Grows into a big tree in moderately wet areas or on limestone with good root penetration*

PRICKLY-OAK

(b) Holm-oak, Quercus ilex: ○ *confined to cliffs,* ● *growing also in accessible places,* X *place name* azyláki *without the living tree. Land over 800 m is hatched.*

HOLM-OAK

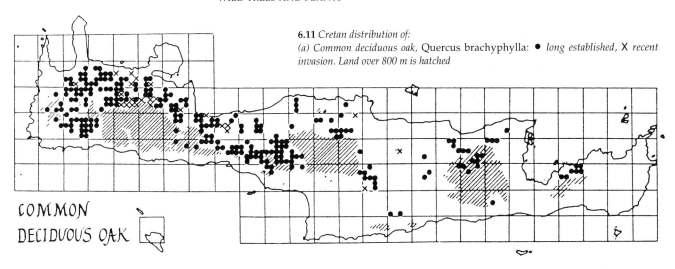

6.11 *Cretan distribution of:*
(a) Common deciduous oak, Quercus brachyphylla: ● *long established,* X *recent invasion. Land over 800 m is hatched*

COMMON
DECIDUOUS OAK

(b) Valonia oak, Quercus macrolepis: ● *long established,* X *recent invasion,* △ *place-name. Known introductions are omitted. Frainetto oak,* Quercus frainetto: ⊙

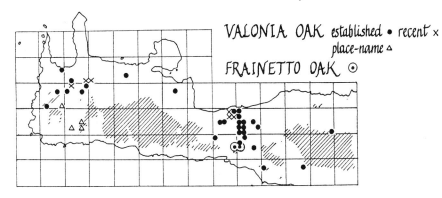

VALONIA OAK established ● recent ×
place-name △
FRAINETTO OAK ⊙

known . . . The dwarf palm (*khamairripheîs*) . . . is common in Crete [and is used for baskets and mats].

History of Plants, II, vi, 9, 11

The dwarf palm could be *Chamaerops humilis*, now confined to the west Mediterranean; it is more likely that he is referring to *Phoenix theophrasti* in a dwarf state. Two ancient place-names in Crete allude to the tree: the city Phoenix (Sf), mentioned in the *Acts of the Apostles* (p. 102), and Phoenix in Séllia (AV), mentioned by Strabo.[10] The tree still grows in both places 2,000 years later (Plate 6.12), and at other places called Phoenix or Vaï, both of which mean 'palm'.

The Venetians noticed the Cretan palm. Buondelmonti in 1415 describes the Almyrós of Gázi (T), 'on whose banks palm-trees without fruit proliferate'; they still survive precariously. Boschini in 1651 depicts another group nearby, which we rediscovered at the place Vayiá 330 years later. The grove at Vaï (Si) in east Crete already existed by 1562 when the place-name is recorded. Monanni in 1631 shows palms, still surviving today, in the river-mouth at Siteía (Si).

Other evergreen trees

Phillyrea media is a tree-or-shrub related to the olive; it looks much like prickly-oak, but has leaves in opposite pairs. It often occurs with prickly-oak, and replaces it near the sea.

The wild olive looks much like the cultivated, but has smaller leaves and is often a thorny bush. It is common especially near the sea and on cliffs. Sometimes people find wild olives and graft them to cultivated varieties; conversely, many wild olives are the remains of neglected olive-groves.

6.12 *Cretan palm* (Phoenix theophrasti) *growing, as is fitting, on the site of ancient Phoenix (Loutró (Sf)). July 1987*

6.13 *Distribution of Cretan palm,* Phoenix theophrasti.
*Inset is the known distribution outside Crete. Palms in
inland gardens, some of which are probably* theophrasti,
are omitted

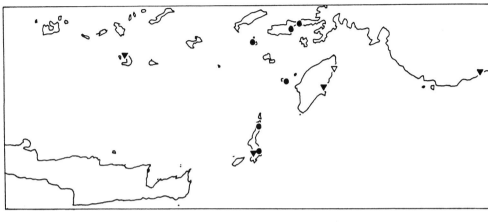

CRETAN PALM

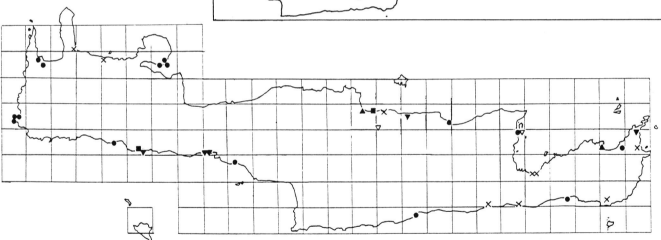

Historic record, place-name, & living plant ■ Place-name & living plant ▼ Place-name without surviving plant ▽

Historic record & living plant ▲ Living plant in natural context ● Living plant with other cultivated plants ✕

Strawberry-tree (*Arbutus unedo*) is the common tree on phyllite-quartzite in west Crete. It is the only Cretan tree that is native to the British Isles (west Ireland). The strawberries ripen in autumn and winter, and a strong drink is distilled from them. Its much less common relative, andrachne (*Arbutus andrachne*), grows locally on limestone; it is one of the few European trees to have a red peeling bark.

Bay-laurel (*Laurus nobilis*) is a small tree mainly on cliffs in the wetter parts of Crete. In up-country Apokórona it is locally the commonest tree.

Carob (*Ceratonia siliqua*) can be either wild or cultivated; it can be a big, ancient tree. It is a legume, with big pinnate leaves and clusters of blackish pods, which often sprout from the trunk. The pods used to be, and intermittently still are, gathered to feed animals, or to be exported for feeding children, for making a delicious flour to bake cakes, or for use in photographic emulsions. Some countries call them 'locust-beans' or 'St John's Bread' in the misbelief, due to squeamish Biblical commentators, that the locusts which John the Baptist ate with his wild honey were really these pods. This mysterious tree has been in Greece since antiquity, but was probably introduced from Palestine.[11] It has no proper Greek name, being referred to as either *kharoúpi*, from its Semitic name, or by the nickname *keráti*, 'little horn'.

Lentisk (*Pistacia lentiscus*) is usually a shrub, but can be a small tree with pinnate leaves. It is the most coastal of common trees-or-shrubs, going right down to the surf. It is resinous and very unpalatable.

Other deciduous trees

Cretan maple (*Acer sempervirens* – it is not, however, evergreen) is a small tree-or-shrub. It forms woods and thickets in the mountains down to 900 m altitude; it goes down gorges almost to sea-level.

Terebinth (*Pistacia terebinthus*) is a tree-or-shrub often growing on cliffs, or in west Crete on the ground. It has pinnate leaves like its sister the lentisk, but they are deciduous; its fruits are often distorted into conspicuous galls. It is resinous like lentisk, but much more palatable.

Plane (*Platanus orientalis*) is a huge and stately tree, the biggest in Crete in terms of girth. It is a constant sign of ground-water; it grows around springs all over the island, in wet areas, forming continuous ribbons along valley bottoms. Vast ancient plane-trees overshadow the springs in village squares; the finest is at Krási (Pe), but there are two even bigger trees (11.5 m girth) by a mountain spring above Thérisso (Ky) (Plate 6). Planes are often pollarded or coppiced.

The Cretan elm is a variant of *Ulmus minor*, a group of elms extending across Europe to eastern England. It grows from root-suckers, forming thickets. It is an aquatic tree in Crete, growing along spring-lines and streams along the northern foot of the mountains (Figure 6.14a). Occasionally it suffers from Dutch Elm Disease, which (in a place so remote from other elms from which the infection might spread) must be indigenous.

Willow (*Salix fragilis*) is an uncommon aquatic tree, principally along the Koiliáris River (Ap).

Wild pear (*Pyrus amygdaliformis*) is a non-gregarious tree, and usually occurs as scattered individuals. It is very drought-resistant, being the only tree in many arid localities, and it is also the principal tree in the floors of mountain-plains. Often people graft cultivated varieties of pear on pollarded wild trees. There is also a wild almond (*Prunus webbii*). Hawthorn (*Crataegus heldreichii* and *monogyna*) is prevalent in mountain-plains.

Crete's most specifically alpine tree is *ambelitsiá* (*Zelkova cretica*), one of the world's rarest trees.[12] It is best seen in the south-east corner of the Omalós Plain and on the heights above. We have discovered a wood of it in the remote upper Eligiás Gorge; it is almost the highest tree in the island at 1760 m (Figure 6.14b). It can be a big rugged elm-like tree with a shag bark; the biggest are ancient pollards. It suckers copiously. Even this rarest of trees has a specific use: all the shepherds' crooks in west Crete are made of it. (Middle and east Cretans, who have very little *ambelitsiá*, use oaken crooks.)

Herbs — medicinal and aromatic
Crete is aromatic. The pungent scents of thyme, savory, cistus and lavender are our invisible companions, especially as they are crushed when we tramp the phrygana. Many aromatic herbs belong to the mint family; their volatile oils, which livestock disdain, give smells and flavours admired by the human species.

Most herbs are gathered and dried in early summer. Thyme (*Thymus capitatus*) and summer savory (*Satureja thymbra*) are characteristic of phrygana in drier localities, while savory and lavender (*Lavendula stoechas*) favour sandier soils. Sage (*Salvia triloba*) and rigany (oregano, *Origanum heracleioticum*) require a little more moisture or light shade, as along the fringes of maquis. A common medicine is camomile (*Matricaria chamomilla*), a daisy-like weed of fallow fields or disturbed ground.

The most famous of Cretan endemics is the herb *dhíktamo* or

érota (*Origanum dictamnus*). It occurs in gorges, especially on north-facing cliffs (Figure 6.2b). It has little round woolly leaves, with a most exquisite scent, and racemes of purple flowers. Theophrastus, the father of botany in the fourth century BC, tells this tale:

> *Díktamnon* is peculiar to Crete. … It is rare: the place which bears it is limited, and the goats bite it down because they love it. The story of the arrows is said to be true, that if they eat it when they have been shot it drives out [the arrow].
> *History of Plants*, IX, xvi, 1

However, unwounded goats are ravenously fond of *dhíktamo*, and never let it survive where they can reach it. The plant has been famous in medicine since antiquity: to judge by Dioscorides's account, any number of unrelated plants were being sold by herbalists as counterfeits. One can now buy bags of cultivated *dhíktamo* to use as tea.

Another Cretan speciality is *ladanum*, the dried exudation of *Cistus creticus*. It is one of the constituents of incense. It is collected with

> a sort of Whip with a long handle, with two Rows of Straps… the Straps whereof, by rubbing against the Leaves of this Shrub, lick'd up a sort of odoriferous Glue sticking on the Leaves … When the whips are sufficiently laden with this Grease, they take a Knife, and scrape it clean off the Straps, and make it up into a Mass or Cakes …

This description is from Tournefort in 1700, but the same tool is described by Belon in *c.* 1550. Both travellers saw ladanum-

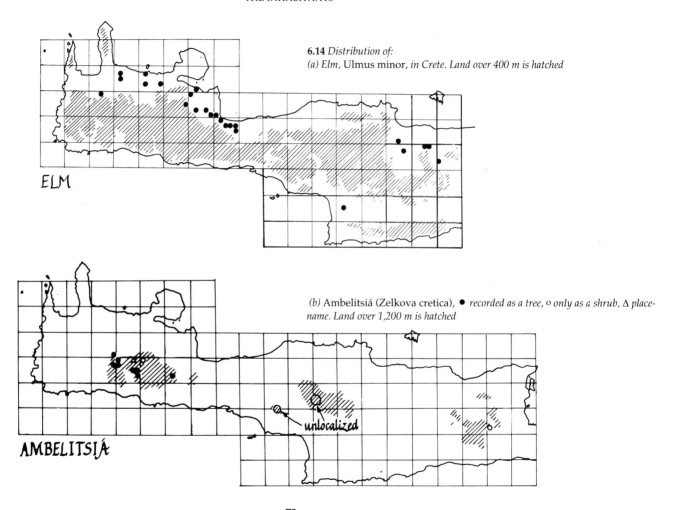

6.14 *Distribution of:*
(a) Elm, Ulmus minor, *in Crete. Land over 400 m is hatched*

ELM

(b) Ambelitsiá (Zelkova cretica), ● *recorded as a tree,* ○ *only as a shrub,* Δ *place-name. Land over 1,200 m is hatched*

unlocalized

AMBELITSIÁ

gathering around Melidhóni (My), where it can now be seen from the new main road, using the same tool, on hot summer days. As far as we know, the plant is the same as grows all over west and middle Crete; it is a mystery why the gathering should be restricted to one area.

Notes

1 W. Greuter (1967), 'Beiträge zur Flora der Südägäis 8-9 [*Phœnix theophrasti, Bupleurum kakiskalae*]', *Bauhinia*, **3**, 243-54.

2 These questions are discussed by W. Greuter (1972), 'The relict element of the flora of Crete and its evolutionary significance', D. H. Valentine (ed.), *Taxonomy, Phytogeography and Evolution*, London, Academic Press, pp. 161-78.

3 W. Greuter (1971), 'L'apport de l'homme à la flore spontanée de la Crète', *Boissiera*, **19**, 329-37.

4 *Natural History*, XIII, xlvi, 134.

5 *History of Plants*, I, x, 6.

6 E.g. Dionysius Periegetes, *Geography*, 503; Callimachus, *Hymn to Artemis*, 192.

7 MCV: Cicogna 1767 c.125.

8 The map includes records in Turland and in P. H. Davis (1984), *Flora of Turkey and the East Aegean Islands*, **8**, Edinburgh, Edinburgh University Press.

9 Greuter (1967, note 1).

10 *Geography*, X, iv, 3.

11 Theophrastus, *History of Plants*, I, xiv, 2.

12 G. P. Sarlis (1987), 'Zelkova abelicea (Lam.) Boiss, an endemic species of Crete', *Webbia*, **41**, 247-55.

7

Domestic animals and plants

Malvesye and Muskadelle thase mervelyous drynkes
Raykede full raythely* in rossete cowpes.

Morte d'Arthur, c. 1400

*served very swiftly
[Malmsey and muscatel were the chief Cretan wines
exported to England]

All the domestic animals of Crete, and all the major crops except olive, pear and almond, are exotic. The animals were all introduced before the Roman period, but new crops have continued to be brought; Cretan life would be hard to imagine without American plants such as potato, tomato and tobacco. Within living memory Crete has almost lost cattle and cereals, which used to be everyday sights throughout the island.

Livestock

Sheep and goats

Almost since their introduction in the Early Neolithic, sheep and goats have been the premier livestock animals. Their feeding habits may have been similar to the indigenous deer, so that after the deer died out, sheep and goats moved into their niche. Early in the Neolithic, some goats probably escaped domesticity for life in the wild and evolved into the Cretan *agrími* (Chapter 5). Contrary to popular belief, sheep and goats have discerning palates (Chapter 10).

Today these animals are of two kinds: flock sheep and goats, which form a separate branch of culture from ordinary farming (Chapter 14), and house-sheep or house-goats. The latter are of distinctive breeds and kept for daily supplies. These cherished animals are taken for walks on leashes by their owners; donkey-loads of foliage are brought back for them at evening.

Cattle

Cattle have been draught animals, beasts of burden, and objects of worship; except in the Early Neolithic, Cretans did not much eat them.[1] The Minoans were fascinated by bulls, the largest animals that most of them ever saw, and were forever depicting them. For example, at the recently excavated Middle Minoan peak sanctuary of Atsipádhes (AV), fragments of cattle figurines were the most frequent finds.[2] From the Archaic period in the Idaean Cave there is a bronze representation of a man milking a cow.

Cattle appear sporadically in Venetian records: for example, in 1370 there was an ordinance against 'wild oxen abandoned without a herder or keeper', and there are occasional references to meat and skins. In 1579 the Governor Foscarini reported a shortage of plough oxen, because many had been eaten or plundered in the recent Turkish war; he forbade any more to be slaughtered.[3]

Within living memory, the average household possessed a yoke of oxen or cows to draw the plough. Raulin in 1847 estimated that there were 63,500 cattle in the island (the third commonest animal), but very few of these small, thin, brown animals are left. The Western traveller who meets a bull will not be tempted to fall down and worship it. Crete is not good cattle country; it would have been a little better before the draining of the fens. There is little opportunity for making hay, and Cretan leaf-fodder is mainly suited to sheep and goats. Cretan breeds of cattle were well adapted to a dry environment and were able to get through the summer on dried-up grasses and stubble; these hardy little animals deserve better than to lapse into extinction unrecorded.

Pigs

The pig appears abundantly in Late Neolithic deposits, and has been constantly present ever since, though never as abundant as other animals. There is no sign that the wild pig ever came to Crete, although its tusks were a favourite exotic ornament.

Demeter, the classical cereal-goddess, liked to have pigs sacrificed to her. At her sanctuary near Knossós (T), pigs formed over 90 per cent of the identifiable bone fragments.[4]

Pigs appear in the medieval regulations for straying animals. In 1847 they were found all over Crete, though not in large numbers. As in most places, Cretan pig-keeping was not dependent on woodland, though we have heard of acorns being gathered for pigs within living memory. Presumably pigs ate rubbish.

Donkeys and horses

Crete does not eat these animals. Nor is it horse country: the horse is a status symbol, charger and mule-maker. The donkey is the ordinary riding and pack animal. The mule is for heavy-duty riding and carrying. In the Venetian period the usual riding animal was the pony or rouncey (Latin *roncinus*), a smaller, tougher, less fastidious beast than the horse.

The donkey may have been present even in the Neolithic, but the horse does not appear until the Late Bronze Age; one was buried in front of a Late Minoan III noblewoman's tomb near Arkhánes (T).[5]

The Venetians and Turks set great store by cavalry, which did neither of them any good. Persons holding lands by knight's service were supposed to maintain war-horses, which could be pastured on public lands. Horses had to be imported from Turkey, and in the middle ages were worth as much as eight donkeys or a very costly slave.[6] There were frequent complaints that knights were turning up to musters on ponies. Another concern was horses, ponies, mules and donkeys straying and eating people's crops. In 1367 farmers were allowed to shoot them if they could not catch them. In 1469 the State forbade horses, etc. to be fed on wheat from the public stores, on pain of amputation of the owner's beard.[7]

In the Turkish period the pony seems to have disappeared –

possibly because Christians were forbidden to ride horseflesh. Raulin reports that in 1847 there were 5,500 donkeys, 12,200 mules and 6,300 horses; a mule was worth 1½ horses, six donkeys, or about a dozen pairs of boots. All but the poorest families would have owned an animal, and could have ridden to work in distant places.

Other animals

The dog appears constantly from the Neolithic onwards, but was not usually eaten. Bronze Age and Early Iron Age owners took their dogs with them into the grave.[8] According to Aelian, a Roman author, 'the Cretan hound is nimble and a jumper and brought up to mountaineering'.[9]

Most Cretan sheepdogs ignore the sheep, and the only wolves the island has ever had are two-legged. We have, however, seen a wonderful dog that could catch partridges on the wing, and another that acted as shepherd without human assistance.

The cat, the last of the main domestic animals, appears first in Europe on the Knossós frescoes.

There are ducks on Minoan frescoes. Hens and geese first appear in the Hellenistic period.

Field crops

Throughout Cretan history the staple foodstuff has been bread. To the English reader this may seem a boring diet, but Cretan bread has not been debased by technology and even now needs no addition to make it edible. Cretans share the odd European habit of preferring wheat bread and despising barley and oats. Rye, rice, sorghum, millet and maize (corn), which call for too much mois-

ture in summer, have never been much grown.

Wheat and barley arrived with the first Cretans, but domesticated oats are not known on the island until the Early Bronze Age.[10] Various legumes have been grown since ancient times. The beautiful blue lupin of Sélinon appears to be an escape from cultivation for seed. Legumes would have added nitrogen to the soil for use by other crops.[11]

In the Late Bronze Age land was commonly measured by how much seed-grain was needed to sow it.[12] In the Venetian and Turkish periods, too, the common unit of land was the *mouzoúri*: the area (about 0.14 ha) which could be sown with one *mouzoúri* (18.4 litres[13]) of seed. The Venetians also thought in terms of the amount of land which could be expected to produce a thousand *mouzoúria* of grain; the idea that this was a fixed area led to endless trouble.

Gluts and shortages, caused by varying weather, have made wheat and barley unsatisfactory subsistence crops at least since the middle ages. In good years (roughly four years out of ten), wheat was exported, chiefly to Venice; in bad years it was imported from Turkey. The main areas for commercial production appear to have been around Candia (Herákleion (T)) and in the Mesará.

The Venetians made the wheat trade a state monopoly. They required feudal lords to sell an annual quantity to the state at a fixed price; they controlled the sale of grain out of the island, and even prohibited the sale of grain from one part of Crete to another. The motives were to secure grain supplies for Venice; to maintain stocks on the island against war or famine; and to make Crete independent of supplies from Turkey, so that Cretans should not be so willing to live at peace with the Turk. This bureaucracy, naturally, made the islanders grow other crops of less interest to the state.

With the approach of the Little Ice Age in the sixteenth century, harvests became more erratic and so did supplies from Turkey. The Venetians did everything they could to encourage the growing of grain, except pay an adequate price for it; Crete continued to be a net importer.

Grain-growing prospered for much of the Turkish period, reaching a peak perhaps in the eighteenth century. From 1930 onward it declined rapidly, the vacant lands being abandoned to phrygana and woodland (p. 118). Small quantities are still grown, particularly in the Askyphou and Lassíthi Plains. Harvest is a leisurely matter, there being little risk of rain. There seems never to have been a functional combine-harvester in Crete. Instead, the annual visit of the threshing-machine, a splendid piece of Victorian technology, occasions a day of hard, thirsty, merry work such as one of the authors remembers from his English childhood. Some grain is never harvested but is eaten in the field by livestock.

Most of the terraced hillsides are a legacy of grain-growing (Chapter 12). A more definite indication is the threshingfloor, *alóni*, an area 3–6 m across, paved (or cemented) and rimmed with upright stones. Most *alónia* are round, but those in the Ierápetra Isthmus are often puzzlingly square or compromisingly D-shaped. They are used in two ways, both Biblical. A group of animals – big mule, small mule, cow and a small donkey on the inside – walks round and round treading the sheaves ('thou shalt not muzzle the ox when he treadeth out the corn'[14]). Alternatively, a person rides round and round on a mule-drawn sledge, its underside set with flakes of iron or chert,

or bits of bandsaw-blade ('a new sharp threshing instrument having teeth'[15]). Grain was often threshed near where it grew, rather than taken home in the sheaf. *Alónia* remain as witnesses to grain-growing even in remote places.

The vine

. . . Hear me, Celia.
Thy baths shall be the juice of July-flowers . . .
The milk of unicorns and panther's breath,
Gather'd in bags and mixed with Cretan wines.

Ben Jonson, *Volpone* (1607)

Crete is a happy land where 'wine that maketh glad the heart of man' has always been an everyday amenity of even the poorest. It has often been the chief cash crop, but is also something that people make for themselves. Cretans delight in offering a stranger their own wine, which tends to be better than any that money will buy. Vines are also grown for eating grapes, for currants and sultanas, and for vine-leaves to wrap up *dolmádhes*, little parcels of meat and rice. Vine-prunings are a favourite fuel for ovens and are sometimes used in the structure of flat roofs.

The vine is an oddity among Cretan cultivated plants. It apparently comes from the north; its wild forebears can still be found in river floodplains in Austria and the Balkans. Of the major crops, it is the least well adapted to the Cretan climate: the last to come into leaf in spring and the first to shed its leaves. All its growing must be done on moisture stored in the soil. The special Cretan varieties of grape flourish surprisingly well, even at low altitudes and in the arid east of the island.

Vines have deep roots and demand a soil with good root penetration. They grow on many Cretan soils, including scree, but the biggest vine-growing areas are on less compact marls and in certain mountain-plains – Zíros and Khandrás (Si) and Askyphou (Sf). Vine-growing is often linked to terracing, which breaks up the bedrock and increases root penetration. It is very labour-intensive. In addition to pruning, gathering and wine-making, vines have to be rigorously weeded – they are very sensitive to competition from weeds which would steal moisture from the soil before the vines start growing. As a labour-intensive cash crop, vines have been more rewarding than grain, especially when dense populations obliged people to make the best use of small areas of land.

Archaeological evidence for vines is rare, and later than for cereals. Grape pips occur at a few Early and Middle Minoan sites, but so far no vine-prunings have been identified.[16] Constructions that may be wine-presses occur in Late Minoan houses throughout Crete, suggesting that wine-making was a household craft. Both Bronze Age scripts have symbols for wine; vineyards are mentioned in Linear B texts from Knossós (T). Cretan wines get only passing mentions from surviving Greek or Roman authors, except for some disparaging medicinal remarks by Galen.[17]

In the middle ages, vines and wine-making are the second most prominent branch of farming, after cereals. Small-scale vineyards and pergola vines appear in descriptions of property, perambulations and regulations concerning stray animals. Buondelmonti in 1415 mentions vineyards which flourished, then as now, around Arkhánes (T). Taxes were levied on wine exported and on wine sold locally from the tap.

Cretan wine gained an international reputation by the four-teenth century, and in the next century overtook grain as the chief export. England, especially, drank a sweet dessert wine which had usually been stewed in great cauldrons. In sixteenth-century Oxford this was known as *vinum Creticum*, but the usual English term was malvesey or malmsey. This word had apparently once implied Monemvasía in the Peloponnese, but by 1420 it had been transferred to Malevyzi in Crete. A decree of the Venetian Senate in 1488, concerning foreign ships taking it to England, makes it clear that Crete was the main source of malmsey.[18] Special ships were commissioned for the trade, and in 1522 Henry VIII appointed the first-ever English consul to Candia.[19]

At times Crete may have been the second biggest exporter of wine to England, where it fetched nearly twice the price of French table wine.[20] Was not the Duke of Clarence, convicted of high treason in 1478, honourably executed by being 'hasteley drowned in a Butt of Malmesey'?[21]

Leonardo Loredan summarised Cretan wine-growing in 1554:

> One year with another, the City [Candia, Herákleion] and its province make 14,000 butts* of wine. Of this, 200 butts of *moscatti* go to Flanders because it is not of too good quality. 500-600 butts of *liatici* are exported to Venice and elsewhere. Chissamo and Bicorna [Apokórona] make about 2000 butts for Flanders. The rest of the aforementioned total of wine is *Logade* and *Cozzifalli*, which are sent to Flanders, to Venice, to Constantinople, to Alexandria . . . to Messina and to Malta.[22]

* A butt was 104 English gallons; the province would thus have made 6.6 million litres, or nearly 10 million modern bottles, a year.

The growth of cities and artistic achievement in sixteenth-century Crete have been attributed to the prosperity of the wine trade.[23]

By 1590 it was claimed that one-third of the cultivable hill-land of Crete was growing vines.[24] The Venetian authorities thought that if people were stopped from growing vines they would grow wheat instead. They prohibited new vineyards, which in practice encouraged people to plant olives. The years around 1600 mark the zenith of Cretan wine-growing. (Was this yet another effect of the Little Ice Age?) English records show that malmsey was consumed up to 1643, when there was a gap while the Turks were warring in Crete. Shipments resumed in 1661 and petered out at the end of the century.[25]

The decline of wine-growing evidently resulted from a changing pattern of trade. This may have come from the introduction of glass bottles and corks around 1600, making it easier to keep other wines drinkable and reducing the demand for the sweet, relatively stable wines of Crete. The English, having made peace with Spain, took to drinking sack and sherry as dessert wines.

Vines were still grown after the Turkish conquest. In deeds of 1659 to 1671 vineyards appear about half as often as fields.[26] Muslim Cretans, contrary to what some travellers claimed, paid some attention to their religious ban on wine, but did not observe it strictly: they owned about one-fifth of the vineyards, compared to one-third of the fields. A century later, wine-making had declined to the point that the traveller Olivier could claim that Cretans drank up their wine in three or four months and then had to make do with water.

Grapes for sultanas and currants demand hot dry summers and are spoilt if it rains while they are drying. In middle Crete this trade goes back to the Venetian period; it is said to have been revived in the 1920s by refugees from Asia Minor.

Distilling *rakí* is apparently an introduction of the Turkish period. It is a festive occasion, taking place around the feast of St George the Drunken (2 November); the still simmers day and night for ten days, and glasses of the fiery liquor are pressed on passers-by.

Raulin in 1847 says that Crete made 8.6 million litres of wine annually (equivalent to 12 million bottles). Added to 580,000 litres of *rakí* and 1,450 tons of raisins, this means that vine-growing was at least equal to that in the Venetian period. The main areas were Kíssamos and Malevyzi; the Candia area was no longer significant.

Vine-growing has never been the same since America gave Europe three disastrous pests: powdery mildew in the 1840s, *Phylloxera* root-aphid in the 1860s, and downy mildew in the 1870s. Crete escaped *Phylloxera* (for a time), but not the mildews: Cretan growers, like everyone else, soak their vines in chemicals, without which they may not get any grapes at all. (Mildew is less troublesome at high altitudes.) In recent years there has been a recurrence of *Phylloxera*. With the trouble and expense of spraying, and the residues that get into the wine, vine-growing is no longer simple.

Most of the grape varieties grown in Crete are peculiar to the island. They differ from one region to another (for example the early-ripening *liátiko* in arid east Crete) and according to the type of wine being made. Some types of wine, such as *logádo,* are made from mixed vineyards. Lists of grape varieties go back to the sixteenth century,[27] and include some still grown today such as *kotsifáli* (Loredan's *cozzifalli*). Other varieties may be more recent. Compared with previous centuries, Malevyzi has declined and Siteía has become an important area.[28]

Although wine-writers find much to discuss in the bottled wines of Crete, the most distinctive are those made by Cretans for themselves. One can buy these on draught in tavernas, but to taste the really best one has to be an honoured guest in someone's home. They are often variants of what visitors call 'Cretan Brown' – a heavy, very alcoholic, sweet red wine with a distinctive 'maderized' flavour that comes from storage in a hot climate. This was probably the malmsey of old. Pashley in 1834 found the best wines in all Crete in the Askyphou Plain, almost the highest vine-growing locality; and here, 150 years later, a friend gave us the best wine we have had in Crete, which we can best liken to an old dessert sherry, worthy of the Duke of Clarence.

The former extent of vine-growing in Crete is to be seen in well-built terraces – those for grain are usually rougher. Around Thryphtí (H) vine-terraces cling to slopes on which the vertical height of the wall may exceed the cultivated area of the terrace; they reach 1,000 m, and were claimed by Raulin to be the highest in Europe.

Another indicator is the *patitíri*, a shallow tank with a spout, built into or against a house for treading grapes. (Earlier, these could be out in the fields, and are mentioned as boundary features.) They are a reminder of Dionysiac Septembers, when friends and neighbours plash knee-deep in the blood of the grape.

The olive

This noble tree is the source of oil for cooking, lighting, lubricating, oiling boots, etc. Olives for eating, although excellent, are a proletarian diet seldom recorded. Soap is made from the worst oil; it is still made on a reduced scale today. The tree is one of Crete's chief sources of firewood; its timber appears in house-carpentry where there is nothing better.

Olive ecology

The olive is perhaps the longest-lived crop plant, and the trees themselves are witnesses to the history of its cultivation. Ancient olives are a special feature of Crete (Figure 7.1), the symbol of endurance and indestructibility. Their age is a clue to things as diverse as climate (Chapter 4), erosion (Chapter 3), and terracing (Chapter 12). It is best estimated, though with difficulty, from annual rings. Only about half the olive-trees in Crete produce countable rings. One can find pruning wounds or the stumps of cut-off boughs from which to estimate the rate of expansion of the stem. Any tree with a trunk diameter of 2 m – and there are some much bigger – is likely to date from the middle ages.

The olive withstands ordinary frosts, but a temperature of -13°C (9°F) kills the tree to ground level, from which it only slowly recovers. The olive limit in Crete is ordinarily 750 m, although occasional wild olives can be found up to 1,000 m. Many of the biggest ancient olives are close to the upper limit, proving that there has not been a severe frost since before the Little Ice Age. Olive-growers in Crete (unlike Italy) do not take risks with their trees.

The olive fruits well only in alternate years, even when irrigated and fertilised. (Greek has a word, ελαιώνα, for the year of the olive harvest.) All the olive-trees in any one area tend to fruit together, which may be tied to the local periodicity of droughts[29] or of *sirocco* winds (p. 37) at the time of flowering. In 1992 there was hardly an olive on the trees of west Crete, except in a small part of Sélinon which had a full crop. This behaviour begets the storing of oil from year to year and speculation on price movements.

The olive is shallow-rooted: its roots just escape ploughing. On terraces, it develops half its roots horizontally under the terrace, and half vertically behind the terrace wall. The tree, though drought-resistant, benefits from removing the vegetation beneath it, which would compete for moisture; this is traditionally done by an annual ploughing. It used to be the practice to grow a cereal crop beneath the trees, as can still occasionally be seen.

7.1 *Olive-tree, one of the oldest in Europe: its annual rings indicate a Hellenistic date. Loutró (Sf), July 1987*

Olive-trees are grafted on rootstocks of wild olive (which continue to sprout from the base of the trunk). There are many cultivated varieties, and old trees can be re-grafted to a different variety. Olives demand little attention apart from ploughing and gathering; but most owners prune them, and the prunings are an important source of fuel. Olive varieties fall into two groups, *khondróelia* and *psilóelia*. The first has a larger fruit and broader leaf; it is a dual-purpose olive, for eating or oil. Most ancient olives fall into this category. The *psilóelia*, with a smaller fruit and narrow leaf, is mainly for oil; these olives are fashionable for new plantings.

The oldest olive-trees are spaced randomly, but from the sixteenth century onwards it has been the custom to grow them in rows. On rocky slopes this may not be possible; olive-groves in such places may have been made by grafting existing wild olives.

Olives are harvested in winter, a laborious task that has confounded all attempts at mechanisation. Harvest is turned into a festive family outing; in many villages children are let out of school to participate. There are three methods: hand-picking, beating the tree with a long pole, and letting the olives drop on their own. Green olives, which are more time-consuming to harvest, produce better oil; ripe olives, which fall on their own into nets strewn below the trees, produce more oil, but more acidic and of worse quality. (The Roman writer Cato took an opposite view.[30])

Machines for crushing olives and squeezing out the oil have been used since ancient times. Olive-crusheries are often mentioned in conveyances of property from the 1650s onwards. In the nineteenth century, every village had one or more oileries, using stone rollers and wooden (or later iron) screw-presses. Processing is now concentrated in fewer, larger factories.

History of olive cultivation

Although it does not appear in the lowest levels of the pollen cores, wild olive is probably native to Crete. It could have survived the glaciations in warm gorges, and afterwards have expanded into coastal woodland. Pollen records suggest that there was olive cultivation on Crete by the Late Neolithic, considerably earlier than elsewhere in the Aegean.[31] Olive stones and possible prunings are known from the Early Minoan site of Myrtos (H).[32] Olives appear as ideograms in Linear A; wild and domestic olives may be differentiated in Linear B texts.[33] (The oil of wild olives is said to be better for perfumery, probably an important 'palace' industry.[34]) In classical times olive oil was used as a cosmetic and in food.

Before 1700, olive-trees were widespread, but in modest numbers, scattered in fields; records rarely mention land set aside for growing them. Olive oil was a relatively minor article of export and import. In 1359 it was regularly imported from the Peloponnese; in 1400 Sicilian pirates relieved a Cretan ship of 100 barrels of oil. Among the evils of the plague in 1348 was the lack of harvesters for grain and vines; olive-picking was not mentioned.[35]

Olive-growing is a story of expansion. The Venetians' efforts to force Cretans to grow wheat caused them to grow more olives (via the Law of Unintended Consequences). Later the Little Ice Age helped Cretan olive-growing: Crete, lying far to the south, escaped the frosts which plagued France and Italy, especially the killing frost of 1709. By the 1730s, Crete was exporting an average of 1,600 tons of oil a year to Marseilles alone, a trade on which much of the prosperity at this time was based.[36]

There was a further expansion from the 1840s onwards.[37] This accounts for trees with trunks some 30 cm in diameter, which greatly outnumber ancient ones. Early photographs, such as those in Sir Arthur Evans's work, show arable fields where these groves now stand.

There has been yet another expansion in the last twenty years, the result of government, and lately European Community, subsidies. Other changes are the bulldozing of new fields and terraces, the use of piped irrigation (not essential but increases the yield), and plastic netting on which the olives fall.

Other crops

Citrus fruits

Our earliest reference is to the sale of *narancie* in Candia (Herákleion) market in the *Book of Bans* in 1360. This probably does not refer to the modern orange (although the name is the same) but to the related bergamot. Bergamots are often mentioned in Venetian and Turkish records, but probably only as garden trees.

Citrus trees are often mentioned in accounts of late Venetian and Turkish gardens. They were also grown for trade: in 1566 nearly a thousand *botte* (450,000 litres) of lemon juice were exported from around Canea to the teetotalling Turks.[38] This anticipated the large-scale citrus orchards around Khaniá (Ky) today, many of them on former cereal fields.

Chestnut

Sweet-chestnut (*Castanea sativa*) is an ancient introduction in Crete. Our knowledge of it comes almost entirely from the trees themselves. The magnificent specimens which delighted Raulin 150 years ago delight the traveller today; some are known from their annual rings to be 700 years old. They are pollards or (less often) coppice stools, sometimes with mysterious little doors in their hollow trunks. Some of these vast and wonderful trees belong to several people, each owning a particular sector of the circumference of the tree.

Chestnut is an orchard tree, grown and grafted for its nuts. Although it grows from seed there are no natural woods in Crete. Most if not all of the coppice poles which are used for telegraph-poles and the like, and the timber for barrel-staves, come from chestnut-woods in north Greece.

Chestnut is very localised to the wet phyllite-quartzite country of west Crete (Figure 7.2). It fits into the landscape more specifically and harmoniously than any other crop. Chestnut-groves line the valleys and go a little way up the hillsides, always in damp (but not too wet) places away from limestone. They have a highly characteristic ground vegetation, dominated by the umbellifer *Lecockia cretica* which grows almost nowhere else in Europe. Primrose, jonquil and the endemic cyclamen are among the beautiful plants that go with chestnut-groves.

Chestnuts are not the staple source of flour in Crete that they have been in parts of Italy, but they perform a social function; autumn festivals are held in honour of this glorious tree at Sémbronas (Ky) and Kándanos (Se). Chestnut-growing flourishes, but not to the excessive degree that olive does.

The chestnuts of Crete escaped the *Endothia* disease that played havoc with those of Italy and the United States in the 1930s. When we first knew them, in 1982, they were suffering from a dieback associated with wet places, perhaps a form of *Phytophthora* ink disease. A run of dry seasons checked its ravages. Chestnut is very tenacious of life; even if three-quarters of the tree is dead it can recover.

Mulberry trees and silk

The 'white' mulberry (*Morus alba*) is a common, very vigorous shade-tree, normally pollarded annually. It is said to be from Asia, and is an ancient introduction, well known in classical times,[39] but never naturalised. The 'black' mulberry (*M. nigra*), familiar in old-fashioned English gardens, is also to be found in old-fashioned Cretan gardens and is grown for its fruit.

Long after the first introduction, white mulberries were grown for feeding silkworms. Silk, and the elaborate methods for preparing it, seem to have come late to Crete. Our earliest record is in 1554 when it was exported to Constantinople.[40] Early Turkish records often mention mulberries and silkworms: in 1658 an inquest was held on a shepherd who fell out of a mulberry-tree while gathering leaves to feed silkworms.[41] In the nineteenth century silk was a minor source of income all over the island. It has now almost died out.

The main use of mulberries is to grow leaves for feeding livestock, especially in the lean season of early autumn. Special leaf-bearing varieties of mulberry are grafted. The trees also produce useful rods and timber.

Other fruit-trees

The carob (p. 70) was originally an orchard tree but has long been wild.

Pears are commonly grafted on to the wild pear (*Prunus amygdaliformis*). Immense pollards can be seen on the Omalós Plain. The quince (*Cydonia oblonga*) is a favourite Cretan tree; in ancient times Cretans imagined that the name of the city Kydónia (Khaniá (Ky)) was derived from that of the tree, or vice versa. Crete is too hot for apples, except at high altitudes.

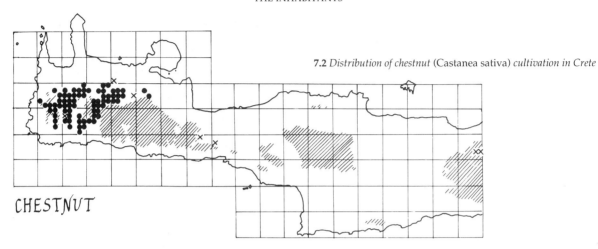

7.2 *Distribution of chestnut* (Castanea sativa) *cultivation in Crete*

CHESTNUT

Figs have been a widespread minor crop since the Bronze Age, as well as a wild tree on cliffs.

Walnut (an exotic tree) is grown mainly at higher altitudes and has probably increased, but the common place-name *Karydhi* attests to the wide distribution of the tree even in arid east Crete. The tree is short-lived. Almonds were recently a major crop, but are now suffering badly from drought and disease.

Cherries are local; there are some spectacular trees on phyllite-quartzite in west Crete. There are several little-known stone-fruits, one of which, the *vyssina*, makes a fine liqueur at Gerakári (Am).

The umbrella-pine (*Pinus strobus*) was originally a sand-dune tree in Italy and perhaps Greece. In Crete it was grown for its edible seeds. Its distinctive umbrella-like silhouette usually indicates a nineteenth-century garden.

The pomegranate is said to come from the south Caspian.[42] It was a favourite of the Greeks and Romans, and is frequent in Turkish documents.

The loquat, *Eriobotrya japonica*, is a Far Eastern tree long grown under the names *dhéspoula* or *moúsmoula*.

The tree *tsítsife* is a mystery. Two places (Ki, Ap) are named after it. It should be the jujube tree (*Zizyphus jujuba*, Rhamnaceæ), cultivated since Roman times. However, Cretans when asked have shown us a species of *Elaeagnus* with an edible fruit.

Bananas are mainly a greenhouse crop, but for many years have been grown in the open in hot, sheltered valleys around Arvi (V).

In recent years some other tropical fruit trees have been grown on a fairly large scale in warm valleys, notably avocado pear (*Persea gratissima*) from the West Indies and kiwi-fruit (*Actinidia chinensis*) from China.

Cotton

Old World cotton (*Gossypium herbaceum*) is native to sub-Saharan Africa; it is a different species from New World cotton. It makes heavy demands on the soil. The classical Greeks knew of 'the wool-bearing tree' from its cultivation in India,[43] but did not grow it themselves.

In the middle ages cotton was less important to Europe than it is now (people used *Cannabis* instead). It was grown by Cretan farmers and sold in Candia (Herákleion) market. Records suggest that cotton was at least the fourth cash crop of the island, as well as being brought from Egypt and re-exported. By the sixteenth century it had declined. Some 80 tons a year were still being grown in the 1840s, mainly in the Mesará and Siteía, but also on the Lassíthi Plain where frost would have cut short the growing season.[44] It is still grown in mainland Greece, but we have never seen it in Crete.

Other herbaceous crops

Flax has been grown since the Bronze Age, at times as a major crop, for fibre (linen) and for linseed. The word *linon* goes back to the Linear B tablets. In the middle ages environmental regulations provided against polluting watercourses by retting flax.

Sesame, another oil-seed, is named in Linear B. The word is said to be Semitic, which would indicate a Near Eastern origin for the plant.

Saffron, the stigmas of *Crocus sativus* or a wild predecessor, is an ancient crop. Saffron-gatherers are depicted on a famous Minoan fresco from Santoríni.[45] In 1402 saffron was among booty seized by pirates from a Cretan ship.[46] Raulin in the nineteenth century found vast fields of it outside Réthymnon.

An unexpected tropical crop is taro or cocoyam (*Colocasia antiquorum*), an aroid with an edible tuber. It was known in ancient Egypt.[47] Tournefort found that at Réthymnon in 1700 'the Natives eat it in their Broth.' The place-name Kolokásia apparently testifies to its presence even in dry Sphakiá. Its huge leaves can still be seen in damp places, such as the springs of Argyroúpolis (R).

The Venetians tried to introduce sugar-cane from Sicily. In 1414 Marco de Zanono was given a ten-year monopoly on the 'mystery of sugar'. This included authority to grow sugar-cane in the Stylos (Ap) area, to process and boil it, and to have an armed guard on the plantations. In 1431 we find him renting more land, building mills, and seeking special powers against arsonists and saboteurs.[48]

The Turkish period was a time of interest in new plants, especially from America. To judge by its appearance in travellers' pictures, the giant aloe or century-plant (*Agave americana*) was introduced in the eighteenth century. Its formidably spiny leaves made it a hedging plant. It is one of the biggest of herbaceous plants; its short-lived flowering stems, 7 m high, are a feature of the Akrotíri Peninsula. Prickly-pear, another hedging plant from tropical America, which yields an edible fruit, has been less enduring. Tomatoes, now the biggest greenhouse crop of Crete, are recorded by Olivier in 1793. (The cucumber, however, was well known to the Ancient Greeks.) The potato, from South America, was still an experimental crop in the 1840s; it now grows mainly in the Lassíthi Plain at high altitude. Tobacco has never prospered in Crete.

Beekeeping

A land like Crete, with an abundance of thyme and similar

undershrubs, rejoices in abundant honey. (However, although flowers are specifically adapted to bee-pollination, *wild* bees are not common on Crete today.) Another kind of honey comes from pine exudations, especially those caused by the processionary caterpillar or bagworm, which is sometimes introduced by beekeepers into pinewoods to stimulate the flow. Pine honey has a resiny taste like retsina.

Honey was the only sugary food apart from onions in antiquity. To the Minoans it was the diet of gods and royalty. The infant Zeus was said to have been fed on milk and honey in the cave on Mount Ida.[49] The Linear B archives reveal that jars of honey were indeed given to the gods. Glaucus, son of King Minos, was drowned (temporarily) in a jar of honey.[50]

Professional beekeepers are mentioned in Linear B. Beekeeping, honey and wax often appear in Venetian and Turkish documents; Raulin lists Sphakiá and Ierápetra districts as producing 90 tons of honey a year in 1847. Today, though in decline, beekeeping may be experiencing a slight revival: there was recently an island-wide symposium on the subject at Prína (H).

Some Minoan pots have been identified as beehives, by analogy with Roman and later ceramic beehives. Archaeological surveys discover great concentrations of broken Graeco-Roman (as well as later) hives, often far from habitation, sometimes within high-walled enclosures to shelter the bees from wind (Chapter 12).

Greece is remarkable for its diversity of beehives. Modern types in Crete include a horizontal, cylindrical pot like a cannon, and a flowerpot-shaped basket, chinked with clay, with a lid. The latter is a form of the movable-comb hive, the key device of modern beekeeping, invented in Greece in or before the Turkish period.[51]

This is the predecessor of the American box-hive, the chief pattern used in Crete today.

Notes

1 M. R. Jarman and H. N. Jarman (1968), in Evans J. D. 'Knossos Neolithic part II', *BSA*, **63**, 241-62.

2 A. A. D. Peatfield (1992), 'Rural Ritual in Bronze Age Crete: The Peak Sanctuary at Atsipadhes', *Cambridge Archaeological Journal*, **2**, 59-87.

3 ASV: DC b.14bis–15 p. 179v. MCV: Cicogna 1767 c.127,132.

4 M. R. Jarman (1973), 'Preliminary report on the animal bones' in J. N. Coldstream (ed.), *Knossos: the Sanctuary of Demeter, BSA supplement*, **8**, 177-9.

5 J. A. Sakellarakis and E. Sapouna-Sakellarakis (1991), *Archanes*, Athens, Ekdotike Athenon Travel Guides, pp. 76-7.

6 E. A. Zachariadou (1983),*Trade and Crusade*, Venice, Istituto Ellenico di Studi Bizantini.

7 ASV: DC b.14 bis c.142v; b.15 c.1.

8 W. Coulson, L. Day, and G. Gesell (1983), 'Excavations and survey at Kavousi, 1978-1981,' *Hesperia*, **52**, 389-420.

9 *On the Peculiarities of Animals*, III, 2.

10 J. R. A. Greig and P. M. Warren (1974), 'Agriculture in the Early Bronze Age of western Crete', *Antiquity*, **58**, 130-2.

11 A. Sarpaki (1990), 'The palaeobotanical approach: the Mediterranean triad or is it a quartet?', in Wells (see bibliography) pp. 62-76.

12 M. Ventris and J. Chadwick (1973), *Documents in Mycenaean Greek*, Cambridge, Cambridge University Press.

13 Y. Triantafyllidou-Baladié (1981), 'Dominations étrangères et transformations de l'agriculture crétoise entre le XVIe et le XIXe siècle', *Greek Review of Social Research, Centre Nationale de Recherches Sociales*, Athens, 180-90.

14 *Deuteronomy*, **25**, 4.

15 *Isaiah*, **41**, 15.

16 J. Hansen (1988), 'Agriculture in the prehistoric Aegean: data versus speculation', *American Journal of Archaeology*, **92**, 39-52.

17 Kühn edition, XV, 648, 862.

18 *Calendar of State Papers Venetian*, **1**, no. 544.

19 *Letters & Papers Foreign & Domestic,* no. 2145.

20 J. E. T. Rogers (1882), *A history of agriculture and prices in England,* Oxford, Clarendon, vol. **3**.

21 Sir Thomas More (1516), *History of Richard III.*

22 ASV: CR b. 82.

23 Y. Triantafyllidou-Baladié (1992), 'The Cretan rural landscape and its changes in late-medieval and modern times', *Petromarula,* **1**, 47-51.

24 ASV: CR b.79 c.5 [Leonardo Quirini].

25 Rogers (1882), *Agriculture and Prices,* vol. **5**.

26 Stavrinidhes (see bibliography), vol. **A**, *passim.*

27 For example, Boschini 1625 in BNP: Ital.383 f.15.

28 M. Lambert-Gócs (1990), *The wines of Greece,* London, Faber.

29 H. Forbes (1992), 'The ethnoarchaeological approach to ancient Greek agriculture', in Wells, (see bibliography), pp. 87-101.

30 *Agriculture,* **65**, 1-2.

31 J. Moody, O. Rackham and G. Rapp (1990), 'Paleoenvironmental studies of the Akrotiri peninsula, Crete: pollen cores from Tersana and Limnes', *JFA,* forthcoming; C.N. Runnels and J. Hansen (1986), 'The olive in the prehistoric Aegean: the evidence for domestication', *Oxford Journal of Archaeology,* **5**, 299-308; Hansen (1988, note 16).

32 J. M. Renfrew 'The plant remains', in P. M. Warren, *Myrtos: an Early Bronze Age Settlement in Crete,* London, Thames & Hudson, pp. 315-17; Rackham (1972), see bibliography.

33 Ventris and Chadwick (1973, note 12).

34 J. L. Melena (1983), 'Olive oil and other sorts of oil in the Mycenaean tablets', *Minos,* **18**, 89-123.

35 Thiriet (see bibliography), no. 351; Noiret (see bibliography), p. 138; Thiriet, no. 214.

36 Y. Triandafyllidou-Baladié (Γ. Τριανταφύλλιδου-Baladié) (1988), *Τὸ Εμπόριο καὶ ἡ Οἰκονομία τῆς Κρήτης (1669-1795),* Herakleion, Βικέλια.

37 Raulin (1868, see bibliography), p.292.

38 VBM: Ital. VII. 701/7694 c.90 [Basadona].

39 Theophrastus, *History of Plants,* passim.

40 ASV: Coll. Relaz. busta 83.

41 Stavrinidhes (see bibliography), vol. **A**, no. 54.

42 D. Zohary and P. Spiegel-Roy (1975), 'Beginnings of fruit growing in the Old World', *Science,* **187**, 319-27.

43 Theophrastus, *History of Plants,* IV, iv, 8; IV, vii, 7.

44 Raulin (1868, see bibliography), B, 410.

45 See I. Douskos (1978), 'The crocuses of Santorini', in C. Doumas (ed.),*Thera and the Aegean World,* London, pp. 141-6.

46 Noiret (see bibliography), p. 138.

47 Theophrastus, *History of Plants,* I, vi, 11.

48 Noiret (see bibliography), pp. 324, 347-8.

49 Hesiod,*Theogony,* pp. 453-67.

50 Hyginus, *Fabula,* 136.

51 E. Crane (1983), *The Archaeology of Beekeeping,* London, Duckworth.

8

People and settlements

We must keep at least two types before our minds. On the one hand there is what we might call the true village … In the purest form of this type, there is one and only one cluster of houses. It is a fairly large cluster; it stands in the midst of its fields, of its territory … On the other hand, we may easily find a country in which there are few villages of this character. The houses … are scattered about in small clusters; here two or three, there three or four. These clusters often have names of their own, and it seems a mere chance that the name borne by one of them should be also the name of the whole parish.

F. W. Maitland, *Domesday Book and Beyond*, 1897 [referring to England]

The Cretan people

There is no such thing as a Cretan race. Crete has always been cosmopolitan. Hesiod, the second earliest Greek writer, thought the Cretans came from three different places.[1] Each successive conqueror of Crete left at least a few people on the island. After the Roman period, when mainland Greece was overrun by northerners, Crete might seem to have escaped through being an island, but place-names and surnames show that some Slavs and Albanians settled here. The medieval Venetians were among the chief colonisers of Crete: they settled their own merchants and nobles, introduced slaves and prisoners-of-war. African slaves continued to be imported until 1859. The biggest influx of colonists may have been Christian Turkish refugees in 1924, amounting to one-tenth of the population of the island.

Cretans are descended, to varying degrees, from Albanians, Argives, Armenians, Bulgars, Dorians, Eteocretans, French, Germans, Hebrews, Minoans, Negroes, Pelasgians, Romans, Saracens, Serbs, Spaniards, Spartans, Tartars, Turks, Venetians and Vlachs. Crete is a fine example of how the distinctive culture and identity of a land do not depend on its people having any specific origin. One wonders how it still has people of such distinctive physique as the Sphákiots, with their high proportion of blue eyes and fair hair.

Crete has had only three native languages. The Minoan language is unknown; so is the Eteocretan, which lingered in far-east Crete into Ancient Greek times and was thought to be aboriginal. Greek has been the language of Crete for over 3,000 years. It has developed in close association with mainland Greek, incorporating Turkish words and French phraseology in the same way.

The Cretan dialect has its own pronunciation (which is an extra complication to the normal difficulties of transliterating Greek place-names). It pronounces Greek as if it were Italian – *kyriakí* (Sunday) is pronounced *chiriachí*, with *ch* as in *church*. Many Cretans do not distinguish *l* and *r*. This is not due to Venetian influence: to judge by the spellings of place-names, Cretan dialect has changed little in 750 years.

Hamlets, villages, towns and cities

To the visitor, Greece seems *par excellence* a land of villages. Everyone lives in a big village of hundreds of houses, packed around the parish church and the coffee-houses in the square. This *nucleated* settlement seems to be the image of a sociable people, who value being near their neighbours more than being near their fields. It is easy to imagine that Greece has always been like this.

Crete is more complicated. There are large villages, 4-5 km apart in an otherwise empty countryside (Figure 8.1b). But there are also parts of the island where people live in *hamlets*, clusters of no more than a dozen houses, a kilometre or so apart (Figure 8.1a). In west Crete the map is black with hundreds of names and still does not include them all. This individualistic landscape, setting less store by coffee-house and parish church, is particularly strong in Sphakiá, with, for example, the eight hamlets of the Anópolis

Plain. The distinction between lands of villages and lands of hamlets runs through Europe. In England it appears that the hamlet landscape (e.g. of Essex) is the older, and the villages (e.g. of Cambridgeshire) are a monument to a period of collectivisation beginning about 1,200 years ago.[2]

The isolated house, standing in its own fields, is a rarity in Crete. Sometimes, in the lowlands, there are 'villas' – upper-class houses of Venetian or Turkish date, not attached to settlements: modest versions of the English manor-house or French *château*.

Crete has other types of settlement. Some villages and hamlets are inhabited only in summer: in Sphakiá the five hamlets of Kallikráti and the seven of Asphéndou are deserted in winter, when the people move down to their other houses in the villages of Patsianós and Vouvás at the foot of the mountains. Elsewhere, there are *field-houses*, set away from the village and lived in for tending vines, olives, etc. These may be grouped into hamlets. For example, Kavoúsi (H), a normal village, has ten hamlets of field-houses (each with its name) in the isolated, fertile valley of Avgo. In the mountains are isolated *mitáta*, places where shepherds live with their flocks in summer, milk their animals and keep equipment for cheese-making.

Settlement hierarchy

In the Old and New Palace Periods there was a hierarchy of four sizes of settlement: hamlets (by far the most numerous), villages, small towns and large towns such as Zákro (Si). In Late Minoan III half the hamlets and small towns were deserted, resulting in a village-dominated landscape punctuated occasionally by a large town. After the Bronze Age rural settlements along the coast all but disappeared, replaced by medium-sized fortified towns on high hills. These may have been the original 'cities' of Homer's Crete (Homer could not make up his mind whether there were ninety or a hundred cities).[3] Small inland settlements continued, much reduced in number. (Much the same happened during the fifteenth and sixteenth centuries AD, when the island was plagued by corsairs (Chapter 18).)[4]

Beginning in the Archaic period, settlements reappeared along the coasts; they became even more nucleated inland. Nevertheless, the seventh-century Law Code of Górtyn refers both to city houses and to country properties where 'serfs' resided, indicating that settlement was not entirely confined to the city.[5] This pattern continued until the Roman conquest. Rural settlement increased throughout the Roman and Early Byzantine periods as a profusion of dispersed farms; the hierarchy of larger settlements of the Minoan period was revived.

How and when this pattern turned into the predominantly hamlet landscape of the early Venetian period is an unsolved problem. Dispersed farms were abandoned in or about the ninth century AD.

Documents and place-names

There are three seemingly complete lists of settlements in the Venetian period: Barozzi 1577,[6] Castrofilaca 1583 (with population figures),[7] and Basilicata 1630.[8] Each names over a thousand settlements (though not the same thousand!). For Canea (Khaniá) province there is a fourth list by Trivan in 1645.[9] Before this time hundreds of settlements are named in documents of other kinds, going back to the twelfth century. These indicate that most Cretan (like English) villages and hamlets are of at least medieval antiquity, *except for those on the coast*. Most inland settlements

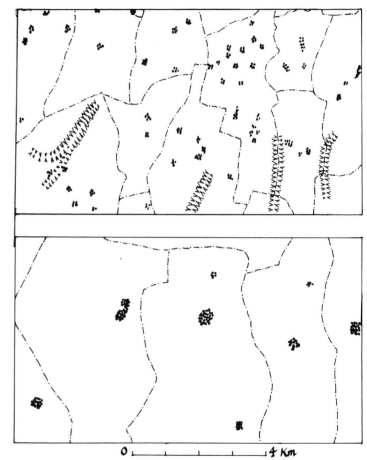

8.1 *Specimens of (a) hamlet territory, around Topólia (Ki), (b) village territory, around Orinó (Si). Settlements, township boundaries, and gorges are shown*

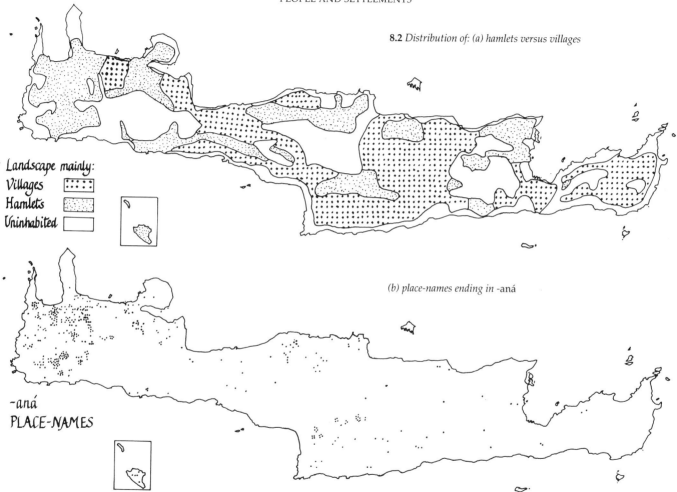

8.2 *Distribution of: (a) hamlets versus villages*

Landscape mainly:
Villages
Hamlets
Uninhabited

(b) place-names ending in -aná

-aná
PLACE-NAMES

existed in 1577, and many (including remote hamlets) much earlier.

To interpret such documents is not straightforward. A document that mentions what is now a village does not prove that it was a village at the time: it could have been a hamlet, or even not a settlement at all. Many coastal villages, for example Pakhyámmos (H), are named on Venetian maps as coastal features long before anyone lived there. Dispersed settlements present another problem. Hamlets were grouped for administrative purposes into townships (Venetian *casali*), and it was a matter of chance which hamlet gave its name to the *casale*. If a hamlet does not appear in a census, this may merely mean that it was subsumed in another place to make up a *casale*. Census-takers often left out places: most major lists omit Frés (Ap). No one list contains anything like all the settlements there were.

Town and village plans

Most villages seem to be haphazard, with houses scattered more or less at random – often in two or more clusters with gaps between. Some are much more tightly packed than others, depending on local styles of architecture and gardening.

In contrast, in the middle and later Bronze Age, most palaces and towns were laid out and extended by people with strong theories of what a town should look like. They conform to a grid in which most walls and streets run parallel and corners are square. Although Roman and medieval towns, set out on a regular plan, are not uncommon in Europe, we know of none of these periods in Crete – except that Herákleion may preserve traces of an unusual circular grid.

Regular plans again became fashionable after 1850. Any settlement planned after that date, especially on the coast, is likely to be laid out on a regular grid. So strong was the fashion that some old towns were re-modelled in its image. For example, at Ayios Nikólaos (Me) the new grid strides relentlessly on, regardless of the old town plan and of the practicalities of the steep terrain.

Deserted medieval villages and hamlets

Our researches show that, as in England, abandoned medieval settlements are roughly as many as those still inhabited. Desertion is not a straightforward matter of an inhabited settlement becoming uninhabited. Settlements can pass through intermediate stages of seasonal use, being demoted to field-house clusters or shepherds' establishments before they are completely abandoned.

Some desertions are recent, such as Samariá (Sf). After a century of decline it was expropriated by the National Park Service in 1962. The similar village in the Trypití Gorge (Sf) was deserted probably in the seventeenth century.

Lophiá in Lambiní (AV) was a small village, with 49 inhabitants, in the census of 1583. It must have been prosperous, for it has an elegant chapel of about that date. In the Turkish census of 1659, however, it had shrunk to two houses;[10] it is not recorded again. All that is to be seen now are this chapel, a medieval chapel and stumps of houses; but the place is still called Lophiá. As with many deserted villages, the fields are still cultivated. A nearby deserted place, Fatrelianá, is also represented by a surviving chapel; no Venetian document mentions it, and it was probably deserted before 1550. Another close by, Korédho, is passing through a phase as field-houses.

We have compared the many censuses for the Ay. Vasíleios district. In 1583 it had nearly a hundred settlements; it now has only fifty. It has changed from a land of hamlets with some villages to a land of villages with a few hamlets. Much of the change was in the seventeenth century; but many deserted hamlets are not in the records, implying that desertion began before 1550.

Middle Crete is more solidly a village country. Here the written record is longer. Out of a sample of 160 places named in various fourteenth-century records, 58 are not heard of again. Although other explanations are possible – the places may have been re-named, or swallowed by the growth of neighbouring villages, or the spelling corrupted – it seems that about one-third of all settle-ments were abandoned in the late middle ages. At least 10 more were lost in the early Turkish period. Of the original 160, about half are still inhabited today.

Kíssamos district is still a hamlet land. Here there are 112 hamlets which are mentioned in medieval (mainly fourteenth-century) documents or which have medieval churches. Sixty-four are still extant, and most of the remainder were lost before 1583. Sélinon tells a similar story, except that there has been less deser-tion: out of 98 hamlets known to be medieval, 76 are still extant.

To summarise, nearly half the villages and hamlets of four-teenth-century Crete are deserted today; most abandonment was before the late sixteenth century. This may seem like a lot of aban-donment, but much the same happened in contemporary England. Nor was it the first time on Crete: previous phases of desertion had occured in the twelfth to eleventh centuries BC and ninth to tenth AD. Two processes seem to be involved: general decline in population, and people migrating from hamlets into villages. There was a second, generally lesser, phase of abandon-ment in the early Turkish period, but there is no evidence to link this with the change of régimes: the plagues of 1678, 1689 and 1703

are an ample explanation. Ayios Vasíleios has changed from a landscape of hamlets into one of villages. In far-west Crete the hamlets remain but have been thinned out. In middle Crete, the village landscape probably goes back into the middle ages, although there were certainly hamlets as well.

There was surprisingly little desertion in the nineteenth century, despite its reputation for sacks and massacres. Desertion was renewed in the twentieth century, especially when the Muslims were expelled in 1923. Many hamlets or small villages with Muslim majorities did not survive. From 1870 onwards new settlements were founded, especially on the coast (Chapter 18).

Settlement and altitude
The upper limit of all-year habitation, with rare exceptions, is only 800 m – much lower than in the Alps, and hardly higher than in Norway. Winter on the Lassíthi Plain is not very different from winter in the English Lake District or at Seattle (Washington State); yet the inhabitants regard this as hardship, and leave if they possi-bly can. We do not understand why.

Desertion is hardly related to altitude: there has not, as in England, been a tendency for settlement to retreat from higher elevations. Nor do we find, as claimed by McNeill for other Mediterranean mountains,[11] an upward expansion of settlement in the last two centuries. The high, remote settlements of Máles (H), Anóyeia (My), and Ay. Iréne (Se) were already the most populous in their districts in 1583.

Cities
For at least 1,000 years Herákleion (T), Khaniá (Ky) and Réthym-non (R) have been by far the biggest settlements on the island.

Khaniá has been the biggest city in the western half of Crete since the Bronze Age – it is probably the oldest extant city in Europe. Although there has been a town at Herákleion since Roman times, the coastward shift from Knossós to Herákleion as the chief city took place in the Arab period. Réthymnon, also of ancient origin, grew into a city in the middle ages.

Most of the 'cities' for which ancient Crete was famous were on the scale of big villages; they were cities only in the sense of being independent. Several of the bigger towns, especially Górtyn (Ka), were in south Crete.

Medieval Canea (Khaniá), Retimo (Réthymnon), and Candia (Herákleion) were quite small, but soon outgrew their thirteenth-century walls. They had the amenities of Italian civic life, with palaces, *loggie,* Gothic churches of the Latin rite, and houses of Franciscan and Dominican friars. Siteía (Si) repeated these features on a smaller scale.

In the sixteenth century the Venetian Senate was alarmed at the growth of Muslim power, especially after Réthymnon was sacked in 1571. They approached the defence of Crete as if it were part of the Italian plain. They fortified Canea and Candia with greatly enlarged circuits of gigantic walls, including all the latest defence technology. (Candia was by then as big as London, but not so populous.) In the event, the walls of Canea held up the Turk for three months, but those of Candia, though by then obsolete, were to withstand the longest siege in history (21 years).

The cities had a chequered history. Siteía was abandoned in 1651 and not reinhabited for two centuries. The Turks, not at first having possession of Candia, set up Canea as the capital city. The three surviving cities were inhabited mainly by Muslims – hence their mosques, and the Latin churches which have been given minarets.

The population, held down by plague, did not fill them, and until the 1910s the Venetian walls towered above barren surrounding landscapes. In the 1920s they were again depopulated by the expulsion of Muslims. Khaniá (Ky) suffered from bombing in World War II, and Herákleion (T) at times from modernistic town councils: one of its great medieval churches was demolished as recently as *c.* 1970.

Towns and giant villages

Towns are places to which people resort for markets, craftsmen or administrative offices, but in Crete they are not necessarily more populous than villages. Voukouliés (Ki) and Kándanos (Se) were markets without having large populations.

There have been minor country towns in Crete since the Bronze Age. Kastélli Kissámou (Ki) and Ierápetra (H) go back at least to the Roman period; Ierápetra then counted as a major city.

The Venetians divided Crete into nineteen castellates (approximately the modern *eparkhíes*). Cretans had various duties at their castellate castles, and this led to markets and thus to towns – some of which, like Kastélli Kissámou, were walled. The town which has become the tourist resort of Ayios Nikólaos (Me) grew up around the castle of Merabéllo (Plate 1); but little remains of its earlier history apart from one of the oldest painted chapels in Crete.

The town of Khóra Sphakíon (Sf) was made by the growing-together of four hamlets, with numerous medieval churches; its castle was not very important. The town's prosperity was continued by a period of shipowning in the eighteenth century. It is now largely deserted, and one can study its ruined houses uncomplicated by later rebuilding.

In the late nineteenth century there was a phase of founding or re-founding towns. Neápolis (Me), whose urban origins go back far into Venetian times, was made the regional capital by the local Pasha in the 1860s. The town of Siteía (Si) was deliberately re-established on the site of the deserted Venetian city, as was Palaió-khora (Se) around the abandoned castle of Sélinon. A little later, Vrysses (Ap) was founded on what seems (despite its great spring) to have been a new site.

There are also 'giant villages', usually in out-of-the-way places, which have no urban characteristics. Kritsá (Me), for example, has been the biggest village in Crete for more than four centuries; others include Máles (H), Anóyeia (My), and Ano Viánnos (V). Some of them have several medieval churches and must already have been big villages by the thirteenth century. Such places are in mountains or relatively barren terrain, and have a strong history of shepherding.

The Lassíthi Plain

This odd place has a peculiar settlement history. In modern times it has had almost the highest year-round settlement in Crete. From Neolithic until Late Roman it had a history of alternating prosperity and decline.[12] Scholars tend to explain these fluctuations in political terms, but a possible alternative is the tendency of the *Khónos* (pp. 27-8) to block and unblock itself, which affects the cultivable area of the plain. Fluctuations in climate may also have been a factor.

It is usually assumed that Lassíthi was inhabited in the early middle ages, but there seems to be not one Byzantine or medieval chapel. The fourteenth-century *Book of Bans* shows that it was used as winter pasturage for horses and mules.

The Venetians had trouble with rebels using Lassíthi as a hide-out, and with their usual heavy-handedness confiscated and depopulated the lands. A famous ban of 1343 forbade anyone to 'dwell, plough, or sow' anywhere on the plain or the inner slopes of the mountains around it, 'under penalty of losing one foot for each contravention'. (Threats of bodily diminishment are common in the *Bans,* but usually in circumstances where they would not have to be enforced.) Pasturage was prohibited on the plain and the inner and outer slopes of the mountains (defined by a perambulation) on pain of a fine of 100 *hyperpera* a time. The preamble refers to the 'fertility and natural fortification' of the plain and ends sententiously by quoting Tacitus, the Roman historian, 'they make a solitude and call it peace'.

The rebels seem at first not to have done what they were told; the ban is said to have been repeated in 1363 (although the pages for that dread year have been torn from the *Book of Bans* in Venice). Buondelmonti in 1415 found that the plain was pastured but not cultivated, although people had forgotten the reason.

In 1463 the Venetian Senate decided to lease the plain to cultivators in order to increase the amount of wheat grown under the government's control, but the experiment was only partly successful. In 1548, the Senate, having on its hands refugees from the mainland cities of Monemvasía and Náuplion, lost to the Turks, decided to settle them in Lassíthi.[13] Originally the refugees were not supposed to live in the plain but only to grow wheat there; but to cultivate it at all required field-houses, and the refugees might have had nowhere else to live. Hence the peculiar, probably planned, settlement-system of Lassíthi arose (see Figure 12.8).

The settlements were not on the plain itself, but were a necklace of hamlets on the base of the slopes all round. Castrofilaca in 1583 lists 49 of them, only eleven of which are given as having any population. The other 38 had been deserted after a run of disastrous harvests. The settlements revived in the Turkish period. Some hamlets have grown into villages; the smaller ones have been deserted or absorbed.

Conclusions

In Crete, as in England, hamlets are the earlier of the present settlement patterns, and villages are more recent. The current cycle of nucleation, however, is the third in the island's history. Why nucleation happens is a matter of much debate and little evidence. It is often regarded as a response to insecurity, but in its modern phase it would have been helped by the appearance of the coffee-house and the parish church as the cement of village society. The hamlets that remain are survivors of an earlier and more distinctively Cretan way of life.

Numbering the people

Our island of Crete is underpopulated for lack of people, and for this reason some settlements remain uncultivated. [An interest-free loan was to be given to whoever should bring into Crete the greatest number of male slaves, not being Turks nor Roman Catholics.]

Decree of the Venetian Senate, 1393 [14]

The study of human population is important to landscape history, because the number of mouths to feed is one of the factors that determine pressure on land, which in turn is a factor in deciding how far cultivation and shepherding extend on to difficult land.

The idea of carrying capacity – the number of people or sheep that a landscape will support – is well known to population scholars, as is the notion that carrying capacity diminishes over the centuries. Soil nutrients are exhausted, and the soil itself may be lost through erosion.[15] Where people are not individually responsible for their land, they are tempted to get more out of their shares in it than the land will sustain – the supposed 'Tragedy of the Commons'.[16] These ideas are true (within limits) and useful, but are only part of the reality.

Carrying capacity can be increased by technology and by work put into the land. In Crete, plant growth is much limited by root penetration, especially on marl. Breaking up the bedrock, especially in terracing, increases root penetration and extends the cultivable area – a permanent gain which accumulates over the centuries. Soil nutrients taken from the landscape as a whole tend to accumulate, in the form of manure, on the most easily cultivable land, which becomes more productive. Over-use of common-land may be averted, either by the land being privately owned (as with mountain pastures in west Crete), or by the commoners agreeing to be sensible.

Trade enters the balance in two ways. In Mediterranean countries, harvests are unreliable, with gluts and failures. To be sure of surviving the worst year in twenty it is necessary to sow enough to produce a large surplus in an average year. This encourages diversification of crops; it also encourages trade with areas distant enough, maybe within Crete, for the good and bad years to be different. Secondly, for a person with little land, the best way to use it is not to grow cereals for subsistence, but to put more labour into it: growing a high-value crop which responds to more attention (especially vines) and which can be traded for the essentials of life.

Other factors are warfare and disease. Historians find war exciting; they exaggerate its effects in limiting population, and play down those of pestilence. The reality, as our own enlightened century has demonstrated, is that it takes an exceptionally savage war to reduce a population by 10 per cent. Bubonic plague, however, can easily kill one-third of the people without attracting so much attention.

The founding of Crete

Crete, like other Mediterranean islands, remained uninhabited long after there were boats capable of reaching it. Successful colonisation called for some degree of organisation and experience in transporting livestock and seed crops.[17]

The earliest well-documented human population is at Knossós (T) around 6100 BC. (It is incredible that this really was the original colony – much as if the earliest settlement in England should turn out to be London!) These first Cretans probably came from somewhere between west Turkey and Palestine.[18]

The archaeological evidence does not reveal any large influxes of people until the Venetian period. Nor (before the twentieth century) is emigration known to have played much part in getting rid of excess population.[19]

Ancient population [20]

To calculate population on archaeological data alone is very uncertain. Four methods have been tried:

1 Assuming so many square metres of floor-space per head (but how can we know how much of a settlement was living space, or how much of the living space was occupied simultaneously?).

2 Identifying a modern situation supposedly constrained by similar ecological and cultural factors to the ancient one. Modern settlement sizes are then measured and correlated to their populations to set up a formula for population density.

3 As a variant of this method, by setting up this formula for regional population:
number of known habitations x average population per habitation x correction factor for habitations not detected x correction factor for discontinuity of habitation.

4 Assuming a constant growth rate from a 'known' base population.[21]

Each method involves obvious uncertainties. Nevertheless, when these four approaches are applied to a survey area around Khaniá (Ky) for the Palace Period, the results are rather close, indicating a Middle Minoan II – Late Minoan I population density between 67 and 84 people per sq. km for the Khaniá plain (excluding the city) and the Akrotíri peninsula. In 1961 the rural part of this area had a density of about 94 per sq. km. If the Minoan densities are extrapolated to the easily cultivable portion of Crete (about 30 per cent of the island) the resulting population is 173,000 to 217,000, indicating a total population of Palatial Crete between 216,000 and 271,000. This is similar to the total population of Venetian and Turkish Crete, and rather more than the *rural* population today.

Diseases

Before written records, knowledge of ancient diseases is limited to those that leave lasting effects on bone, which epidemic diseases like bubonic plague do not. Arthritis, anaemia, spina bifida, and bone cancer have been identified in the Late Minoan III cemetery at Arménoi (R). Entire families seem to have been wiped out by tuberculosis; there was also malnutrition. Life expectancy for both sexes declined from the Palatial to the Post-Palatial period, perhaps because of worsening diet.[22]

The influence of malaria is hard to assess. As recently as 1947, Allbaugh found malaria very common all over Crete (which means that there must still be Cretans harbouring the parasite). It was not linked to marshes, being transmitted by *Anopheles super-pictus*, the mosquito of mountain streams. As in England, it died out, but not for lack of mosquitoes: one of the writers still regularly uses a mosquito-net in Crete. It is usually supposed that malaria was prevalent in classical Greece; this is based on medical writings, the skeletal evidence being ambiguous. Roughly one Cretan in twelve now possesses the gene for β-thalassaemia, an abnormality of the blood which protects against malaria; this confirms that malaria was present for many human generations.[23] Chronic disease could have been responsible for the lethargy which some travellers attributed to Cretans in the Turkish period; but, if so, why did this not apply to earlier, supposedly more industrious and creative, periods?

The Black Death of 1348 – bubonic plague – hit Crete particularly hard. Plagues followed in 1398, 1419, 1456, 1523, 1580, 1592, 1678, 1689, 1703 and 1816, and some of these were credited with killing one-third of the population.

In 1947 Crete was still full of strange 'Third World' diseases. Leprosy, for which Crete (along with Norway) was notorious, died out only in the mid-twentieth century.

The last six centuries

The Venetians thought Crete was underpopulated, even though it did not consistently grow enough to feed itself. They encouraged various nations to set up colonies. In 1363 they invited Armenians to settle.[24] In 1416 they transported to Crete a large number of Turkish prisoners-of-war, who two years later were encouraged to send for their families and settle down in the island. (The Venetians may have settled more Turks in Crete than the Turks did.)

In the later Venetian period we find a remarkable set of censuses. Governors' reports give apparently exact counts for the whole island or for its four provinces or nineteen districts (excluding Sphakiá). The earliest, that of Geronimo Zane in 1534, puts the population of Crete at 175,268, about one-third of what it is today.[25] The most complete census is that of Castrofilaca in 1583, which gives the number of *huomini da fattion*, 'men of action' (aged between 15 and 60), of boys, old men, and females, in the cities and in each of 1,073 *casali*. There are further lists of the number of men owing public services.

Can we believe the lists and numbers? According to Bernardo's census of 1536, the village of Gavalokhóri (Ap) – to take a typical example – comprised two *casali* with a total of 172 action-men. Of these, 59 were named Gavalla, including eleven Constantin Gavallas, eight called Janni, and seven called Manoli. It can have been no light matter to keep track of all these Gavallas; and they themselves may not have been over-meticulous about giving information, since being inscribed could have led to an uncomfortable spell at the oar or digging ditches.

To number the people of Crete can never have been a light task, because settlements are not neatly aggregated into villages and

Cretans often have second or third homes. There is no sign that the Venetians understood these problems: successive lists of *casali* differ. Whole *casali* could be left out; even Castrofilaca seems to have overlooked the town of Ierápetra. It seems best to assume that even the highest count is too low. Fluctuations over short periods are more likely to result from changing efficiency of counting than from real changes in population.

Nevertheless, there is a consistency in the Venetian censuses indicating that they bear some relation to reality (Figure 8.3). The earliest figures appear to show a rapid rise in population, which could be a recovery from the terrible plague of 1523. The maximum figure of 270,000 is from a census of *c.*1560 of which we have not seen the original; if true, it implies an actual population of some 300,000, a remarkably high figure especially since much of the best land was uncultivated (p. 197).

Next comes a well-attested fall by about one-quarter; this can be explained by numerous disasters, including three plagues, between 1570 and 1600. The terrible bubonic plague of 1592-93, chronicled by Filippo Pasquaglio, killed 38 per cent of the population of Candia.[26]

Recovery set in at the end of the Venetian period. The population grew to the 254,040 'souls' in the *relazione* of Civran (1639), implying an actual population not much less than 300,000.

Statistics for the early Turkish period, though incomplete, indicate that the population fell considerably by 1700.[27] There is no reason to suppose that the war of conquest was destructive enough to account for the difference. Plague was said to have killed 78,000 in 1678. The traveller Savary guessed in 1788 that there were 350,000 Cretans and Olivier in 1795 that there were 240,000; we do not know how either figure was arrived at.

In *c.*1820 it is said that there were 28,330 Christian and 24,941 Muslim 'households'.[28] What is meant by a household is not stated, but if it averaged four persons (as in the 1881 census), this would make the total population 213,000. Pashley in 1834 was given figures totalling 16,133 Christian and 5,402 Muslim 'families', plus the populations of the three cities. He thought that this implied a total population of 130,000. There can be no doubt that there was a severe fall, brought about by the last of the plague epidemics and helped by the great revolt of 1821-28. However, it is questionable that Muslims should have fared so much worse than Christians.

Since then the population has gone consistently up, regardless of the great revolt of 1866-68, World Wars I and II, and the influenza epidemic of 1919. It reached 279,000 in 1881, 400,000 by about 1930, and 500,000 in 1980.

Another important figure is the degree of urbanisation, for city-dwellers are likely to be less dependent on the products of the island itself and more susceptible to disease. Statistics in the later Venetian period put the total population of the four cities between 30,000 and 50,000 (between one-sixth and one-eighth of the population of Crete); the fluctuations may be real because of plague. In the nineteenth century the degree of urbanisation was much the same.

The balance between cities and countryside drastically altered after World War II. The four cities have gone on increasing, and some country towns have become urban (Ay. Nikólaos (Me)). This is difficult to put into figures because of problems of definition, and because recent censuses appear to overestimate the rural population. The rural population (of settlements up to small towns) seems to have reached a maximum of 350,000 – probably the highest ever – about 1950, and is little more than half of that now.

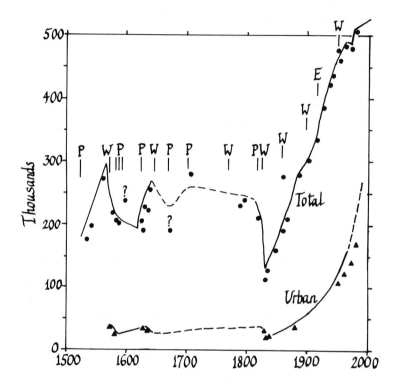

8.3 *Population of Crete. The points indicate actual census figures; the curves are our estimate of the true population. The lower points and curve are for the urban population; in the later twentieth century this becomes increasingly vague, owing to uncertainties in defining a city and defining residence in it. P = plague, W = war or revolt, E = expulsion and refugees*

On surnames

Nearly all surnames in Crete (as in the Máni, the southern tip of Greece) end in -*ákis*, which is a diminutive, as in Moodykin, Rackhamkin, etc. This is popularly supposed to have been a disparagingly familiar form of address, accepted by Cretans in order to be humble before their masters the Turks (as if any Cretan would do such a thing!). In reality, as contemporary records show, the -*ákis* fashion began in the middle ages, but did not become predominant until the nineteenth century.

Cretan surnames are remarkably stable. In 1082 the Emperor Alexios Comnene supposedly sent twelve noble families to be lords of Crete; every one of those names – Gavala, Skordhylis, Khortatzos, etc. – is still in the Cretan telephone book today, often in an -*ákis* form. At least one-third of the names of the thirteenth-century Venetian nobility are still extant in their own cities, including families illustrious in Venetian history. There are Falelákis (from Falier) and Tsagarákis (from Zancarol) in Khaniá (Ky), Kornáros (Corner) and Dándolos in Réthymnon (R), and Kallérgis (Callergi) and Dhemetzákis (De Mezzo) in Herákleion (T). The others either died out in the middle ages or (if they still had Venetian connections) left at the Turkish conquest.

In the countryside there is less local stability. Gávalas no longer live in Gavalokhóri (Ap) or Gavalomoúri (Ki). The Papadhópoli, Venetian chieftains of Sphakiá, are not represented there now; their rivals the Patéres live just outside. However, the Tzérmias family still flourishes in Tzermiádhon (L).

Cretan surnames have the same sort of meanings as English ones. Some are patronymics: Giannákis and Petrákis are roughly the same as Johnson and Peterson. Some are descriptions: Makry-giannákis is a descendant of Long John, Mavromatákis means Black-Eye. Others indicate a place of origin: Kounenákis from Kounéni (Ki), Foufouridhákis from Foufourás (Am), Naxákis from the island of Naxos, Smyrnákis from Smyrna. Armenákis indicates a Cretan of Armenian descent, and there are similar forms for Bulgars, Albanians, Spaniards and Vlachs. Among names derived from trades and vocations, Papadhákis (equivalent to Mr 'Priest') is the commonest, followed by Dhaskalákis ('Teacher'), Grammati-kákis ('Clerk'), and Psarákis ('Fisher'). Dermitzákis (Turkish *dermi* 'iron' + -*ci* 'worker') is much less prolific than Smith is in England or the United States. Others include Vamvakákis (someone to do with cotton), Zografákis ('artist'), Varelákis ('cooper'), and Kafetzákis ('coffee-house-keeper'). The prefix *khatzi-*, as in Khatzi-konstandinákis, was evidently adopted by Christians who had made pilgrimages to Jerusalem, in emulation of their Muslim friends who called themselves *hajji* after they had been to Mecca.

Notes

1 *Aegimius*, 8.
2 O. Rackham (1986), *The History of the Countryside*, London, Dent.
3 *Iliad*, II, 649; *Odyssey*, XIX,174.
4 J. Moody (1992), 'The continuity of settlement and land-use systems in west Crete', *Petromarula*, **1**, 52-9.
5 Column IV, two-thirds of the way down.
6 BNP: Ital. 384.
7 BMV: Ital. VII.1109 (8880); a less good MS is BMV: Ital. VI.156(6005).
8 *Mn*, 5, pp. 113-38.
9 BNP: Ital. 2091 f.110-13.
10 Stavrinidhes (1984-87), no. 163.
11 Chapter 3, note 10.

12 L. V. Watrous (1982), 'Lasithi: a history of settlement on a highland plain in Crete', *Hesperia supplement*, **18**.
13 S. G. Spanakis (Σ. Γ. Σπανάκης) (1984), *Σύμβολη στην Ιστορία του Λασιθιού*, Herákleion, Σφακιανός.
14 Noiret (see bibliography), p. 54.
15 This idea is much promoted (though not for Crete) by J. R. McNeill (see Chapter 3, note 10).
16 G. Hardin (1968), 'The tragedy of the commons', *Science*, **162**, 1243-8.
17 J. F. Cherry (1990), 'The first colonization of the Mediterranean islands: a review of recent research', *Journal of Mediterranean Archaeology*, **3**, 145-221; C. Broodbank and T. Strasser (1991), 'Migrant farmers and the Neolithic colonization of Crete', *Antiquity*, **65**, 233-45.
18 J. D. Evans (1971), 'Neolithic Knossos – the growth of a settlement', *Proceedings of the Prehistoric Society*, **37**, 95-117.
19 G. W. M. Harrison (1988), 'Background to the first century of Roman rule in Crete', *Cretan Studies*, **1**, 125-55.
20 For studies of ancient population and disease see: R. Sallares (1991), *The Ecology of the Ancient Greek World*, London, Duckworth.
21 J. Carothers and W. A. McDonald (1979), 'Size and distribution of the population of Late Bronze Age Messenia: some statistical approaches', *JFA*, **6**, 433-54; A. C. Renfrew (1972), *The Emergence of Civilization: the Cyclades and the Aegean in the Third Millennium B.C.*, London, Methuen; M. Wagstaff and J. F. Cherry (1982), 'Settlement and population change', in C. Renfrew & J. M. Wagstaff (eds.), *An Island Polity*, Cambridge, Cambridge University Press, pp. 136-55.
22 P. J. P. McGeorge (1990), 'A comparative study of the mean life expectation of the Minoans', *Πεπράγμενα του ΕΤ΄ Διεθνού Κρητολογικού Συνέδριου*, **A1**, 419-28.
23 D. Loukopoulos, quoted in D. Weatherall and J.B. Clegg (1981), *The Thalassaemia Syndrome*, Oxford, Blackwell.
24 Thiriet (1978), no. 407.
25 ASV: CR b.79.
26 *Mn*, 3, 64-114.
27 O. Rackham, forthcoming in *Petromarula*, **2**.
28 N. Stavrakis (1890, Chapter 2, note 11).

9

Place-names

The more part advised to depart ... if by any means they might attain to Phenice, and there to winter; which is an haven of Crete, and lieth toward the south west and north west.

St Paul's last recorded voyage, *Acts of the Apostles*, **26**, 12

[The remarkable double harbour can be identified; the place is still called Phoenix (Sf), and the special Cretan palm, *Phoenix theophrasti*, after which it was named, still grows there.]

The place-names of a country record its successive peoples and languages, and the vegetation, land tenure and land-uses of the past. There are *major place-names* – in Crete about 3,000 names of towns, villages, hamlets, rivers, mountains, etc. – and *minor place-names* which are the names of springs, rocks, trees, etc. Cretan fields are too small to have individual names; instead each township is divided into twenty or so units called *topothesíe* which form the bulk of the minor place-names.

In a country overwhelmingly Greek-speaking for more than 3,000 years, the great majority of place-names are apparently in Greek. Sometimes they still have a meaning in Modern Greek: for instance Stérnes, 'Cisterns', or Azogyré, the name of the poisonous shrub *Anagyris foetida.* Most, however, have lost their original meaning: Kándanos (Se) and Alikianoú (Ky) mean as little to modern Cretans as the name Miami does to modern Americans.

Place-names can acquire a false meaning. We may smile at the Venetians, who misinterpreted Melidhóni (My) as *Mille Donne*, 'Thousand Ladies', but the same happens less obtrusively in Greek. Sidhéro, the north-east cape of Crete, would be assumed to have something to do with iron (*sídheros*) if Buondelmonti had not told us that there had been a chapel of St Isidore there. Pandanássa (Am) is a recent corruption of what appears in Venetian documents as Endanasso or Andamasso: evidently a place-name from Bronze Age Crete, confused with the word *Pandanássa*, 'Ruler of All', a title of the Blessed Virgin Mary. How often this has gone on we cannot tell. In England, the original meaning can often be recovered by looking at how the name is spelt in documents from nearer the time when it originated, but in Crete we lack records from appropriate periods.

Many Cretan place-names are in the plural, such as Khaniá (Ky). Often they are written in the genitive case – 'Kambanoú' instead of 'Kambanós' – though this tradition is dying out. Crete seldom feels the need to differentiate between places of the same name. There are pairs of places called Ano and Káto (Upper and Lower) or Éxo and Mésa (Outer and Inner), but one looks in vain for parallels to Northampton and Southampton, or to Ayot St Peter and Ayot St Lawrence. There are four places called Azogyré, eleven called Papadhianá, and innumerable places called just Ayios Geórgios (St George). No trouble seems to have been caused by the two places called Falerianá (Se), 4 km apart – unless this was a trap to confuse Venetian taxgatherers.

The student has to reckon with the modern fashion for changing place-names that were inelegant or politically incorrect, supposed to be Turkish, or alluded to donkeys or other indecent animals. This has particularly happened with large towns. In the nineteenth century, the distinctive name of Merabéllo town gave way to Ayios Nikólaos (Me), already the name of dozens of other places. More recently, Koprána (Ap) 'Dunghill' was turned into Aspro 'White' – dunghills now call for euphemism. Another complication is the practice of reviving extinct ancient names, or archaising the spelling of surviving ancient names. Knossós and Herákleion (T) are revivals of illustrious names that had died out.

Kaloí Liménes (Ka) ('Fair Havens') is not the extraordinary unaltered survival of a Biblical place-name, but a rationalising of what in the ordinary course of linguistic development would have become Kalouslimiónas. Re-namings and rationalisings are mainly a feature of the last hundred years, but there are occasional earlier examples.

Few interpretations of Cretan place-names can be certain. We try to tread a middle path: we shall satisfy neither the over-credulous nor the despairingly diffident among place-name scholars. Others with a greater knowledge of Cretan dialect, especially of plant-names, will find meanings that have escaped us.

Pre-Greek place-names

Linear B tablets from Knossós (T) contain between fifty and a hundred place-names.[1] Their identification is difficult and controversial, because there is no good evidence of where they were. Twelve or fifteen names have been identified with Graeco-Roman places. These include the name Knossós itself (*ko-no-so*); Kydonía, the ancient name of Khaniá (Ky), (*ku-do-ni-ja*); and Aptara (Ap), (*a-pa-ta-wa*). All these names died out in post-classical times: the only place-name in the tablets which has certainly been used down the millennia and is still used today is that of the village of Tylissos (Ma) (*tu-ri-so*). (Linear B contains no *l*; Cretan dialect confuses *l* and *r*.)

Other places named in the tablets are problematical. It would be nice to think that *ma-sa* was the village of Máza (Ap), or that *pa-na-so* was the present Panasós (Ka), or that *se-to-i-ja* was the city of Siteía, but there are too many coincidences and duplications of place-names to be sure. Most of the places in the tablets are not heard of again.

Other Bronze Age place-names may perhaps be recognised from the present or historic form of the word. The Minoan language had many words in -ssos and -nthos; whoever mentions cypress or terebinth (kyparíssos, terebínthos) still utters this mysterious speech. There are still a few places with these endings, and in Venetian times there were a few more. One of the most exciting is Zóminthos, a topothesía high in the mountains above Anóyeia (My), which must surely be the original name of the Minoan villa recently excavated in this unlikely place. However, as the tablets show, most Bronze Age place-names did not have distinctive endings, and cannot be distinguished from later names.

On present evidence, surviving pre-Greek place-names in Crete are about as rare as Welsh place-names in England or Indian place-names in Texas. Many others, however, may survive undetected.

Greek and Roman place-names
Venetian scholars amused themselves by trying to construct lists of the hundred cities of Crete. Well over a hundred Cretan place-names are mentioned in ancient authors, but many are mere names, with no indication of where they were. Others have come to light, with some evidence of location, from coins and inscriptions.

Not many definitely Minoan place-names were then remembered; an example was Berekynthos, the place near Aptara where fire and metals were invented, perhaps the Maláxa Ridge.[2] Most of the names are vaguely Greek, but would probably have meant no more to the ancients than they do to us.

Roman place-names are few. Examples must include Praitória (Mo) and Augústa (now the remote valley called Deré (Ky)), although at neither is anything known to justify an Augustan or a Praetorian connection.

We have been through a list of sixty names of Greek or Roman settlements in known locations. A little under half of the names are still in use. About one settlement in four survives under its ancient name: for example Réthymnon, the city of Malla (now the great village of Máles (H)), and the little ancient 'cities' of Araden and Anópolis (Sf). The name may have evolved, as with classical Oloús turned into Oloúnta, then Byzantinised into stin Eloúnda ('in Eloúnda'), then Venetianised into Spinalónga, which has the false meaning of 'Longthorne'. Sometimes, particularly with coastal settlements, the place is now inhabited under its ancient name, but after a long interval of desertion: as at Soúyia (Se), whose ancient name of Suia survived as that of a coastal feature through all the centuries of piracy.

With the 60 per cent or so of Graeco-Roman place-names that have died out, the commonest cause is that the settlement itself was deserted, sometimes to be revived later under another name. Alternatively, the settlement continued but changed its name. Ancient Láppa was so great that it was known in the middle ages simply as Stímpolis, 'In the City', later as Pólis, mysteriously turning in the mid-nineteenth century into its present name of Argyroúpolis, 'Silver City' (R). Sklavopoúla (Se) may be a translation of Doulópolis, 'Slave City', known to have been somewhere near.

The survival rate of ancient place-names is probably reduced because most of the locatable ones are on the coast, where settlements were particularly liable to be abandoned. Most of the desertion and re-naming took place in the Byzantine period: for example Knossós (T), when it re-emerged from oblivion in the thirteenth century, was still quite an important place, but was called Makryteíkhos, 'Long Wall', after some ancient ruin. (The bishops of Górtyn called themselves Bishops of Knossós until the nineteenth century.) Only a few ancient place-names, such as Práisos (Si – now revived), died out in the Venetian or Turkish periods.

Many more place-names might be known to be ancient if documents survived that dealt with the details of Crete. In the story of the infant Zeus, the future god was snatched from his cradle near Knossós by the nymph *Néda* and taken to a cave on Mount Ida, and his umbilical cord fell from his navel (*ómphalos*) into a plain near Kydonía which was thenceforth called *Omphalos*.³ Is it a coincidence that today the *Nídha* Plain lies before the cave of Mount Ida, and the similar plain above Khaniá is called *Omalós*?

Arab and Byzantine place-names

The most obvious legacy of the Arabs to Crete is Candia, which lasted until recent times as the name of the chief city (now Herákleion (T)) and of the island itself. The word is from Arabic *handax*, 'ditch', referring to the city moat. Other Arabic place-names seem to be few, suggesting that there was little rural colonisation, but some may be disguised as Greek words. The name Ayiá is said to come from an Arabic word for 'water'; there is an Ayiá (Ky) by the great springs near Khaniá, and another in Mylopótamos. Although Ayiá is not to be confused with Ayia, 'female Saint', the mysterious Ayia Rouméli may signify 'Water of the Romans' (meaning Greeks); there is no Saint Rouméli known to the calendar. The name Atsipádhes, which occurs in four places, is said to come from an Arabic word for 'lord'. The Arabs or Saracens themselves seem to be commemorated in the six places called Sarakína.

The Byzantine Empire left little mark on the place-names of Crete. Being Greek, place-names created then would be hard to distinguish from those of other periods. The place-names Polemárkhi and Strategianá (both Ki) appear to perpetuate titles of Byzantine officials.

There are a few Slav place-names. Topólia (Ki) looks like the Slav word for 'poplars' (which still grow there), and Vlátos (Ki) is probably Slav for 'fen'. There are four places called Voulgáro or Vourgáro, indicating Bulgarians. The meaning of places like Sklaverokhóri (Pe) is uncertain because of confusion between Slavs and slaves.

Another people apparently giving rise to place-names are Armenians. Five places are (or were) called Arménoi or Armenokhóri ('Place of Armenians'), the earliest known (Ki) being recorded in 1322, before the Armenian colonisation of 1363. Vlachs – that mysterious people, related to Romanians, who now inhabit north-west Greece – also seem to have reached Crete, if we believe place-names like Vlakheronítissa (Ki) and three others.

Place-names of the Venetian period

After the Venetian conquest there is abundant evidence for major and occasionally minor place-names. Very many settlement-names in Crete today, except on the coast, existed by the fourteenth century if not earlier. (We emphasise that the first written record of a place-name is no guide to when it originated.) When one gets used to the rules of Venetian spelling, most of the place-names are instantly recognisable, and often display all the nuances of Cretan pronunciation (e.g. 'Ciefala' for Kephála, pronounced Chiefála). The linguistic development, and the separation of place-names from their meaning, had evidently already taken place by the fourteenth century.

The Venetians themselves contributed few Italian names. Most are of castles: Malevyzi (*malo vicino*, 'Bad Neighbour'), Monofátsi (*Bonifacio*), Belveder, etc. A villa in Kaláthenes (Ki) was called Retónda, although it is not really a rotunda.

A characteristic of Crete, especially the west, are place-names in *–aná*, for example Kharkhaletroudhianá (Mo) and Loukoumi-kheliáná (Ki) (Figure 8.2b). The names are plural (less common equivalents are *–anós* (singular) and *–ádhon* (plural)). With few exceptions these are the names of hamlets, not villages, and are not the name of the principal hamlet after which a township is named. They are derived from personal names: the very common place-name Papadhianá comes from the very common surname *Papadhákis*; Pondikianá and Zouridhianá could come from *Pondikákis* and *Zouridhákis*, Mr Mouse and Mr Marten; and Dhouliá (Ap) alludes to a Mr Slave. Hamlets named after families are common in France (les Cachouds, les Bertholets) and can be found in England (Rackham's Corner) and Texas (Moody).

Place-names ending in *–aná* occur in Venetian and Turkish documents, but not commonly, doubtless because they were names of minor hamlets less likely to be recorded. They begin occasionally in the fourteenth century, and gradually become more frequent. Some are formed from Italian surnames (for example Falerianá, Travisanianá and Tzagaralianá from the noble Venetian families of *Falier, Trevisan* and *Zancarol*). A few allude to connections outside Crete: Ragousianá (Mo) means somebody from *Ragusa*, now Dubrovnik. The great majority are from Greek parent names, mostly of humble families but including illustrious ones such as *Skordhylis* and *Kallérgi* (Skordhyliáná, Kallergianá).

We have a few apparent Turkish parent-names, e.g. Avdhouli-aná (Se) from *Abdullah*, but this does not prove a post-1645 origin, since there were Turks in Venetian Crete (p. 98). The evidence points to the middle Venetian period as the time when these place-names were being most actively formed.

Turkish place-names

The Turkish conquest of Crete made little difference to the place-names. Most Muslims in Crete were Cretans, spoke Greek, and were content to live in places which had inherited Christian names. Some places called Panayía ('All-Holy', a title of the Virgin Mary) or Ayia Trías ('Holy Trinity') were wholly or mainly Muslim. Most Turkish place-names were in or near cities, and were sometimes translations of Venetian names; thus Koúm Kapí, a quarter of Khaniá (Ky), renders *Porta della Sabbionara* ('Sand Gate'). Others were the names of khans, hostelries on main roads, for example Bábali Khaní (now Ayioi Pándes (Ap)). A very few towns were re-named: the castellate town of Témenos became Kanlí Kastélli ('Bloody Castle'). Whether the blood was human we cannot tell, but it was shed at some time after 1671. There are rare Turkish place-names in remote places: for example, Deré (Ky) (Turkish *dere*, 'valley') replaced Roman Augusta.

The Turks were fascinated by Christian monasteries and had nicknames for them. The monastery of Our Lady of the Cape (Panayía Akrotirianí (Si)) was dubbed 'The Gun' (Toploú, from *top*), and is still so called. Balí (My), the Honeyed Monastery (Turkish *bal*, 'honey'), has replaced the ancient Atali. Vrondísi (Ka) was called Santrivanli ('Fountainy') from the Adam-and-Eve fountain which can still be seen outside the gate.

However, most of the major place-names which have been altered in the belief that they are Turkish appear in Venetian records. For example, Moukhtári (now Evangelismós (Pe)) seems to be derived from *muhtar*, a Turkish official, and yet is recorded back to 1328.[4]

Meanings of place-names

Most Cretan major place-names are too old to have a meaning in the language of today, and we lack the documents which would decode the apparently meaningless ones. Where there is a meaning it often seems bizarre or unsuitable for a place-name. How is it that for centuries a place was called Kakó Khorió (Mo), ('Bad Town')? How can a place have lived with the name Katsogrídha (twice in AV), ('Cockroach')? Why should minor place-names often be Mélissa ('Bee' – just one bee) or Pyróvolos ('Firearm')? Why were hamlets called Phonés (Ap), ('Murderers') or Phónissa (AV), ('Murderess'). We suspect that there are layers of meaning now lost, in the same way that Ugley in England is named after someone called Ucca and has nothing to do with the word 'ugly'.

Minor place-names, and decipherable major ones, are concerned with certain classes of things. Saints figure abundantly, but there is no memory of the old gods. There is a great interest in wild plants, especially trees, but no bias towards the useful or commercial ones. Cultivated plants and domestic animals are under-represented.

Among antiquities, a place called *Goulé* (Turkish *kule*, 'castle') will always reveal a Turkish fort (most names of individual forts, if they had any, seem to be lost), while *Kástellos* is usually a Venetian or Byzantine castle. The common place-name *Pyrgos* ('tower') can mean a more ancient fortification, although often there is nothing now to be seen. The place-name *Éllenes* or *Elleniká* normally means a site of Hellenes, that is Ancient Greeks or Minoans.

The name Neokhorió ('Newtown') is common, and (as throughout Europe) indicates an old settlement; we have two dating from before 1314.

Place-names often mention mills (*myloi*). There are few that allude to roads, despite the importance of roads in the written record. There are several mentions of baths (*loutró, loutráki*). Terraces are extremely rare; but in 1630 there was a place Pesuglia (lost in Ki), ('Terraces') , which is a welcome addition to the meagre written evidence for terracing (p. 143).

Kephála ('head') means a spring or a cape; *Vryssi* is an alternative word for a spring; *Pigí* is a well. Among vegetation, *Livádhi* ('grassland') is common especially in west Crete.

Among trees, the commonest in major place-names is plane. We know of sixteen settlements called Plátanos or the like; plane-trees and settlements are both attracted by water. There follow olive (*elía*), prickly-oak (*prínos*), walnut (*karydhi*), mulberry (*mourniá*) and myrtle (*myrtiá* – another aquatic tree). Among the other oaks, the best represented is the rare holm-oak (*azyláki*) (p. 64). Valonia oak (*velanídhi*), although a commercial tree, has given rise to only two place-names known to us, both outside its present distribution. The common deciduous oak (*dhrys*) is under-represented in place-names, as are chestnut (*kastaniá*) and cypress (*kyparíssi*).

There are a few names of rare cultivated plants such as *kolokásia* (p. 85) and *tsítsifes* (p. 84). If Crete gave the cauliflower (*kounoupídhi*) to the world,[5] it is satisfying to find the name of a Mr Cauliflower perpetuated since Venetian times in Kounoupidhianá (Ak).

Animal names are relatively few. The wild goat (*agrími*) and buzzard (*vytsilos*) enter into many mountain place-names. We cannot explain Elaphonísi ('Deer Island'); there have been no deer since Roman times.

Conclusions

Place-names lead to a surprising historical conclusion. Most Cretan village and hamlet names are certainly at least 400, and many at least 700, years old. Since when first heard of they had already developed nearly into their present form, they are likely to be much older than this. If we had only the place-names to go on, we would infer that Venetians and Turks played a small part in the Cretan landscape, hardly greater than Slavs, Armenians, Saracens and Vlachs. To some extent this redresses a bias in the written history. It looks as if the Byzantine and Arab periods were a formative age in the landscape, to an extent which the meagre documentation does not reveal. Most of the place-names were then established and there was not much scope for later alteration. Except for those on the coast or named after families, the average Cretan major place-name, like its English equivalent, may be rather more than a thousand years old.

Place-names are of value for what they tell us about the uncommon. We learn less about the ubiquitous olive than about maple, which is relatively rare but well represented in place-names like *Asphéndou*. The names *Phoénix* and *Vaï* have often led us to find the rare Cretan palm (p. 65). The few places called *Pévkos* are around the strongholds of the Cretan pine before it had expanded to its present extent. *Priniás* ('prickly-oaks'), although generally a common place-name, first led us to discover the remarkable alpine occurrence of this tree high in the Samariá Gorge. *Ambelos* ('vine') is still the site of the only vineyard on Gávdhos.

In general, the landscape of place-names is not strikingly different from what there is now. Certain classes of things, such as roads, terraces and anything to do with cultivation, are under-represented, but we rarely find evidence of features that have disappeared: there is no parallel in Crete to the English place-names that record vanished heaths. Place-names support the view that Crete has had a stable landscape in historic times.

Notes

1 Ventris and Chadwick (1973, Chapter 7, note 12).
2 Diodorus Siculus V.64; P. Faure (1969), 'Sur trois sortes de sanctuaries crétois', *BCH*, **93**, 174–213.
3 Callimachus, *Hymn to Zeus*, 33–54.
4 *Book of Bans:* Vidulich (see bibliography), no.184.
5 *Flora Europaea*, **1**, 337.

10

Vegetation

For the battle was there scattered over the face of all the country: and the wood devoured more people that day than the sword devoured … And Absalom rode upon a mule, and the mule went under the thick boughs of a great oak, and he was taken up between the heaven and the earth; and the mule that was under him went away … And a certain man saw it, and told Joab … And [Joab] took three darts in his hand, and thrust them through the heart of Absalom, when he was yet alive in the midst of the oak.

*2 Samuel, **18**, 8–14*

[This could easily happen today in the wood-pastures of the Lassíthi Mountains, with a clear space under the trees.]

The present holds the key to the past. In this chapter we give an outline of Cretan vegetation as it is now (mainly omitting the high mountains, coast and islets). We discuss which land-use factors hold the vegetation in its present state, and what happens when each factor is intensified or diminished. We then consider the great changes that have happened in the past 150 years. The object is to define how the landscape may have responded to changes in the factors in the more distant past.

Present vegetation

Woodland and savanna

The ordinary visitor, like visitors down the centuries, probably does not think of Crete as a wooded land. The island hides its woods in places where it takes effort to see them; some we have found only with the help of satellite images. We shall not guess at how much of Crete is wooded. Cretan woods have no sharp edges

10.1 A hedgehog-plant: *Acantholimon androsaceum*

Table 10.1. *Differences between typical shrubs and typical undershrubs*

	Shrubs	Undershrubs
Colour	Bright or dark green	Grey-green
Habit	Potential trees	Never become trees
Palatability	Variable	Unpalatable
Rooting depth	Deep	Shallow
Combustibility	Moderate to high	Low to moderate
Effect of fire	Survive	Usually killed
Life-span	Centuries	Decades
Growth from seed	Difficult	Easy

but shade off into maquis (shrubland), into savanna (pasture with scattered trees), into olive-groves; the answer depends on where we draw three arbitrary lines determining what is or is not a wood. Greeks use *dhásos*, 'wood', to cover at least the taller shrublands, but seldom agree as to what exactly is included. Official statistics of the extent of *dhásos* vary from 4½ per cent of Crete in 1981 to 33 per cent in 1992 – it all depends on what you include. (Orchards of mulberries, chestnuts and olives go far to redressing Crete's apparent scarcity of woodland.)

The great mountain ranges are girdled with woods and wood-pastures. In the White Mountains the woods are of cypress and pine (Figure 6.8), with admixtures of prickly-oak, maple and *ambelitsiá*. The woods descend the gorges to the south, making Sphakiá the most wooded part of Crete. Psilorítis is predominantly girt with prickly-oak, pine and cypress woods occurring sporadically. The common trees on the Lassíthi Mountains are prickly-oak in the north and west, pine in the south and east. The Siteía Mountains are wooded with pines on the south-west, which sweep down to the coast.

At lower elevations the variety of woods defies description. Each part of Crete, almost every gorge, has its characteristic tree. Cypress forms extensive lowland woods in Apokórona, pine in Ierápetra, and juniper around the Gulf of Merabéllo. Deciduous oaks frequently form groves among cultivated land in west Crete, decreasing eastwards. The most extensive low-altitude woods, clothing the phyllite mountains in far-west Crete, are of arbutus mixed with tree-heather and sometimes with holm-oak or deciduous oaks. This type of woodland cannot be separated from maquis.

3 *The Amári in spring*

1 [above left] *The town of Merabéllo (now Ay. Nikoláos) seen from the north-west in 1631*

2 [below left] *The topographer Raffaele Monanni sketching Réthymnon in 1631*

5 *The endemic* Petromarula pinnata *on a Venetian wall*

4 *Arádhena Gorge*

6 *Immense pollard plane-tree, probably of Byzantine date*

7 [above right] *Pollard* ambelitsiá (Zelcova cretica)
8 [below right] *Vegetation mosaic: maquis*

9 *The High Desert, seen from Mount Svourikhtí*

10 Anchusa cespitosa, *a flat-plant, endemic to the High Desert*

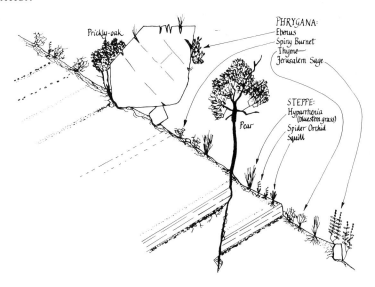

10.2 *Maquis, phrygana and steppe in relation to root penetration:*
(a) on hard limestone, with poor moisture retention but good root penetration along fissures: mainly maquis
(b) on marl, with good moisture retention but poor root penetration: mainly phrygana

To the English visitor (but not the American) the woods of Crete look rather neglected, as they are nearly always grazed and rarely have any defined boundary. This should not hastily be construed as a lack of conservation, for even vineyards are not always walled (Chapter 12).

Cretan woods have little distinctive woodland flora. Deciduous woods are often jungles, tangled with greenbrier (*Smilax aspera*) and wild madder (*Rubia* species). A few plants, such as the orchid *Limodorum abortivum*, seem to be bound to trees, but most shade-bearing plants are drought-sensitive, preferring the shade of rocks to that of trees. Woods, additionally, contain a selection of plants from the surrounding phrygana.[1]

Maquis, garigue (phrygana), and steppe

About half of Crete is roughland covered with some combination of shrubs, undershrubs and herbaceous plants. The distinction between shrubs and undershrubs is more fundamental than between trees and shrubs; it was recognized by Theophrastus in the fourth century BC.[2] Most shrubs in Crete are trees reduced to a shrubby form (Chapter 6), whereas undershrubs are woody plants which can never grow into trees.

Table 10.1 summarises the differences between shrubs and undershrubs. However, not every shrub or undershrub has all these properties. *Ebenus cretica* (p. 54) is clearly an undershrub, but is very palatable and sprouts after a fire. Heathers and some forms of spiny broom thrive after fires.

It would take long to enumerate all the undershrubs of Crete. Many of them, aromatic members of the Cistaceae and Labiatae, produce the typical scents of Cretan summer: three species of *Cistus*, sage (*Salvia triloba*), thyme (*Thymus capitatus*), savory (*Satureja thymbra*), and many others. Others are spiny legumes: spiny broom (*Calicotome villosa*), *Genista acanthoclada*, and *Anthyllis hermanniae*. There are **'chicken-wire plants'**, their leaves and flowers protected by intricacies of spines diverging at 120°: spiny burnet (*Sarcopoterium spinosum*), spiny euphorbia (*Euphorbia acanthothamnos*), spiny restharrow (*Ononis antiquorum*), etc. Jerusalem sage (*Phlomis fruticosa*) is a tall undershrub, protected by a nasty fluff that sets most people sneezing; it is replaced in many areas (especially in the east) by the smaller, endemic *Ph. lanata*. **'Hedgehog-plants'**, cushions defended by spines bristling outwards, as in *Genista acanthoclada* and the endemic *Verbascum spinosum* (p. 57), become more numerous at high altitudes (Figure 10.1).

Herbaceous plants are of three principal kinds. The most numerous are annuals, often clovers, medicks and other legumes, or grasses, which usually grow in winter and dry up in May, leaving their curiously-shaped dry fruits to continue next year. Perennials with bulbs, tubers or deep rootstocks leaf in winter, flower usually in spring, and dry up by summer: examples are asphodel (*Asphodelus microcarpus*), yellow asphodel (*Asphodeline lutea*), and the many orchids. Other perennials, mainly grasses, persevere throughout the year: the commonest is *Hyparrhenia hirta*,

the nearest European equivalent to the bluestem grasses of America.

Plant communities composed of shrubs (trees in shrubby form) are traditionally called **maquis** by most Mediterranean ecologists. Those composed of undershrubs are termed **garigue** or its Greek equivalent **phrygana**. **Steppe** is the name for communities of herbaceous plants. Ruined Landscape theory claims that maquis was produced when forests were degraded through browsing, burning and woodcutting. Further ruination led to garigue, and yet more ruination produced steppe.

In Greece and Crete, maquis, phrygana and steppe typically do not cover whole tracts of country on their own, but are

10.3 *Sheep devouring polythene bags and their contents. Palaiókhora (Se), March 1982*

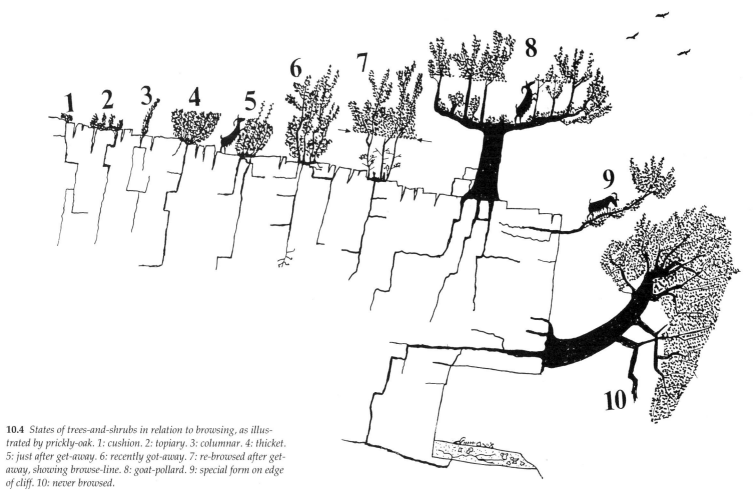

10.4 *States of trees-and-shrubs in relation to browsing, as illustrated by prickly-oak. 1: cushion. 2: topiary. 3: columnar. 4: thicket. 5: just after get-away. 6: recently got-away. 7: re-browsed after get-away, showing browse-line. 8: goat-pollard. 9: special form on edge of cliff. 10: never browsed.*

intermingled in mosaics (Plate 8). A hillside is speckled with patches of dark-green maquis, grey-green phrygana, and steppe – the last being pale-green in winter and spring, yellow in summer and autumn. The proportions vary widely, and it is clear that in most cases climate and soil determine them, not land-use. Maquis is often nearly continuous in west Crete, with little phrygana or steppe; in east Crete, steppe is more predominant, with varying amounts of phrygana but often only the occasional maquis shrub or none.

Already this aspect of Ruined Landscape theory begins to look thin. More intensive land-use may reduce tall maquis to low maquis, but no amount of cutting, burning or grazing will turn maquis into something else. (Grubbing-out is a different story.) When land-use ceases, shrubs do indeed grow back into trees (provided there is enough moisture), but steppe remains steppe, and phrygana often dies out.[3]

There are many different kinds of each of these plant communities. With maquis, a mixture of carob, wild olive and lentisk near the coast often gives way to prickly-oak inland. This contrasts in turn with arbutus–heather maquis (a reduced state of arbutus–heather woodland) on schist, or with the combination of prickly-oak and maple at higher altitudes. Maquis is woodland in miniature and may have associated herbaceous plants, like greenbrier and wild madder, or the climbing grass *Brachypodium retusum*. Garigue can consist of any of twenty undershrubs, alone or in various combinations. Steppe is equally variable, depending particularly on slope and rooting depth. To some extent all three vary independently, so that the number of possible combinations is very large. Garigue, being short-lived, can change several times during the lifetime of the maquis component.

10.5 *Effects of food preference. A mosaic of maquis of prickly-oak (in its topiary form) and of phrygana has lately been invaded by pine. Browsing by goats and sheep is enough to hold down the oak to about 50 cm high, but has no effect on the much less palatable pine. Anópolis (Sf), July 1987*

Factors affecting vegetation

Moisture – the importance of roots

The real determinant of roughland appears to be moisture. This involves (1) rainfall; (2) the amount of moisture retained by soil and bedrock; (3) the degree to which roots can penetrate and get at the moisture. Where all three are favourable, as with much of the phyllite of west Crete, continuous maquis results. Further east, rainfall tends to diminish and maquis becomes patchy. On marls, even though rainfall is not particularly low and much of it is held by the rock, poor root penetration favours undershrubs, which have shallow roots and endure drought. (Sections of rock in road-cuts show no sign that root penetration has been better in the past.)

In Crete, roots of plants are at least as important as tops. Many an apparently barren hillside is really a closed plant community underground: an upside-down forest where roots fill all the accessible space. On hard limestone, every shrub occupies a particular rock fissure (Figure 10.2). On marl, the occasional shrubs occur where a geological fault, or a Minoan tomb, or even the underside of a big boulder allows roots to penetrate. For the same reason, trees tend to occur around the edges of screes and at the bases of cliffs. As we shall see, root penetration is also essential in agriculture.

Changes in stature alter the balance of root competition. When shrubs grow into trees, they use more water, which they take from the neighbouring steppe and particularly phrygana.

Altitude

Contrary to what most books say, Crete has very little altitudinal zonation. Deciduous trees do not form a zone above evergreen broadleaves, nor do conifers form a zone above deciduous trees. The highest and lowest trees in Crete include all three classes. The only clear difference is between the alpine zone, which is above the highest trees (typically about 1,500 m), and the rest. As one ascends a mountain, certain trees and plants drop out one by one; but in general appearance, and in many of the species, vegetation at 1,400 m is not systematically different from that at sea-level.

Browsing

The roughlands of Crete are browsed by something like 300,000 goats and 700,000 sheep, a proportion which (as far as the evidence goes) is typical of much of history.

Animals have likes and dislikes. A favourite food of Cretan sheep is polythene bags and their contents (Figure 10.3); they also feed on grasses and herbs (living or dead) in preference to trees and shrubs. The efficiency of these sheep in flourishing and giving milk on meagre herbage never fails to astonish; the various dandelion-like steppe plants (species of *Crepis* and *Leontodon*) are critical.

Goats prefer shrubbage to grasses. They are indifferent to harsh textures but dislike strong flavours. A goat will swallow the most ferocious thistle and enjoy prickly-oak, but spits out cypress, and will not touch pine unless pressed by hunger. The order of palatability to goats and sheep (and presumably elephants and hippopotamuses) has been critical in determining what grows where in Crete (Table 6.1).

Most grazing in Crete is watched. As in the Bible, a shepherd (sometimes armed) guards the flocks and leads them to pasture and water. Animals are not allowed to feed in one place long enough to destroy their favourite plants. Weeks or months can pass between visits, allowing plants to make new growth.

The degree and history of browsing can be estimated by looking at shrubs (Figure 10.4). The severest degree is when prickly-oak is bitten into a flat layer a few cm high. With less it grows into cushions 20–50 cm high. With less browsing still, it forms irregular shapes looking like topiary (Figure 10.5). The next degree is marked by columnar shapes. At this point shrubs are liable to *get away:* to reach a height at which goats cannot browse, and thence to grow into trees. If grazing should be resumed, there results a wood with a *browse-line:* a sudden termination of the tree canopies, about 1½m above ground, below which there is no foliage. These stages are different for palatable and unpalatable species; they also vary with moisture and temperature, which determines the amount of yearly growth.

Much of the roughland in Crete is wood-pasture or savanna. The trees are big, scattered, and usually of only one or two ages – corresponding to times in the past when a slackening of browsing allowed new trees to grow up. Often they are pollarded in distinctive styles. Pollard boughs are cut as iron rations when other pasturage fails. In the Lassíthi and Skinávria Mountains there are *goat-pollards*, in which the foliage forms a topiary-like platform into which a goat climbs to eat the leaves. Many of these trees are several centuries old.

Woodcutting

At present there is very little woodcutting of natural trees. Almost all the timber used in Crete is imported, and almost all the wood and charcoal come from olives, walnuts and vines. However, there can be no doubt that until about 1950 wild trees, shrubs and even undershrubs were much used. Most wild trees that are older than this are in the form of pollards or coppice stools (Figures 6.5, 6.6, 6.7); often they are ancient trees which were cut every few years for centuries.

Wildfires – the natural history of burning

Crete, unlike most of Britain but like much of North America, is a combustible country. Fires in Greece, although they occur every summer, are regarded as a tragic abnormality. Rumour and the Press attribute them to shepherds or to colourful causes such as 'foreign agents', 'right-wing politicians', madmen, or beekeepers smoking swarms. The visitor, noting the profusion of matches and cigarettes, wonders why the whole of Crete does not burn down every year.

Let us not be led astray by the causes of ignition. All over the world, fires occurred long before human history, and plants and animals became adapted to resisting, evading or recovering from them. As a rule, wherever trees and other plants are combustible they are adapted to fire in some way.

Whether or not a fire can happen depends on weather – hot windy days in late summer being the most risky – and vegetation. Some plants burn easily and will support a fire on their own; others burn only if ignited by their neighbours. Pine is the most ferociously combustible Cretan plant: it is full of resin and flammable oils; its persistant litter of loose-knit fallen needles adds to the fuel; its light shade encourages undershrubs which catch the needles so that they do not compact. Cretan pine is not flammable by misfortune: these features are adaptations to promoting fire. It is the business of this, as of most of the world's pines, to ignite from time to time and burn up its less fire-adapted competitors. Most Greek fires reported in the Press involve pine.

Arbutus and tree-heather belong to another combustible plant family (Ericaceae). Most evergreen trees and shrubs are combustible to a lesser degree. They are easily killed to ground level by a fire, but sprout from the base just as they do after being cut down. Juniper and cypress (non-resinous conifers) are less combustible than the other evergreens, unless mixed with more flammable trees. They are not fire-adapted: when burnt (unless very lightly) they are killed completely and do not easily return. Most Cretan undershrubs are less combustible than evergreen shrubs, although fires can occur in phrygana alone (especially heather). Deciduous trees are difficult to burn, although fires can occur in the persistent leaf-litter of oak and plane.

Not even the fiercest fire consumes everything. It is a myth that people have 'cleared' land for cultivation merely by setting fire to woodland. Leaves, herbaceous plants, leaf-litter, and small logs burn; the trunks remain standing and are no easier to get rid of than they were when alive.

We have witnessed several fires in Greece and Crete. A fire not involving pine usually starts low down and burns uphill for several hours on a gradually widening front. It goes out when it reaches a ridgetop, or less combustible vegetation, or an area previously burnt, or rocks or cliffs. Such fires damage olive-groves, which although not killed are easily scorched and take years to recover.

A big pine fire, such as happened above Monastiráki (H) in 1987, is an awesome phenomenon. When stoked with several square kilometres of young pines, fallen needles, sage and spiny-broom, it releases as much energy as a small atomic bomb. Much of this comes out as gusts of red-hot air which sear cliff-plants and jump gorges to ignite phrygana on the other side. The very rocks are calcined at the edges. In the heart of such a fire even big pines are killed (but not consumed), and after the fire the charred cones gape open and release seeds which may start the pine-and-fire cycle over again.

Not all pine fires are so destructive. In many pinewoods in Sphakiá the charred bases of the trees show that they have been burnt at least once. If pines escape burning until they have all lost their lower branches, a fire may then run along the ground, burning the dead leaves. The pines are saved from injury by their thick bark, but any thin-barked trees among them, such as cypresses which might eventually compete with the pines, are killed.

After an ordinary fire, the land comes quickly to life again. Lizards and ants are on the move, and some underground plants are stimulated into growth by the heat. Within three days we have seen squills emerge from their charred bulbs, grow a metre high, and come into flower; the mysterious little endemic *Euphorbia dimorphocaulon* had also come up from its deep tuber and was blooming. If the fire is early, the trees sprout the same year and some of them, such as prickly-oak, can be a metre high by autumn. The next spring, there is often a profusion of flowers, especially orchids and hollyhock, much as in an English wood after it is felled. Grasses and other steppe plants flourish.

What happens next depends on whether the site is grazed. Browsing can hold back the maquis and allow steppe to remain dominant for several years. Recovery of undershrubs varies. Many species take several years to re-establish themselves, but *Cistus* species may come up at once from buried seed. In Crete the common large form of spiny-broom is characteristic of phrygana that has not recently been burnt.

In America, fires are often caused by lightning striking hollow or dead trees; we have been told by foresters in north-west Greece that this happens there. Near the Arádhena Gorge, we once found a group of pines bearing the fresh scars of a lightning strike, one of which had been set on fire but without, as it happened, igniting anything else. If all shepherds, arsonists, madmen, beekeepers and smokers could be locked up, fires would get worse. They would be less frequent, but all the fiercer and more extensive for the fuel accumulated since the previous fire. Experience with the similar vegetation of California shows that suppressing ordinary fires results in tremendous conflagrations.[4]

Occupational burning

In parts of Crete, particularly the continuous maquis of the western schist country, there is a patchwork of triangular areas of different ages of regrowth after burning. The areas are normally narrow triangles. This 'pattern-burning' by shepherds in spring is a traditional, formerly more widespread, type of land management. It causes maquis to sprout at ground level, where the animals can browse the shoots; it revives the steppe, encouraging the growth of grasses, legumes and other nutritious herbs at the expense of inedible undershrubs; it gets rid of big spiny-broom for several years; it recycles phosphate, which remains in the ash and fertilises the new growth.

People unfamiliar with management by burning usually disapprove of it. But burning in Crete is part of a world-wide tradition: Scots will be reminded of the regular burning of heather moors. Cretan shepherds have different styles of burning: the area burnt at one time varies from a single bush (to keep warm in winter) to a few hectares – unless the fire gets out of hand, which most often happens if the burning is too late in the season. Without occupational burning, fires would tend to be catastrophic, especially as they would occur later in the season.

Changes of the last 150 years

What one first notices about early pictures and photographs of rural Crete is how much less vegetated, indeed more 'desertified', the landscape used to be. This is clear from the views drawn by Pashley in 1834 and Edward Lear in 1864, or archaeological photographs by Harriet Boyd in the 1900s or Gerola and Evans a little later. In nearly two-thirds of such pictures there has since been an increase in wild or cultivated trees or in other plants (Figure 10.6); in the remainder there has been no change. We have found rare instances in Greece where vegetation has decreased, but virtually none in Crete.

The reasons are abundantly clear. In 1850 Crete was very extensively exploited. Agriculture has now retreated to the better land. Terraces – covering something like one-quarter of the whole island – are rarely used for grain. Some grow olives or other cultivated trees, but a large fraction have become grazing land. There can be little doubt that the number of livestock has decreased, whereas the area available to them has increased. The 120,000 cattle, mules and donkeys that Raulin found in Crete in 1847 are now far fewer. Reliable figures for sheep and goats are difficult to arrive at (Chapter 14); but according to all the indicators of browsing, such as the occurrence of *Ebenus*, wide areas particularly in east Crete are not now browsed at all, and this is not made up for by increased browsing of the remainder.

The changes are corroborated by other lines of evidence; for example, for all the common (and some rare) trees, young individuals now outnumber middle-aged and old.

Cypress-woods

Cypress has roughly doubled in the last hundred years (Figure 6.8a). This appears from every old illustration of cypress country and from the trees themselves: many cypress-woods are on old terraces, and young cypresses are abundant. Dead cypresses, except where there has been a fire, are quite rare, even on cliffs where they would be allowed to remain: this is another mark of an expanding population. Cypress is unpalatable, and the least relaxation of browsing allows it to get established. (It appears that *agrímia* eat it less reluctantly than domestic goats.)

Although cypress has increased in almost all its mountain strongholds, its most dramatic spread has been in the lowlands off the hard limestone, where it did not form woods in historic times. The view of 'Psilorítis from Frés' sketched by Edward Lear in 1864 can no longer be seen: the few cypresses shown by Lear have multiplied in their thousands and fill the landscape. These woods cover much of Apokórona, on former terraces and olive-groves. Much the same is happening at Ayios Ioánnes (AV), and on a small scale at Kavoúsi (H) where there is no historic record of cypress at all. These expansions start from sacred cypresses (round chapels) or field trees. Even the Palace of Knossós has been invaded by children of the cypresses planted by Evans.

Pinewoods

Pine has very greatly increased. In most pine areas (Figure 6.8b) young trees greatly outnumber middle-aged, and often are on former fields. For example a pinewood more than 1 sq. km in extent has arisen since the 1950s in the north of the Anópolis Plain (Sf). Pinewoods, which were certainly not there in Raulin's time, have engulfed most of the ex-cultivated land on the island of Gávdhos. Around Myrtos (H) this increase was noticeable in 1968, and pines have since gone from strength to strength; they are no longer confined to north-facing slopes. There is now at least twice as much pine in Crete as eighty years ago.

In the Gorge of Samariá (Sf), where pine and cypress overlap, both have increased, but pine more than cypress. We have sat on the rock where Pashley sat sketching the 'Iron Gates' in 1834. Some of the cypresses which he drew are still recognisable, but have been joined by many, more recent, pines. We suspect, from the over-abundance of young trees and the rarity of old or dead ones (even in inaccessible places), that pines have been increasing for at least 200 years.

The increase in pines brings an increase in fires. There have been five major pine fires since 1986, each burning mainly young pines. Old terraces have often emerged from under the burnt pines.

Maquis into woodland

New woods of prickly-oak are particularly easy to form. The oaks are already there as maquis shrubs, which turn into trees if browsing relaxes for a few years. This happens more easily if the oaks grow fast, as they then may reach the get-away point before the goats return. A couple of wet seasons can make all the difference between maquis and woodland.

This point is illustrated by the cypresses, oaks and maples round the Omalós Plain. It is clear from Diamantopoulos's photographs[5] that these trees have much increased since 1909 (Figure 10.6). The cypresses are of all ages, which is consistent with their power to get established under moderately severe browsing. The maples are mostly young upstanding trees; until recently they were bitten down, like the oaks, into 'topiary' shrubs. The oaks are still in the 'topiary' state. Maple is about as palatable as oak, but at this altitude (1,100 m) grows faster. About twenty years ago, browsing declined and could no longer hold down maple; it still holds down prickly-oak.

Most maquis shrubs behave in this way. In west Crete much of the arbutus–heather maquis has turned, or is turning, into woodland. Lentisk is the least changed: being very unpalatable, it has not much responded to the decline of browsing. It has sometimes invaded abandoned farmland.

10.6 *Omalós Plain, showing increases in trees:*
(a) 1909, from a Diamantopoulos photograph in Trevor-Battye. The foreground is covered with low maquis, and the mountains behind are dotted with small cypresses
(b) April 1982. In the foreground cypresses and maple have grown into trees, but most of the prickly-oak is still in the form of topiary. The cypresses on the mountains are bigger and have been joined by the maples, oaks, and occasional ambelitsiá

Deciduous woods

Deciduous oaks (in Crete) start from acorns rather than from bitten-down shrubs. As cultivation recedes, they form woodland on terraces and even on level farmland. There are fine examples around Spíli (AV), in western Amári, the eastern Khaniá plain, and (with valonia oak) around Arménoi (R). Less commonly, deciduous oak invades heather on former pasture.

Maple-woods are increasing around many mountain-plains. Plane-woods by rivers and in valleys are extending, and their coppice stools are growing into big trees.

Phrygana and steppe

In the drier parts of Crete, although maquis has increased in stature, there is still not much of it. Without maquis competition, phrygana tends both to expand and to grow up into taller states of phrygana. Those few undershrubs that are sensitive to browsing have often increased at the expense of the others. In much of Siteía *Ebenus cretica* has become a dominant undershrub. Its abundance ends suddenly at fences, proving that browsing is the decisive factor. Occasionally, where there has been no browsing

10.7 *Myrtos (H), showing increase in vegetation:*
(a) July 1968: the foreground has only scattered low lentisk bushes. The hills behind are scattered with pine; the hill to the left has land-juniper
(b) August 1988: the foreground is dense with Atriplex halimus *and is beginning to be invaded by pines. The hills are nearly continuous with pinewood, except where bull-dozed for plastic greenhouses. The junipers are bigger but scarcely more numerous*

for twenty years, *Ebenus* has grown almost into a tree with a thick erect trunk. Near the sea, *Atriplex halimus*, also very palatable, has increased and grown into big bushes.

The greening of Myrtos

The Myrtos area (H) is arid and marly, with little maquis but some

pines. In the summer of 1968, one of us (O.R.) made detailed observations. These were repeated exactly twenty years later (Figure 10.7), and compared with air photographs taken by the Germans in 1941.[6] The village of Myrtos is a somewhat extreme example of the changes in Crete. The years from 1968 to 1988 were a time of prosperity. Agriculture, already shrunken by 1968, was replaced by greenhouse horticulture confined to the coastal plains. Grazing, severe in 1941, almost ceased shortly before 1968.

Pines, somewhat increased by 1968, have since almost doubled at the expense of phrygana and terraced land. This brought Nemesis in the shape of great fires in 1984 and 1994. Juniper has also increased, but other shrubs have done little more than hold their own.

121

Undershrubs much increased from 1968 to 1988, covering great areas which had been bare rock or tenuous steppe. Much of the increase was of *Ebenus* and *Atriplex*. There had been much turnover of the other, short-lived, undershrubs in twenty years. The least altered place in the area was a hard limestone cliff: several small trees were almost unaltered after twenty years.

Conclusions

The increase in wild vegetation is consistent, some of it due to abandoned cultivation and some to reduced browsing and wood-cutting. (The possibility of a run of wet years, reducing the time to get-away, cannot yet be excluded.) All the widespread Cretan trees have multiplied in their former areas and sometimes have colonised new areas. Even the rare *ambelitsiá* has increased (despite a recent author's pessimistic view of its future[7]): most individuals have been released from browsing within the last eighty years. Increases in undershrubs are more difficult to establish, but the Myrtos observations do not leave them in doubt.

Crete is emerging from a period in which browsing, woodcutting or cultivation held down even pine and cypress. There can be little doubt that such relaxations have happened in the past. This is confirmed, for browsing, by our observation that trees in wood-pastures tend to be of one, two or three ages, rather than of a continuous range. However, this sort of thing is most unlikely to be noticed and recorded in writing. In all Cretan documents, ancient and modern, we have found only one mention of an increase of vegetation: Filippo Pasquaglio, in his history of the Lassíthi Plain, says that in 1514 part of the plain was grubbed out, 'having become enwooded by the length of time' since cultivation had been prohibited 150 years before.[8]

Cretan vegetation, therefore, is resilient. The idea of progressive deforestation, on which Ruined Landscape theory depends, has been falsified.

Notes

1 For an attempt to being the woodland of Crete into a West European style of vegetation classification see: M. Barbero and P. Quézel (1980), 'La végétation forestière de Crète', *Ecologia Mediterranea*, **5**, 175–210.
2 *History of Plants*, I.iii.1.
3 Rackham (1983, see bibliography).
4 R. A. Minnich (1987), 'Fire behavior in southern Californian chaparral before fire control: the Mount Wilson burns at the turn of the century', *Annals of the Association of American Geographers*, **77**, 599–618.
5 Trevor-Battye (1913, see bibliography).
6 Rackham (1972, see bibliography). O. Rackham (1993), 'The greening of Myrtos', *Petromarula*, **2**, forthcoming.
7 G. Sarlis (1987, Chapter 6, note 12).
8 *Mn*, **3**, 58.

11
Vegetation history

Pausanias says that the grove of Poseidon at Onchestus existed in his time. Strabo says that there were no trees in it. Where is the inconsistency between these statements? Strabo wrote in the reign of Augustus [27 BC – 14 AD]; Pausanias wrote in the reign of Marcus Aurelius [161 – 180 AD]. Did trees cease to grow after the time of Strabo?

J. G. Frazer, *Pausanias's Description of Greece*, London, 1898, **1** xcii

Crete before settlement

Up to 9000 BC we can only make informed guesses, based on indirect evidence, about Cretan vegetation. On Santoríni, fossil remains of lentisk, terebinth, olive, tamarisk, and two palms (*Phoenix* and *Chamaerops*) have been found, preserved by successive eruptions of the volcano at different dates in the Pleistocene.[1] Sparse pollen from deep-sea cores suggests that the vegetation from some warm periods during the last glaciation was not very different from today.[2]

On Crete, vegetation for the last two million years would have been very much determined by the peculiar animals. During glaciations, the altitudinal limits of species would have been shifted downwards; they must also have been compressed, since very low-altitude endemics (e.g. *Phoenix theophrasti*) were not driven into the sea.

The pollen record

Many trees and other plants produce vast quantities of pollen grains, which may be preserved for millions of years. They can be identified to some extent under the microscope. Crete is not a good place for a pollen record: the conditions for pollen preservation – a permanently waterlogged place in which layers of peat or mud, containing pollen grains, are built up year by year – seldom occur (Figure 2.1).

The only evidence from Crete for this period is from a core from the lowland of Ayia Galíni (AV), analysed by S. Bottema.[3] The area is now dry, vegetated mainly with phrygana, and has no oak. In the pre-Neolithic, things were very different. Trees included evergreen and deciduous oaks, hazel, alder, elm and lime (= linden or basswood). The last three are trees of north and middle Europe: alder and lime are now absent from Crete, and elm is rare (Figure 6.14a). We interpret this as indicating that the climate was less arid than today. However, the land was not all woodland. Although tree-or-shrub pollen amounts to a little more than half the total, it is inflated by a large amount of pine, which is a prolific pollen producer. Much of the pollen comes from plants – Leguminosae, Umbelliferae, Compositae – which could not have produced pollen in shade. Asphodel is well represented: this is a steppe plant, a poor pollen producer, and is often regarded as an indicator of over-grazing. Garigue species are poorly represented.

The Ay. Galíni record, although meagre, is consistent with pre-Neolithic pollen diagrams from mainland Greece. These all contain northern trees and show that, although trees were abundant, the lowlands were not continuously wooded. (There are no pollen cores from the mountains.)

We infer, cautiously, that the first settlers of Crete would have found the island rainier than today. The wetter parts would have had near-continuous woodland; the drier parts would have been a mosaic of maquis and steppe. Garigue was less extensive than now, perhaps limited to coastal areas (see later). The woods were most likely dominated by evergreen oaks on hard limestones, deciduous oaks where there is now cultivation, and perhaps decid-uous oak with holm-oak and arbutus on schist. There were patches of pine. All this would have been browsed by native mammals at least as severely as it is today by sheep and goats. Lime and elm would have been common on cliffs.

Plane is remarkably rare (at most a grain or two) in all the cores from pre-Neolithic Greece. Some pollen analysts argue that Neolithic and later people somehow made the tree abundant, or even introduced it, but in Crete this is most unlikely: some plane appears in the pre-Neolithic, and the tree today is common and is not related to human activity. The present plane-woods along Cretan streams would then, in part, have been alder-woods.

Cypress, too, is scarce in the pollen record, although it produces a great deal of pollen. It may have been almost confined to the mountains, as it was until recently.

The first human impact

The native mammals disappeared. They were replaced by domes-tic animals, but these did not come at first in large numbers, nor were they specifically adapted to Cretan vegetation. It is possible that there was a lull in browsing between Crete populated by deer and hippopotamuses and Crete populated by sheep and goats, during which the island might have become more wooded than ever before or since. The pollen record (for what it is worth) suggests that woodland did increase until the mid-Neolithic.

Neolithic vegetation

Pollen evidence

The Ay. Galíni core continues, and is supplemented by the Tersaná core from the Akrotíri peninsula near Khaniá.[4] The vegetations of the two areas diverged much as they do today. Throughout the Neolithic the south coast continued to be a mosaic of steppe and woodland. Pine declined, but deciduous oak increased: a long enough interval may have elapsed between fires for the less flammable species to take over.

The history of the north-west coast was rather different. At the beginning of the Neolithic it was a mosaic of phrygana and wood-land. One might have expected more woodland, given the higher rainfall here, but tree growth may have been stunted by strong coastal winds, allowing phrygana to develop. Since we do not know how long the native mammals persisted, we cannot say for sure if this vegetation is partly a product of browsing – although it seems likely. The woodland was made up of much the same Mediterranean and Central European trees as the pre-Neolithic forest: deciduous and evergreen oaks, lime, hazel and hornbeam (*Ostrya*).

During the Middle Neolithic olive pollen begins to appear in small quantities at Tersaná (Ak). By the Late Neolithic it is abundant enough to indicate local cultivation (Chapter 7). It is then that land clearance for agriculture begins noticeably to affect the wild vegetation at this site. Oak woodland decreased, while phrygana and steppe increased.

There was a temporary decline in agricultural evidence during the Final Neolithic, but evidence for burning increases. Charcoal is present in the sediments, and fire-related plants flourish (pine, Ericaceae, Cistaceae, asphodel, etc.). An increase in pine suggests that fields were no longer kept clear for cultivation. It is therefore possible that burning was intended to maintain pasture. Simultaneous declines in lime, hornbeam, hazel, elm and poplar – all well-known fodder sources – are suggestive. However, this scenario may be peculiar to the Akrotíri.

Archaeological evidence
In general, bones and charred plant remains from archaeological excavations have little to say about the landscape at large. Exceptional are the carbonised fragments of a wooden stake from Early Neolithic Knossós, which have been identified as deciduous oak.[5]

Minoan vegetation

Here we return to speculation. The amount of direct evidence on the Minoan Cretan landscape is small, though rapidly growing, and until recently most scholars either were silent or tried to eke out inferences from scraps of indirect evidence. Few scholars have approached the matter with an open mind. All too often they start from the assumption that Minoan Crete was very different from modern – much more wooded – and clutch at any straw that can be made to point in that direction. The right questions to ask are: (1) is a piece of evidence definitely inconsistent with the vegetation of early-modern Crete (the only Crete that we thoroughly know about)? and (2) with what range of conditions would it be consistent?

Pollen evidence
Pollen evidence becomes less abundant: the Early Bronze Age is covered by two Cretan pollen cores, the Middle Bronze Age by one, and the Late Bronze Age by none.

The beginning of the Bronze Age brought striking changes. At Ay. Galíni (AV) steppe and phrygana dominated the landscape for the first time. Surviving woodland was still mainly of deciduous oak, but lime and hazel disappeared, never to return except as garden trees. On the north-west coast olive cultivation peaked in the Early Bronze Age, implying substantial land clearance. Pine increased, but not to a degree implying local woods of the tree. As on the south coast, oaks (probably deciduous) and hornbeam dominated local woodland. Lime disappeared by the end of the period.

The Tersaná core provides our only pollen data for the Middle Bronze Age. Agriculture seems to have declined in the local area, allowing natural woodland to increase, but the vegetation did not revert to a phrygana-woodland mosaic; instead it reverted to *steppe* and woodland. In spite of a general increase in wetland and Central European trees, lime did not reappear (nor does it occur at this time in any other pollen core known to us from southern Greece).[6] Although changes in land-use were probably responsible for the fluctuations in olive pollen, they cannot account for the shift from garigue-woodland to steppe-woodland, nor for the *complete* disappearance of lime even on cliffs. This indicates that the climate became drier, perhaps by rainfall concentrating in fewer months. These changes probably mark the development of the Mediterranean dry season for the present interglacial (Chapter 4).

It is difficult to know what was happening in Late Bronze Age Crete. Pollen cores from low elevations in mainland Greece show an increase in trees towards the end of the period, including the occasional reappearance of lime.

What of the mountains during the Bronze Age? Since Middle and Late Minoan I settlement patterns are very similar to Early Byzantine, it is tempting to extrapolate backwards from the much later Así Goniá core (see below). This would suggest that a little over half the north-facing slopes of the White Mountains were wooded during the Bronze Age. Whether or not these woods were filled with timber trees we cannot say. But an extensive shepherding tradition, as is implied in the Linear B tablets, does not require large-scale removal of natural woodland above 700 m. Trees could have been pollarded or shredded for leaf-fodder.

Archaeological evidence

Plants are depicted on pots, seals and walls; these tell us about gardens, lilies and olive-groves, but little about wild vegetation.[7]

All we can definitely say is that Bronze Age Crete had non-woodland trees. Bones and charred remains of crops, again, give quite a good picture of animal and plant husbandry, but have little to say about the landscape at large.

Linear B tablets say much about the products of husbandry, but only indirectly about the landscape. From Knossós (T) there is a large archive of shepherding tablets, enumerating at least 80,000 sheep, nearly all males kept for wool.[8] These alone indicate at least 160,000 sheep in Crete, compared to at least 500,000 in modern times. There is no indication of what fraction of the island's sheep these were. If there were tablets not preserved, sheep kept for other purposes, or sheep in which the Palace was not interested, the amount of browsing in Late Minoan Crete could easily have been comparable to what it is now.

Many scholars have claimed that in Bronze Age Crete timber and wood were more plentiful and of larger sizes than they are today; some go on to claim that the Minoans used up the supply and got into difficulties. Sir Arthur Evans even supposed that they were so lavish with timber that finally they had to use gypsum as a substitute.[9]

Many ordinary Minoan buildings used rather more timber than vernacular Cretan buildings today. However other Bronze Age settlements, such as Myrtos (H), were composed of tiny rooms with internal piers, needing only short timbers. This may be regarded as a style adapted to a land where a tree 5 m high is a big tree (like the modern Cyclades).

The great beams in the Palace of Knossós are supposed to have come from bigger trees than any that grow in Crete today. The longest were apparently 7½ m long, and the thickest at least 40cm square. Charred fragments survived, and Evans had them identified by an anonymous expert as cypress,[10] although Spyridon Marinatos claimed that they were fir (a tree never known to have grown in Crete).[11] It is important to know who was right, since a fir identification would prove that the timbers were imported, but without the microscopic details we shall never know. If the timbers were cypress, they would not prove Crete was more wooded than it is now. Trees of this size grow in Sphakiá today. The architects of Knossós, the grandest building in south-east Europe, could presumably have fetched timber from anywhere in the Aegean. Like cedar in King Solomon's palace, the lavish use of a scarce material could have been a symbol of grandeur.

One hears it argued that the Minoans had a sea empire; they therefore possessed a fleet; they therefore built ships; they therefore had plenty of timber in Crete. None of the links in this chain have been tested. We hardly even know that the Bronze Age Cretans had ships of their own, still less how many, how big, how long they lasted, or where they were built. If the Minoans did not have enough timber, they could have bought timber or ships from elsewhere, as classical Athens did later. Shipbuilders can more easily import their raw material than any other trade.

It has been argued that Crete exported timber to Egypt. This rests on the Egyptian records of timber brought by ships of 'Keftiu', which may or may not have been Crete; where the ships got the timber from is not stated.

One of us (O.R.) has had a first look at charcoal samples from the Royal Road excavations at Knossós (T).[12] The material included evergreen oak, a little deciduous oak, olive, cypress and probably juniper, and occasional plane and pine, distributed as follows:

Middle Minoan I	few pieces, predominantly olive
Middle Minoan II, Late Minoan I	evergreen oak > cypress or juniper >> olive
Late Minoan II and III	cypress (+ juniper) > evergreen oak > olive
Hellenistic or Roman	mainly evergreen oak

These do not match the modern vegetation, in which the nearest evergreen oak is 6 km away, deciduous oak farther still, cypress is only a field tree, and there is no juniper. We do not know whether they came from burnt buildings or furniture or fuel. Olive would have been a first choice for firewood.

Conclusion

The evidence indicates that until the end of the Early Bronze Age the vegetation was very different from the present. Lime grew side by side with olive on the low, exposed northern peninsulas of the island, which would be unimaginable in the present environment. Today lime survives in middle and south Greece at high altitudes on north-facing cliffs: the high elevation and north aspect prove that it is limited by climate and not just browsing. Several other trees of Neolithic and Minoan Crete no longer grow wild: alder, hornbeam, hazel. Deciduous oaks were also much more abundant then – though they are now again on the increase. Prehistoric Crete was more extensively tree-covered than the present, although never wet enough for continuous forest at low elevations. The differences are partly due to a change in climate: if they had been wholly due to human activities, the central European trees would still survive on cliffs, which they do not. The change to the present climate was roughly equivalent to a move of 500 km southwards (Chapter 4).

Woodland in the foothills and coastal plains has come and gone with agricultural activity since the Late Neolithic, if not before. If the Tersaná core is typical, it has fluctuated by 30 per cent during the Neolithic and Early to Middle Bronze Age. What happened in the Late Bronze Age or at higher elevations can only be conjectured.

The age of the Greeks and Romans

The written record

The imagination of scholars fills Ancient Greece with vanished forests. The claim that Crete was very wooded has become 'true by repetition'; few authors bother to document it. As far as we can tell, it rests to a great extent on a single word of Strabo (first century BC): 'The island is mountainous and wooded, but it has fertile valleys.'[13] The Greek word *daseía* means just 'wooded', but scholars cannot resist the temptation to translate it '*thickly* wooded'. Its meaning is relative: modern Crete would be 'wooded' to an Arab but not to a Finn. A huge inverted pyramid of argument has been built on this one vague word.

Even today, not all the juice has been squeezed out of the ancient texts. Homer, in a rare passage genuinely evocative of landscape, sang of a pig-sticking:

> . . . they lodg'd a Bore, of bulke extreame,
> in such a Queach,* as neuer any beame
> the Sun shoot, pierc'st. Nor any passe, let finde
> The moist impressions of the fiercest winde:
> Nor any storme the sternest winter driues;

> Such proofe† it was; yet all within, lay leaues
> In mighty thicknesse . . .

> *Odyssey*, XIX. 439–43

* grove   † impenetrability

This evokes the dense heather–arbutus–ilex maquis (p. 29), with its dark, dry interior crackling with dead leaves; growing on phyllite, it would have been full of small springs (p. 42), and therefore (on the mainland) an excellent habitat for wild boar, as similar maquis is today in Sardinia.

Three authors from whom we can infer something of what Ancient Greece looked like are Theophrastus the botanist, Xenophon in his fourth-century book on hunting, and Pausanias in his guide to mainland Greece in the Roman period. At almost every point but two (terraces and fens), what these authors say is consistent with the early twentieth-century landscape. Pausanias writes of a land in which woods were unusual and worth taking notice of. Where he mentions a wood, sometimes there is a wood today and less often not; but there also exist woods today (e.g. on Mount Taygetos in the Peloponnese) which Pausanias would surely have mentioned had they then existed. Xenophon looked for hare or boar not in noble forests but in 'oak-groves, depressions, roughs, meadows, fens, and waters'.[14]

In Attica and Boeotia, probably the best-documented part of Greece, records show clearly that the great woods, if they ever existed, had been destroyed in the Iron Age or earlier, leaving a landscape no more wooded than it is today.[15] There is no need to fill Ancient Greece with vanished forests; nor is there real evidence anywhere in Greece of a reduction in woodland during the

Classical-to-Roman period.[16] What one misses, comparing Xenophon's landscape with the present, are not the woods but the fens; one notices also the lack of mention of terraces (Chapter 12).

So much for Greece. On Crete, the information in ancient authors does not provide a connected account, such as we might have hoped for had Pausanias visited the island.[17] Crete was famous for cypress, which probably grew nowhere else in Europe except as a planted tree. From the fifth century BC onwards cypress was a symbol of Crete.[18]

Theophrastus, the greatest surviving Greek botanical writer (370–c. 285 BC), never went to Crete and was not always well informed about it, but much of what he says is convincing:

> They say that in Crete on the mountains of Ida and on those called the White Mountains the cypress is found on the peaks whence the snow never disappears; for this is the principal tree both in the island generally and in the mountains.

> The cypress in most regions grows from seed, but in Crete from the trunk also, for instance in the hill country about Tarra* . . . when cut it shoots in every possible way, from the part which has been cut, from the ground, from the middle, and from the upper parts; and occasionally, but rarely, it shoots from the roots also.

* At the mouth of the Samariá Gorge, still the chief heartland of cypress.

> In some places, if the ground is merely lightly worked and stirred, the plants native to the district immediately spring up; for instance, the cypress in Crete.[19]

Theophrastus knew, though inaccurately, about cypress's coppicing behaviour; as a botanist, he was impressed, for conifers ought not to coppice. He also knew about its invading arable land. All he says is consistent with cypress in Crete today. It is still the principal wild tree of the island (unless pine or prickly-oak has recently overtaken it), and chiefly abundant in the White Mountains.

Theophrastus does not support the notion that Crete was an exporter of timber. It does not appear in his lists of countries from which Greece got shipbuilding or carpentry timber.[20] An inscription records that cypress from Crete went into the roof of the Parthenon, and Pliny says it was used for statues. Both of these uses imply a precious wood rather than ordinary timber.[21]

Ancient plane-trees existed in Theophrastus's time, including the famous one at Górtyn (Ka), which was evergreen in memory of Zeus having lain with Europa under it.[22] He also mentions two endemic plants: *díktamnon* (p. 71) and *tragion*, the latter now unidentifiable.[23]

A few of Theophrastus's records are dubious. He mentions black poplar in the Idaean mountains, including a sacred one at the Idaean Cave, and in the mountains of east Crete.[24] Black poplar is not otherwise known from Crete, and the localities are most unsuitable. Pharmacological writings mention 'berries of Cretan black-poplar',[25] which real black-poplar does not have. We suspect confusion with some other rare tree such as *ambelitsiá*.

The *Stadiasmós*, an undatable guide to the Mediterranean coast, describes the Díktynna peninsula as 'high and tree'd down' – the rare word *katádendron* could mean 'very tree'd' or 'sparsely tree'd'. Today the peninsula is arid and looks barren, but with small hidden woods of lentisk, and big olive-groves at its base.

The medical texts of Galen, Hippokrates and Pliny show that in

Hellenistic and Roman times Crete was regarded as the best source of herbal remedies. The most famous were *díktamnon*, juniper berries (p. 63), and *skórdion* (probably *Teucrium scordium*, water-germander). They were exported by professional pharmacists, such as Andromakhos the Cretan, and prescribed even to Caesar himself.[26]

Plato, in an oft-forgotten passage, implies that Crete had inadequate shipbuilding timber: little fir, pine or plane, and not much cypress.[27] This would be an important piece of evidence if we could believe what Plato said about Crete.

A few perambulations of boundaries are recorded in east Cretan inscriptions. They can approximately be traced on the ground, and indicate a landscape of mountains, rocks and caves, no more wooded than what is there now.[28]

So much for the good evidence; now for the bad. The most tenuous allusions have been taken to 'prove' that ancient Crete was forested. Every mention of trees is taken to imply woods, and is re-quoted to imply forests. Plato's *Laws* are cast in the form of a conversation between three aged philosophers on an afternoon stroll from Knossós to the Cave of Mount Ida, during which they expect to enjoy the shade of roadside trees.[29] This does not prove that Crete was forested; all it proves, to anyone who has ever done the long and arduous trip, is that Plato did not know Crete.

Ancient lexicographers thought Mount Ida had once been wooded because its name happened to resemble *ídi*, an obscure word for 'tree'.[30] This could hardly be less appropriate for a mountain whose bald summit soars far above any elevation at which trees could conceivably have grown. More plausibly it is a Minoan mountain-name of unknown meaning. (The medieval name Psilorítis may indeed mean 'bald mountain'.)

Diodorus Siculus (first century BC) mentions a grove of cypress at Knossós;[31] this grove, magnified in successive re-tellings, has doubtless turned into the 'cypress forest' which some modern authors claim was there.

The claim that cedar once grew in Crete appears to be based on a statement by Vitruvius, architectural writer of the first century BC, that the island was a source of cedar and juniper.[32] Vitruvius does not appear to have visited Crete, and did not know his trees; he may have been misled by the Cretan name for juniper being *kédros*.

Conclusions

Fragmentary though it is, the evidence comes from several independent directions, and can be combined to tell a definite story. The main types of wild vegetation in Crete today would be recognised by any Cretan from Late Minoan times onwards. Their proportions and distribution may have fluctuated down the millennia, but not overwhelmingly. Most of the evidence for the historic period could be reconciled with the recent landscape. Archaeology indicates that the classical period may have been a low phase in the fortunes of the islanders; Theophrastus, writing at the end of it, implies a landscape not very different from the present.

How much woodland was there in ancient Crete? Crete never became a major producer of ordinary timber, which it would have done had it been as wooded as France is today. On the other hand, if it had been less wooded than in the nineteenth century, people would have stopped writing about its trees. We conjecture that woodland on Crete has fluctuated between about three times and one-half of its present extent.

11.1 *Peat-bog on the borders of Sphakiá and Réthymnon, the site of the Así Goniá pollen core. The trees are planes. April 1991*

Crete never had any large fuel-using industry comparable to the metal-smelting of Attica, Cyprus or Elba. We do not as yet know the significance of this. Metal-working may, naïvely, be assumed to lead to the 'exhaustion' of woodland;[33] it could, however, encourage the conservation of a resource for future use.

There are still huge gaps in our knowledge: for instance, we have no idea when coppicing and pollarding were practised on wild trees. Were there goat-pollards in ancient Crete?

The Byzantine periods

Archaeological survey on Crete indicates that rural settlement during the Early Byzantine was more extensive than at any time since the Late Bronze Age. We may conjecture a somewhat similar state of affairs in the lowlands to that which prevailed in Minoan times, albeit with a drier climate.

From the mountains, one good piece of evidence comes from this dark period. In 1982 we discovered the southernmost peat-bog in Europe, in the White Mountains between Así Goniá (Ap) and Myrioképhala (R). It is surrounded by phrygana and savanna with patches of big trees (Figure 11.1). From it we took a core 4.5 m long, which gave six good radiocarbon dates; it has been analysed by Jean Hall and Margaret Atherden.[34]

The bottom of the core probably dates to the sixth century AD. It depicts a mountain landscape of evergreen and deciduous oak, with occasional maple, alder and hornbeam. Plane is significant throughout, and still grows around the bog today. Olive pollen is also present throughout – in small quantities – and either indicates cultivation at a distance or occasional wild olive in the natural woodland.

It is curious that this mountain area seems little affected by human activity: woodland was stable or increasing, and evidence for burning (in terms of charcoal fragments in the sediment) is low compared to later periods. One must be careful, however, in equating evergreen oak pollen with oak forest, since prickly-oak maquis produces pollen when less than 1 m tall. The charcoal dust – rarely over 20 per cent of the total pollen count – may be due to natural fires, but occupational burning (producing a low, continuous oak maquis) cannot be ruled out.

A possible human impact may be seen in the decrease of decid-uous oak. This is unlikely to be related to agriculture, since neither olive nor cereal pollen increases. The trees could have been shred-ded or pollarded for fodder; they would remain alive, but their pollen production would decline dramatically. Such a reconstruc-tion implies substantial shepherding at this elevation, but without a strong tradition of burning the vegetation to maintain pasture (Chapters 10, 14).

During the Late Byzantine period the vegetation changes dramatically. Tree pollen (chiefly prickly-oak) suddenly drops from 80 to 30 per cent, but without a definite increase in charcoal. This could mean felling for timber.

The Venetian period

The documents: woods, wild trees, timber
The earliest medieval records consist of incidental mentions of woods in other contexts. In 1328 there was an armed affray 'on the way in the middle of the wood on the way from . . . Muctaro [Moukhtári *alias* Evangelismós (Pe)] to the castle of Pedhiádha.' In 1332 someone was found knocked on the head 'in the grove of Pyrgiotissa'.[35] These two are the only examples we can find in hundreds of pages of the *Book of Bans*. Perambulations across the middle of Crete in 1333, 1342, and 1364 mention many vineyards, meadows, etc., but not a single wood. We infer that woodland was as scarce in middle Crete (the area mainly covered by these docu-ments) as it is today.

Buondelmonti, on his travels in 1415, took particular account of woods. The most notable were in the White Mountains, where 'cypresses innumerable reach for the stars' on the south coast and around the Anópolis Plain. In Sphakiá:

> The countryfolk … never sow because of the dryness of the mountains; but they live by making boards of cypress and by the multitude of their goats …

> We departed … along very high cliffs of cypresses and nests of falcons …

> The woolly countryfolk slide many trunks of cypress down from the mountains, thrown headlong into the [river] Massala; thence, with little trouble, they bring them to the sea. From here we had on our right vast rocky clefts, from which great cypresses reach up without moisture from the earth …

These and other allusions indicate that there was, then as now, a ring of trees, mainly cypresses, all round the middle elevations of the White Mountains. He gives similar information about the pines, mainly on the south and east sides, of the Lassíthi and Thryphtí mountains.

The export of cypress timber was already long-standing by 1359.[36] A year before Buondelmonti's visit, Venice was concerned about reports that the tree was diminishing. In the secret registers of the Senate is to be found a decree of 1414:

> Since the cypress timber of the Island of Crete is consumed from day to day, and is diminishing because of the great quantity … exported from the Island … and also because of the fires which are set by countryfolk in the groves and

mountains where all the cypresses are; And the said cypresses are now coming to such a state that the mules which go to load up such wood … can hardly go to … the mountains in which they are found, because all that was in accessible places has been consumed and cut down; … because the trees are of such a nature that the roots and stumps of burnt or cut trees do not sprout, and also those which begin afresh take a long time to grow. From which … the Island of Crete will have a great scarcity and loss of the said cypress timber, both for building houses and for constructing ships & other necessary works.[37]

Export of *unworked* cypress was forbidden, on penalty of confiscation of the logs plus a fine equal to their value. The export of cypress articles was expressly allowed, as was the movement of logs from one part of Crete to another. Export of cypress was de-restricted by 1471.[38]

Cypress boards and chests are among the products of Crete most often mentioned by travellers. 'Venetian' cypress chests are still found among antique furniture in Europe. A simple one, perhaps of Buondelmonti's time, is in a church in Norfolk (England) where one of the authors was brought up. It is made of planks from short and crooked trees, cunningly joined at the edges with secret nails in a manner which we have found otherwise only in Cretan ikons. It has a chip-carved scene of the Annunciation and paintings of ships; after 500-odd years it still has the beautiful scent of cypress. The trade continued until the end of the Venetian period.

The wording of the 1414 decree shows some attempt at understanding the ecology of cypress. Unlike almost all writers on 'deforestation' down to the present, the drafter took regrowth into acount. Cypress was evidently used both as a precious timber for furniture, and for ordinary construction.

In 1555 the traveller Belon was the first to describe the woods of Mount Psilorítis. He gives the impression that they were rather more extensive than now on the east side, but some details have not changed, for example the restriction of cypress and pine to the south side.

Public works in Crete depended almost entirely on timber shipped from Venice. In 1356, 100 oak beams were ordered to be shipped to Candia for use in repairing the harbour,[39] and the import of oars for galleys is recorded from 1430 onwards. There are numerous lists of beams, planks, etc., in stock, which are either larch or fir (*albeo*), neither of which grew in Crete; only occasionally are small quantities of cypress mentioned.[40]

Cretans got timber for ordinary purposes, with more or less difficulty, from local woods and trees. This is usually beneath the notice of the kinds of people who left archives, although many of the timbers must still survive in buildings. In 1633, a proposal for taming the outlet of the Lassíthi Plain (p. 150) involved cutting 1,000 piles, each 6–7 feet long and 6 inches thick, from evergreen oaks such as grow today around the plain.[41] How the many woodless and treeless places got timber we are not told.

Crete, a land of oil and wine, and whose galleys had large and thirsty crews, was very dependent on barrels, which demand the best oak timber, and seem always to have been imported. In 1395 a tax was imposed on barrels imported other than from Venice.[42]

Leather was tanned with the bark of deciduous-oak roots before the introduction of the use of valonia acorn-cups.[43]

All this implies that Crete, throughout the Venetian period, was rather less wooded than it is today, except perhaps with deciduous oak. Its reputation among modern authors as a wooded island rests on the argument that the Venetians maintained galleys there, which implies shipbuilding which implies local timber. In reality galleys were normally built in Venice from Venetian timber, and sent out empty to Crete.[44] The Arsenals in Crete could seldom do more than fitting-out and repairs.

Crete's shipbuilding capabilities, however, were not entirely negligible. Some of the more able governors tried to train up shipwrights in the Cretan arsenals. Benetto Moro, governor *c.* 1600, built three galleys of timber from Corfú and Crete, but this was a rarity.[45] Galleys were flimsy craft, merely enormous rowing-skiffs, and would not have demanded much timber except for oars. More important was commercial shipbuilding, which went on sporadically. In 1603 there was a vessel on the stocks of at least 600 tons, an average-to-large size for the cargo ships of the time, but noted as an unusual event in Cretan shipbuilding.[46] The timber, of course, was not necessarily Cretan.

Governors' reports are inconsistent about the woodland of Crete. Giacomo Foscarini in 1579 was disparaging,[47] but was followed by an enthusiastic successor:

In my judgement, they [woods] are one of the great riches of this Island. From them can be cut timber to build every kind of warship and merchant ship. ... Although the woods are mostly sited on the property of private persons, they are nevertheless common to everybody, and anyone, without restriction, can cut whatever quantity he needs.[48]

The people of Sphakiá owed much of their independence to owning the only extensive woods in Crete, yielding timber of cypress, and of Pine which they cut from the Woods that are there, and take them to sell in Canea, Rettimo, and in Candia . . .[49]

They were the main shipbuilders in Crete, and at least until the eighteenth century had shipping of their own.

Benetto Civran, almost the last Governor, established about 170 shipwrights in Candia and Canea. He claimed to have discovered sources of timber in the island:

This shortage of timber ... in the Arsenals, through the difficulty of sending it from the City [Venice] ... there being in the Realm [Crete] many woods, I sent practical personnel, who with all diligence reviewed, marked and catalogued the trees suitable for this purpose ... from which in future this need may be abundantly supplied at little expense; except for masts and the like, which it will still be necessary to send from the City.[50]

The Venetian dockyards had therefore not previously been in the habit of commandeering timber in Crete. Six years later Crete fell to the Turks.

In the early Turkish period, Cretan shipping apparently increased, with shipyards at Khaniá (Ky) as well as Loutró (Sf). Local timber was used as well as timber imported from Turkey, Epirus, Albania and France.[51]

All these lines of evidence (for which we have much more material) point in the same direction. Fourteenth- to seventeenth-century Crete was less wooded than it is today. The amount of woodland in the mountains may in places have been more than today, in places less. In the lowlands there was no more woodland than before the twentieth-century expansion. Sphakiá was the only well-wooded area, and the only one that exported timber or used it in shipbuilding.

The oft-repeated claim that the Venetians strictly controlled the use of woodland is unfounded. The Office of Woods in Venice was exclusively concerned with nearby woodland. There were only two official interventions in the woodland of Crete: one weak and short-lived, the other right at the end of the period.

Other roughland

In Venetian times, as in antiquity, maquis, phrygana and steppe were taken for granted and not mentioned. In the Venetian period, at least after the Black Death, the cultivated area was less than in the nineteenth century. The authorities compiled lists of uncultivated lands including several coastal plains. On the other hand, very few inland areas were without villages and hamlets.

Given all this area for pasture, shepherds might not have been able to keep enough animals to hold down the vegetation, so that tall maquis and woodland might have been widespread. There is no hint of this in the documents, and there are two negative indications: accounts of revolts nowhere suggest that rebels took to the woods, like French *maquisards;* nor is there any mention of setting fire to the maquis to flush them out.

In the seventeenth century, pictures show a landscape a little less vegetated than now. This is clear in Monanni's watercolours of 1631 (Plates 1 and 2). Myrtos (H), for example, had a tree'd plain, corresponding to the present orchards, between bare hills with no hint of the pines that now grow there. Merabéllo (now Ayios Nikólaos) has an indication of hillsides covered with trees like the junipers and pines of today. At Retimo the countryside had groves of trees around hamlets; in the foreground Monanni depicts himself, in doublet, hose and sword, sketching between two squills.

Grass may have been more prevalent than today. Grasslands were reserved for cattle and horses. One such was close to medieval Candia, while others were in the mountain-plains. On the Anópolis Plain, Buondelmonti found 'the flocks shaving the flowery meads' where, as in Lassíthi, cultivation was banned. Later, to the Venetians' disgust, the Omalós Plain was not cultivated because the men of Sphakiá claimed rights of pasture over it.

Burning and the pollen record

In the Así Goniá diagram, the fall in tree pollen in late Byzantine times leads to a predominance of heather, rushes, grasses and bracken throughout the Venetian period. The remaining woods or maquis were of prickly-oak and arbutus, with some deciduous oak, olive and a little hornbeam. Charcoal fragments increase steadily until the late Venetian. All this indicates great pressure on land, and (since most of the plants respond well to fire) increased burning.

In Early Venetian times oak pollen briefly increased from a low of 5 per cent to about 30 per cent, perhaps as a response to rebellions and plagues (Chapter 8) – bad times for men being good times for trees. From about 1400, however, tree pollen dropped to about 10 per cent.

If the burning was done by shepherds, this implies a change in herding tradition from the Byzantine to the Venetian – at least for the local area. The 1414 decree gives occupational burning as a reason for the decline of cypress, which is sensitive to fire. However, the only regulations about burning known in the *Book of Bans* relate to arson as a crime.

That some fires got out of hand is implied by place-names incorporating *kapso*. Kapsódhasos (Sf) apparently means 'Burntwood'; the village is now several km from the nearest woodland. The name must be older than 1397 when someone was called by it.[52] In 1612 there was a famous fire in the cypress and pine woods[53] near Sphakiá town. It is supposed to have burnt for a year, which is highly improbable; in a later retelling this grew to three years.[54]

A slight increase in tree pollen (especially evergreen oak and plane) at Así Goniá (Ap) near the end of the Venetian period may be related to the plagues, famines and unpredictable weather that beset the island from the late sixteenth century on.

Early botanical records

There are two lists of plants in St Mark's Library by visiting botanists at the end of the Venetian period.[55] Each covers about thirty localities. Many of the plants are in the same localities 350 years later. The golden henbane, *Hyoscyamus aureus*, 'Tusgriano con fior d'oro', was found on the walls of Candia (Herákleion (T)); it still grows in the same spot, almost its only locality in Europe. *Petromarula*, then as now, was a speciality of the Venetian walls of Khaniá (Ky). Other endemics were *Valeriana asarifolia* and *Cyclamen creticum*, both from the Apokórona coast. On the sacred cliff of St John the Stranger (Akrotíri) the travellers found *Dianthus creticus* (an endemic shrubby pink), and *Ebenus*. (We pride ourselves on having spotted *Origanum dictamnus* there, which they failed to see in Crete.) A visit to Mount Ida gave the endemic *Chionodoxa cretica* and two hedgehog species of *Astragalus*. In the Lassíthi Mountains they noted *ambelitsiá* ('Apelica'), which we have never found there.

The impression is one of extreme stability, of plants then in exactly the same places as now; but there are some questions. Why did the botanists in Sphakiá miss yellow asphodel, now so prominent there, although they recorded it elsewhere?

The Turkish period

Travellers' accounts

Where these are sufficiently detailed for retracing routes, they show, in general, much more cultivation and less wild vegetation than today. Many features of the wild vegetation are still visible. For example, Tournefort in 1700 was as impressed by the wood-pastures above Máles (H) with their mighty prickly-oaks as one of us was in 1968.

Raulin in 1847 found the schist mountains of Kíssamos and Sélinon covered, exactly as now, with arbutus, heather, bracken and Spanish broom. Unexpectedly, he fails to mention burning, although he knew about it elsewhere.

Captain Spratt in 1852 went to the Omalós Plain by a route now followed by thousands of bus-loads of tourists visiting the Gorge of Samariá. After reviewing the cultivated terraces of Lákkoi (Ky), now abandoned, partly pastured and partly wooded, he went on:

> for three-quarters of an hour's distance we wound up a rocky zig-zag path too steep to ride, and thus reached a little shelf on the side of the mountain, where there was a well to quench our thirst, and a large ilex tree to give shade during our rest.

Beside the road today there are four great 'ilexes' – that is, prickly-oaks – near a well. Next he came to the large upland plain of the Omalo, enclosed in a wall of mountains on every side, and looking like a green lake from the lateness of the fresh-springing crops growing in it, every part of the plain being tilled with oats . . . At the summit of the pass descending into the plain the ilex and yellow broom were in full flower, the one tinging the mountain with gold, and the other with a blood-red hue, while here and there the hill was enlivened by a shrub or two of Cretan sage . . .

The Omalós was more cultivated than today. The bitten-down cushions of 'ilex' are still blood-red with new leaves in April; but the big change is that the summit of the pass is now largely over-grown with cypress and maple trees (p. 119), which restrict the view of the plain described by Spratt.

Trees and woods

Cypress disappears from the records of trade and manufacture. The Venetians had almost no cypress outside Crete, but the Turks had plenty in Asia Minor. The main evidence comes from the trees themselves, many of which date back to the early Turkish period if not before. Cypress was a workaday tree of beehive-lids, coppic-ing for firewood, and ordinary carpentry; Raulin in 1847 thought it the most important such tree in Crete. Sphakiá continued to send timber to the western Mesará until within living memory.

Raulin states that Crete imported two-thirds of its structural timber and firewood (for cities and soap-boileries). Charcoal was made from evergreen oak and arbutus; in places oleander was regularly coppiced. He claimed that 1,300 tons of charcoal were made a year (which seems too little) mainly in the Lassíthi Moun-tains. Réthymnon (R) drew much of its wood from the valonia-oak area to the south. He says that woods of prickly-oak and maple were 'disappearing more every day' from the mountains. The ages of surviving trees confirm that trees and woods were at their lowest extent about this time. Raulin, however, records the existence of 'rather sparse' deciduous oakwoods around Voukouliés (Ki).

The pollen record

Non-woodland plants continued to dominate the Así Goniá (R) landscape. The only noticeable change in the early Turkish period is a slight increase in fire-tolerant plants. Later there appears to be a more wooded phase, which could be related to the rebellions that plagued the island from 1770 to 1898. Olive pollen also increases in the second half of the Turkish period, and charcoal is abundant throughout the period.

Alder and hornbeam, most unexpectedly, hung on until the late Turkish period, but are probably extinct in Crete today.

General conclusions

The aboriginal vegetation of Crete was very different from the natural vegetation today. There can be little doubt that important transformations took place in the Neolithic and again in the Bronze Age. Partly these were due to human activities: extermination of native mammals; destruction of natural vegetation for cultivation; modification of the remaining natural vegetation by woodcutting, occupational burning, and the browsing of a different set of mammals. However, many of the changes were due to a change in climate independent of human affairs.

Since these early changes, most of the direct evidence points to a history of stability, the proportions of woodland, maquis, phrygana and steppe fluctuating within fairly narrow limits for millennia. This may, however, be an illusion. The last 150 years show that Cretan vegetation is resilient, and recovers in only a few decades of reduced pressure. Reduced pressure is most likely to occur through declining population, instability and war, episodes of which have occurred thoughout Cretan history. When cultivators are rowing galleys and armies have eaten the goats, the trees can come back. The Así Goniá pollen core, which covers several such periods, does indeed reveal increases and declines of vegetation of the kind that we might expect. However, there is no means of telling how typical this one site may be.

Notes

1 W. L. Friedrich (1978), 'Fossil plants from Weichselian interstadials, Santorini', in C. Doumas (ed.), *Thera and the Aegean World* 1, London, Thera Foundation, pp. 741–5.

2 F. McCoy (1980), 'Climatic change in the eastern Mediterranean area during the past 240,000 years', in C. Doumas (ed.), *Thera and the Aegean World* 2, London, Thera Foundation, pp. 79–100.

3 S. Bottema (1980), 'Palynological investigations on Crete', *Review of Palaeobotany and Palynology*, **31**, 193–217.

4 J. A. Moody (1987),*The Environmental and Cultural Prehistory of the Khania Region of West Crete: Neolithic through Late Minoan III*, Ph.D. dissertation, University of Minnesota; Moody et al. (forthcoming, Chapter 7, note 31).

5 A. C. Western (1964), 'Timber from Neolithic Knossos', in J. D. Evans 'Excavations in the Neolithic settlement of Knossos, 1957-60, Part I', *BSA*, **56**, 239-40.

6 Moody (1987, note 4).

7 O. Rackham (1978), 'The flora and vegetation of Thera and Crete before and after the great eruption', in Doumas, note 1, pp. 755–64.

8 J. T. Killen (1964), 'The wool industry of Crete in the Late Bronze Age', *BSA*, **59**, 1–15.

9 *Palace of Minos*, II, 565.

10 *Palace of Minos*, I, 344.

11 S. Marinatos and M. Hirmer (1960), *Crete and Mycenae*, London, Thames & Hudson, p. 12.

12 By kind invitation of Mr Sinclair Hood and permission of the British School at Athens.

13 *Geography*, X, 4.

14 *Kynegetika*, X, 19.

15 Rackham (1983, see bibliography).

16 The assertions of J. D. Hughes (1983, Chapter 2, note 18) fail to take regrowth into account.

17 Many authors are quoted by A. S. Zakharis (Α. Σ. Ζαχάρη) (1977), *Τά Δάση τῆς Κρήτης από τῆν Αρχαιότητα εῶς Σήμερον*, Athens, Ἡ Ὑπερεσία Δασικῶν.

18 E.g. Hermippos the Comic, *Phormophóroi*, I. 14; Pindar, *Paean*, 4. 31–44.

19 *History of Plants*, IV. i. 3, II. ii. 2, III. iii. 4.

20 *History of Plants*, V. ii. 1, VII. i–4.

21 As far as we know, the only balanced and critical account of timber growth and supply in Antiquity is: R. Meiggs (1982), *Trees and Timber in the Ancient Mediterranean World*, Oxford, Oxford University Press.

22 *History of Plants*, I. ix. 5.

23 *History of Plants*, IX. xvi. 4.

24 *History of Plants*, III. iii. 4.

25 Hippokrates (Littré edition), VII.350.2, VIII.182.2.

26 E.g. Galen, *On Antidotes*, **1**, XIV.9–10.

27 *Laws*, IV. 704D.

28 H. van Effenterre and M. Bougrat (1969), 'Les frontières de Lato', *Kretika Khronika*, **21**, 9-53; P. Faure (1967), 'Aux frontières de l'état de Lato: 50 toponymes', W. C. Brice (ed.), *Europa: Studien zur Geschichte und Epigraphik der frühen Aegaeis*, Berlin, Brice, 94–112.

29 *Laws*, I. 625B.

30 Hesychos, *Lexicon*.

31 V.66.

32 *De Architectura*, II. ix. 13.

33 T. A. Wertime (1983), 'The furnace versus the goat: the pyrotechnologic industries and Mediterranean deforestation in antiquity', *JFA*, **10**, 445–52 [which fails to take growth-rates into account].

34 J. A. Hall, M.A. Atherden et al. (1992), 'A pollen diagram from the White Mountains: a preliminary interpretation', *Petromarula*, **1**, 40–1.

35 ASV: DC Bandi b. 14 c.48v, 78; Vidulich, p.184.

36 Thiriet (1978), no.351.

37 ASV: Misti registro 50 c. 131v.

38 Noiret (see bibliography), p. 522.

39 Thiriet (see bibliography), no. 288.

40 For example VAS Provv. da Terra e da Mar b.728 (1554).

41 *Mn*, **3**, 74.

42 Noiret (see bibliography), p. 62.

43 MCV: Cicogna 1767 c.125 (G. Foscarini *relazione*, 1579).

44 F. C. Lane (1965), *Navires et constructeurs à Venise pendant la Renaissance* (2nd ed), Paris, SEVPEN.

45 ASV: CR b.79 c.52v.

46 ASV: CR b. 79 c.41 (Priuli *relazione*).

47 MCV: Cicogna 1767, p. 175.

48 BMV: Ital. VII. 918 (8392) c.31 (anonymous *relazione* 1582).

49 VAS: Coll. Relaz. b.80 (Contarini *relazione* 1636).

50 ASV: Coll. Relaz. 80 c.9v.

51 Y. Triandafyllidou-Baladié (1988, Chapter 7, note 36), further information from Dr J. Grove.

52 Noiret (see bibliography), p. 88.

53 Spanakis's version has *carpini*, 'hornbeam', but the word in the original is *Zappini*, 'pines'.

54 Iseppo Civran, VAS: Coll Relaz. 80 c.15v-16. A. Cornelius, *Creta Sacra*.

55 BMV: Ital.VI.340(5750); Ital.VI.2393(11724) c. 372–4.

12
Terraces, fields and enclosures

He found him sitting in the front of his [field-]house, where the fine great high enclosure was built in a place with a view around, with a passage round it. This the swineherd himself had built for the pigs of his absent lord ... dragging boulders and coping it with thorns.

Odyssey, XIV, 5–10

[Just such dry-stone walls, with spiny bushes on top to deter climbing animals, are to be seen in Crete today.]

'Stranger, would you want to work for me, if I should employ you, on an outlying farm ... gathering [stones for] walls, and planting great trees?'

Odyssey, XVIII, 357–9 (our translations)

There are many styles of dry-stone walling in Crete. Some walls are one stone thick, but many have two faces, sometimes with an infill between. A distinctive style of wall consists of big slabs set on edge at intervals, the gaps being filled with smaller stones. If walls are to keep out livestock, the tops may be defended by a coping of spiny bushes, as in Homer's time. Very thick walls also have the function of using up stones taken from the land – an alternative to making stone-piles – especially around ploughed fields, vineyards and vegetable gardens.

Terraces

Terraces are the most abundant and conspicuous cultural features in Crete. They were a means of extending the cultivable land, but with the retreat of agriculture few old terraces are still cultivated. The best area to see the different kinds still in use is probably Ayios Vasíleios district, but the Enneakhoriá valley (Ki) contains beautiful terracing, with irrigated gardens. Surprisingly small and remote patches of soil, up to at least 1,300 m, have been terraced –

often around seasonal habitations.

Construction and incidence of terraces[1]

There are three types of terrace plan (Figure 12.1):

1 **Stepped terraces**, which are parallel (either straight, or more usually curving round the contours). Access is either from the terrace below (often by steps in the terrace wall) or by a track intersecting the terraces.

2 **Braided terraces**, which zigzag up the slope, being joined by switchbacks at the ends.

3 **Pocket terraces**, providing roothold for individual olives or fruit-trees.

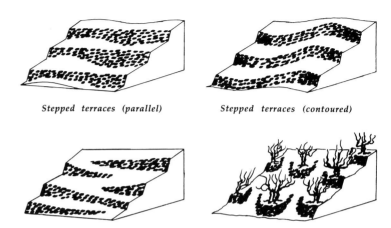

Stepped terraces (parallel)   Stepped terraces (contoured)

Braided terraces   Pocket terraces

12.1 *Types of terraces*

Nearly all historic terraces are held up by dry-stone walls, which may now be buried or inconspicuous. Terrace walls may be built of stylish masonry, but (unlike enclosure walls and the stumps of buildings) they have only one finished face.

Most terraces were deliberately dug into the hillside, the boulders taken out and used to build the retaining wall, and the spoil piled behind. In making a terrace the original soil structure is buried or dispersed, but this matters less in Crete, which seldom has well-developed soils. Some terraces are in the nature of check-dams: the wall was built first and the sediment, washing down the slope, was allowed to accumulate behind it.

Terraces are occasionally on slopes of 45°, e.g. the amazing vine-yard terraces of Thryphtí (H) (Figure 12.2), whereas in the Frangokástello Plain they are built on slopes of less than 2°. They occur on all types of bedrock, but are rather more prevalent on

hard limestone. The decision whether or not to terrace a slope depends on local custom. In some areas, for example Sakhtouriá (AV) and the south-west Amári, unterraced fields are ploughed on slopes up to about 15°, accumulating a terrace-like *lynchet* by soil-creep at the bottom. Anything steeper is left uncultivated.

Purposes of terraces

Makers of terraces assumed that everyone knew why they were made and did not leave an explanation. We suggest some combination of six reasons.

141

1 To redistribute sediment. This may be the main reason on limestone, where cultivable soil occurs locally in small pockets.

2 To increase root penetration. This may be the main reason on marls, especially for olives, fruit-trees, and vines whose roots cannot penetrate the solid rock. Making a terrace breaks up the bedrock and enables them to get at moisture in the rock. The trees are planted in the broken-up bedrock at the front of the terrace.

3 To make a less steep slope on which to cultivate. This may be the main reason on phyllite-quartzite.

4 To make a wall out of the stones which would otherwise interfere with cultivation.

5 To increase absorption of water by the soil in times of heavy rain. In Crete, however, terraces are not more prevalent in low-rainfall areas where this would be an advantage.

6 To control erosion. This reason appeals to modern agriculturalists and is popularly believed in Crete today. Its importance, however, is easily exaggerated in a land where the problem of erosion is largely created by the bulldozer (Chapter 3). Terraces control sheet erosion; they may control gully erosion if well designed; they have no effect on wind erosion. They may aggravate slumping, both by cutting into a slope and by increasing the absorption of moisture to lubricate slip planes within the rock. It may be significant that terracing is avoided in parts of Crete where there is a risk of slumping.

Almost any kind of crop can be grown on terraces; the crop grown within living memory is not necessarily what they were built for. Pocket terraces are most commonly associated with olives and other orchard trees. Well-built terraces – high, and with good

12.2 *Terraced vineyards, Thryphtí (H), without enclosure-walls*

craftsmanship in the walls – go with vines, or with irrigated gardens for which a nearly horizontal surface is essential.

Poorly-built braided terraces, especially in remote places and on thin soils, often have threshing-floors nearby, indicating grain or legumes. (If they had last been used for olive-trees, we would expect to find remains of the trees.) Braided terracing may go with arable cultivation: the switchbacks enable the plough – like the bulldozer – to work continuously from one level to another. Olives and cereals could also be mixed on the same terrace.

History of terracing

Agriculture has been in retreat from terraced terrain for at least a hundred years. People still know how to build terraces and occasionally make new ones, but the great majority are nineteenth century or earlier; nobody now alive remembers when they were not there.

We find it very difficult indeed, by looking at a terrace, to say how long it has been out of use, and impossible to say how long it was in use before it was abandoned. There are three possible lines of argument: documents, trees and archaeology.

The whole corpus of Ancient Greek writing mentions no structure that is certainly a terrace, and has no definite word for it. (Cretans today speak of *pezoúla, paravolí,* or *tráphos,* words not to be found in most Modern Greek dictionaries.) *Haimasiá* (normally meaning 'enclosure wall') and *óphrys* (normally meaning 'eyebrow'[2]) may occasionally have been used for terraces.

It may be that terraces existed but were too commonplace to mention, being beneath the notice of poets or philosophers. But it is curious that Hesiod did not mention repairing terraces among the tasks of the farm; or that defeated troops never escaped the cavalry by taking to the terraces; or that Xenophon's hunted hare, hart or boar did not get away by leaping up terraces.

Much the same applies to Venetian and Turkish records. There is no definite Venetian word for a terrace, and we know of no picture that definitely shows them. Monanni's view of Merabéllo (Ay. Nikólaos) in 1631 vaguely shows what may be terraces.[3] Sixteenth-century views of the Candia aqueduct depict sloping fields above Knossós (T), where sloping fields are still the norm.[4] There is a mysterious word in Turkish perambulations which could mean 'terrace' but is more likely a baulk, an uncultivated strip between fields.[5] Nor did travellers often notice terraces: Tournefort in 1700 does not mention them for Crete, but was impressed by the terraces of the Cycladic island of Kéa.

Archaeology

Terraces are difficult to date in isolation: the sediments and artefacts in them may be either older or younger than the terraces.[6]

Some systems of terraces are relatively late. We find that the shallow terraces of the Frangokástello Plain (Figure 12.3) belong to the second and third phases of the post-Roman field-system.

The earliest well-dated terrace system in Crete is on Pseíra (Si). This islet was settled only in the Bronze Age and the Byzantine. There are massive terraces of the check-dam type, which Julie Clark shows, from stratification of Minoan sherds within the terrace, soil development and other evidence, to belong to the Middle Minoan period.[7]

Trees

Historians and archaeologists have little to say about dating terraces: let us ask the trees. Annual rings of invading trees give a *terminus ante quem* for the dates of abandoned terraces.

Ancient trees normally post-date the terrace that they stand on. (An absence of root-buttresses (Figure 3.5) usually reveals those few instances where a terrace has been built round a pre-existing tree.) At Tylissos (Ma), olives datable to the early Second Byzantine period stand on terraces. High above Thérisso (Ky), a very well-built terrace sustains some of the mightiest of all planetrees, of roughly the same date. At Loutró (Sf), an olive-tree whose annual rings indicate a Hellenistic date grows on a terrace-wall (Figure 7.1).

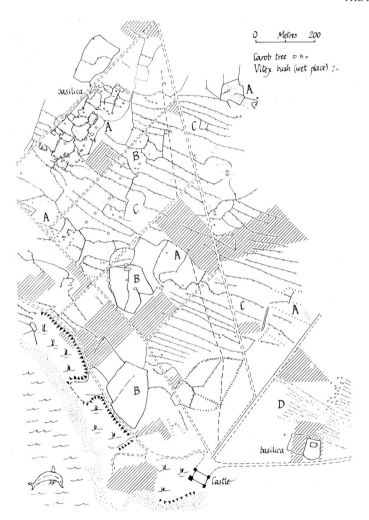

O   Metres   200

Carob tree ○ ○ ○
Vitex bush (wet place) ⸬

basilica

A

C

A

B

C

A

B

A

A

C

A

B

basilica

D

Castle

Conclusions

Terraces are the key to understanding the chronology and development of the whole Cretan landscape. We do not yet have that key. Terraces go back at least to the Bronze Age. The writings of Spratt suggest that they had passed their peak by 1850 AD. We conjecture that terraces were not uncommon in the classical period, since many cities were in places where agriculture would hardly have been possible without them. The pressure for terracing may have been greatest in the late Venetian period, when the rural population was nearly as high as it has ever been, and when much good non-terraced land was unusable because of corsairs. If so, it is remarkable that contemporary documents say nothing about their construction.

Spratt and many other observers stress the enormous burden of labour in making and maintaining terraces. Whether this is true depends entirely on whether it took ten or a thousand years, which we do not yet know. Cretan agriculture seems not to have involved quite the unrelenting hard work that is claimed for other Mediterranean mountain countries;[8] it had its months of leisure as well. Was terracing something to do on otherwise idle mornings? Or something a young man was expected to do before marrying? Or something to keep slaves busy? In our experience, maintaining

12.3 *Fields on the Frangokástello Plain. Late Roman or Early Byzantine farmsteads (A) are marked by stumps of buildings, piles of stones, and clusters of ancient carob trees. Around these are small, irregular fields with massive walls, which may be contemporary. Then there are remains of larger enclosures (B) and walls which meander irregularly across the plain. Next come series of terraces (C) fitted in between the earlier remains, or occasionally on top of ancient sites. Then there are tiny terraces (D) no more than one stone high. The grid of straight roads and the bulldozed areas (hatched) date from the 1970s.*

144

terraces would have been merely a matter of replacing the occasional fallen stone, or of mending breaches after a 75-year flood.

Terraces are the greatest outstanding problem in Greek landscape archaeology. The answer will come from gradually accumulating information, both intentionally (by looking for ancient trees on terraces or for faint terrace systems associated with ancient sites) and accidentally (by observing how terraces impinge on some other, directly datable structure or feature). Archaeologists must seize such opportunities.

Fields

To the outsider, Crete is a land of small fields, often of less than one hectare. This irritates agricultural theoreticians, who call small fields 'inefficient' and suppose that time spent in getting from one field to another is wasted. Successive governments over the last forty years have encouraged Cretans to reorganise their land (where the terrain permits) into large, straight-edged, boring fields, as with the English Enclosure Acts of the nineteenth century. However, Cretans have a different sense of priorities: many such reorganisations are either unfinished or have begun again to be subdivided. Apart from the Lassíthi Plain (p. 149), we know of no historic large-scale reorganisation which might have caused all the fields in an area to be of one date – in contrast to the island of Kéa.[9]

It is often supposed that small fields result from partible inheritance, the custom of dividing a family's land among the children. If this were the whole story, a swift calculation shows that the average size of a field today ought to be measured in square centimetres. In the Turkish records for middle Crete in 1659–71, the sizes of fifty-nine fields are given, the most common size being just under 1 ha; vineyards seem to have been a little smaller.[10] Average field size has remained much the same for the last 320 years. (Ownership boundaries do not necessarily go with field boundaries; a property of half a hectare can easily consist of fractions of four or five different terraces.)

Because of the small size, individual fields are difficult to identify in records, and thus are difficult to date. We know of no early maps that identify fields.

Boundaries
Fields in Crete are bounded by hedges, baulks, terrace-walls or enclosure walls. Wire fencing became common in the 1980s. The enwalling of individual fields is commonest where there are boulders to be got rid of or where patches of cultivation are surrounded by pasture.

Hedges are locally common. In western Ayios Vasíleios district they are almost English in character, usually ragged and irregular, composed of brambles and strips of maquis, not cut or managed; they probably arose by neglect rather than design. Elsewhere rows of fruit trees can act as hedges, and there are remains of what were evidently planted hedges of giant aloe and prickly-pear.

Field-systems
Field shapes are sometimes constrained by topography. On gentle slopes fields may function as shallow terraces. Small limestone sinkholes, as on the Akrotíri or around Khrysoskalítissa (Ki), may be walled off as fields.

Where there is no such constraint, many styles are possible. Rarely are fields quite irregular: an example, probably late Roman, is on the Frangokástello Plain. The soilless, wooded limestone plateau of Arádhena and Ayios Ioánnes (Sf) is covered with walls of irregular fields which have lost their soil by wind and karst erosion; these, too, are probably Roman.

Frangokástello (Sf) illustrates how successive generations have reorganised fields and recycled the stones in the walls, but without completely effacing the earlier fields (Figure 12.3). Each reorganisation, perhaps after a period of desertion, expressed a very different attitude to land-use and ownership. There was evidently a time when people were so fond of terraces that they were prepared to go through the motions of terracing a slope of no more than 2°. The plain has recently been reorganised yet again by people especially fond of straight lines.

As far as we know, Crete has no examples of centuriation – the practice of dividing land rigidly into exact squares, regardless of topography – which was widespread in Roman colonies. (Could there have been any vacant land to colonise in Roman Crete?) The fields around Górtyn (Ka), the chief Roman city, show no trace of rigid planning.

The plain of Khaniá is covered with the remains of a field-system which shows the marks of a different large-scale geometry (Figure 12.4). More or less regularly spaced north-south axes run out from the city, diverging slightly towards the hills. The cross-divisions are at irregular intervals. This area – much of it set with ancient olive-trees – is unexpectedly lacking in pre-Roman sites, and we suspect that the semi-regular fields were laid out after a mud-flow or similar catastrophe had destroyed the previous property boundaries. This type of field-system, planned in one direction

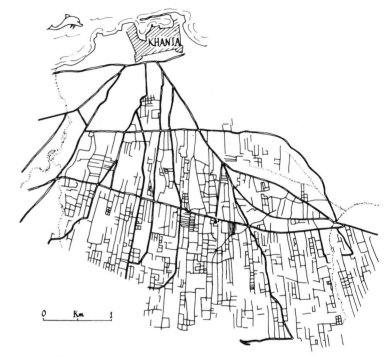

12.4 *Field-pattern on the Khaniá Plain*

but not in the other, is widespread in the British Isles and of various prehistoric dates; in Greece an example is known from Boeotia.[11]

Another evidently planned field-system exists around the decayed village of Monastiráki (H), which was a Roman site of unknown character (Figure 12.5).[12] Here the regularity exists in the

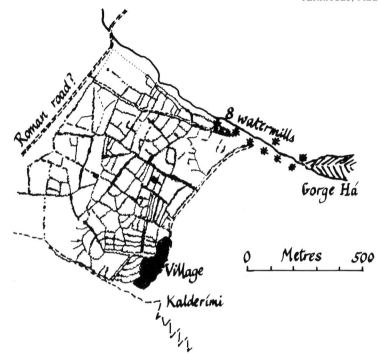

In 1944 an unknown German aerial photographer flew over the Mesará, and recorded for posterity an extraordinary variety of field-systems.[13] There are big rectangles averaging 1 ha; small squarish fields averaging 0.1 ha; and straight or curving strips, from 400 to 800 m long but usually about 20 m wide (Figure 12.6). The kinds of fields occur not intermingled but aggregated into large blocks, each of a few square km and comprising several hundred similar fields. These are not closely related to topography or to township boundaries. They seem to be related to an earlier, more dispersed settlement pattern than the present: each village and each deserted settlement is marked by a patch of tiny fields. Such settlements were regarded by Sanders as successors to Roman villas and farms.

These strips are reminiscent of the open-field strip-cultivation fashionable in medieval Europe, which spread as far as Russia and Connecticut. Forms of strip-cultivation, of unknown date, occur in Attica. The Mesará strips, however, are too long to be comfortable units of ploughing. They tend to be more prevalent in the lower, central part of the Mesará called Livádha ('Meadow'); perhaps they were originally divisions of meadowland rather than arable.

12.5 *Hedges of Monastiráki (H), from air photograph 1 May 1941. The site slopes north-westwards*

Fields in mountain-plains

Askyphou

This plain is divided into squarish fields, all much the same size, used for vines and for some of the last cereals in Crete. The fields turn gradually into terraces in the sloping arms of the plain. They are watered by wells from a shallow water-table.

Askyphou is excellent for the study of hedges and hedgerow

well-defined, squarish perimeter; the internal divisions are less regular. The boundaries here are well-defined walls and hedges with ancient carobs. Where they cross a slope they have acquired a lynchet (a difference of level) which almost makes them into terraces.

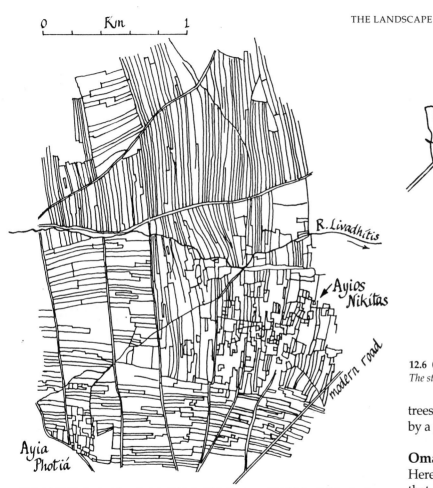

12.6 (a) *Fields in the Mesará: strip fields in Khárakas township (Mo) with islands of tiny, squarish fields around the decayed hamlets of Ay. Photiá and Ay. Nikítas*

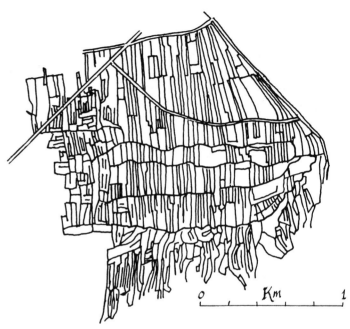

12.6 (b) *Fields in the Mesará: strip-fields in Khárakas and Praitória townships (Mo). The strips in the south appear to be water-meadows by the river*

trees; it has some beautiful quinces. The whole plain is surrounded by a great enclosure-wall.

Omalós

Here, at 1,080 m, cultivation today is precarious; yet terraces prove that cultivation once flowed well up the rocky slopes above (Figure 12.7). The plain is divided between Lákkoi (Ky) to the north

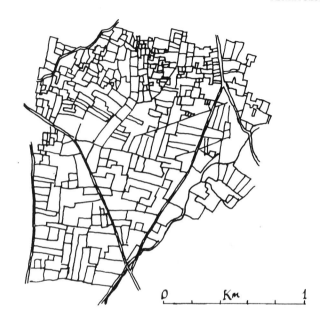

12.6 (c) *Fields in the Mesará: large rectangular fields next the ancient city of Górtyn (Ka), whose site underlies the small squarish fields in the north*
Figure 12.6 is from air photographs of April 1944. Most of the field boundaries are not hedged, and not all can be seen from the air

12.7 *Omalós Plain. The general extent of terracing is shown, not individual terraces*

of the mountains and Ay. Iréne (Se) to the south-west; Samariá in Sphakiá, the other place adjoining, has no share of it. The two field-systems are different: Ay. Iréne has squarish fields, but Lákkoi goes in for strips. The fields are separated by baulks, in which there are some of the most magnificent pear-trees in Crete.

During the late sixteenth century, Venetian governors complained that the men of Sphakiá pastured their animals on the

plain and would not let the rightful owners cultivate it. It belonged, however, to private individuals, so the field-systems may be older.

Lassíthi

The Lassíthi Plain has probably the only old example in Crete of a geometric grid of rectangular fields, such as the Romans loved

(Figure 12.8). There is a grid of ditches, called *liniés*, which define the compartments, each called a *voudéa* (*bovina* in Venetian). There are today, as in Venetian records, 193 compartments, counting fractional ones round the edges of the system. Each *voudéa* is in the shape of an approximate half-square, covering 5.3 ha (13.0 acres), and is subdivided irregularly into about thirty-five individual fields.

The plain is drained by a river which disappears into the *Khónos* (p. 27) at its north-west corner. Air photographs show that the grid of fields overlies an earlier, less regular, field-system, influenced by tributaries of the river. The eastern half of the Lassíthi, called Xerókampos, 'Dry Plain', is slightly higher-lying, and still has irregular fields and no ditches.

As we have seen, the Venetians were over-confident about re-colonising the Lassíthi Plain in 1463 and 1548 (p. 95). Besides bad weather, there were blockages in the *Khónos*; rain and snow-melt backed up and drowned some of the crops (although some claimed that the silt fertilised the land). Only in the 1630s does the problem seem to have been thought capable of solution. A number of reports recommend deepening, widening, straightening, and revetting the river, and deepening [not making] the ditches between the *voudéës*. Why this should have been expected to solve a problem that depended on the capacity of the *Khónos* is not clear, although the need to keep it clear of debris is also mentioned.[14]

It is sometimes claimed that the whole field-system dates from the 1630s,[15] although this is not what the records say. The word *bovina* appears, as a unit in which land was leased, as early as 1465.[16] Like *voudéa*, it suggests a unit of ploughing with oxen (cf. the old English *oxgang*). The angle between north-south and east-west

ditches is 88°, not 90°, suggesting easy-going Venetian, rather than precise Roman, surveying. The fact that the grid is confined to the lowest-lying part of the plain, terminating abruptly to the east and south, suggests that it had something to do with the drainage problem. We cannot tell at what point between 1463 and 1630 it was laid out, nor the date of the underlying fields.

During the Turkish period the inhabitants came to terms with the Lassíthi environment and took up a mixed economy including livestock. Eventually they came not only to till the whole plain but to build terraces far up the hills. The *Khónos* problem mysteriously went away. Either rainfall and snow-melt diminished, or some underground blockage cleared itself. When we last saw the *Khónos* it was full of polythene bags, and nobody seemed to care. Lassíthi now suffers from too little water, not too much.

Enclosures

In a mixed economy enclosures are needed to protect crops from roaming animals. Enclosures in remote areas are connected with transhumance (Chapter 14). There are four main types:

1 *For livestock*. These are strongly built, at least 1½m high, with a well-finished inner wall-face. Livestock-holding pens are usually arranged for shade and sometimes contain water. Milking pens have rounded corners and one narrow exit, so that sheep can be milked as they come out one by one.

2 *For cultivation*. These are at least 2 m high, with a well-finished outside face. They usually contain tender crops – maize, vegetables, cotton, vines – easily damaged by livestock or wind.

12.8 *Lassíthi Plain*

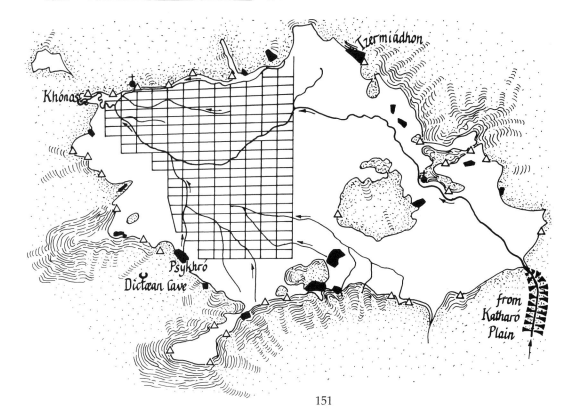

Settlement ● Deserted settlement (approximate position) △
Monastery ☗ Natural watercourse ➤

Edge of plain ⠿ Terraced hillside ≋

Scale 0 ⊢————————⊣ 3 km

Tzermiádhon

Khónas

Psykhró
Dictæan Cave

from
Katharo
Plain

Turkish and Venetian villas in the Khaniá plain have high orchard-walls of mortared masonry. Many cultivated areas are not enclosed, such as the Thryphtí (H) vineyards: it was evidently the shepherds' responsibility to keep their animals out.

3 *Bee-enclosures*. Many high, small, oval enclosures, with well-finished outer and inner faces, and with gates were constructed to contain beehives (Figure 12.9). They often contain narrow paved terraces on which to place the hives. Beehives needed to be protected from careless animals, and the bees needed shelter from strong winds. Bee-enclosures are particularly common in the windy beekeeping region of Sphakiá.

4 *Property boundaries*. Walls intended merely as landmarks are variable; they can be poorly constructed and too low to keep out animals. These include the long sinuous walls that wind up slopes.

Enclosures are no easier to date than terraces, but have a better-documented history. They appear in Minoan art and in Greek writings including the *Odyssey* (though not as Cretan examples). Occasionally they are mentioned in Venetian and Turkish documents: for instance, in 1349 a schedule of fines for stray animals doubled the fine if the animal got into land enclosed or ditched around.[17] Perambulations in the 1670s mention many enclosure walls.[18]

12.9 *Bee-enclosure. Anópolis (Sf), July 1988.*

Notes

1 J. Moody and A.T. Grove (1990), 'Terraces and enclosure walls in the Cretan landscape', in S. Bottema, G. Entjes-Nieborg, and W. van Zeist (eds.), *Man's Role in the Shaping of the Eastern Mediterranean Landscape*, Rotterdam, Balkema, pp. 183–91; O. Rackham and J. Moody (1992), 'Terraces', in Wells (see bibliography), pp. 123–30.

2 R. Baladié (1974), 'Sur le sens géographique du mot grec «ophrys», de ses dérivés et de son équivalent latin', *Journal des Savants*, 153–91.

3 BMV: Ital. VII. 889(7798) p. 129.

4 ASV: Fortezze, Disegni 235–7.

5 Stavrinidhes (see bibliography), vol. A, *passim*.

6 In some parts of mainland Greece terraces are claimed to date from the Classical period: see for example E. Zangger (1992, Chapter 3, note 18).

7 J. A. Clark (1990), *Soils and Land Use at an Archaeological Site: Pseira, Crete*, M.Sc. thesis, Queen's University, Kingston, Ontario.

8 R. McNeill (1992, Chapter 3, note 10).

9 J. F. Cherry, J.L. Davis and E. Mantzourani (1991), *Landscape Archaeology as Long-Term History: Northern Keos in the Cycladic Islands*, Monumenta Archaeologica, **16**, Los Angeles.

10 Stavrinidhes (see bibliography), vol. A, *passim*.

11 Rackham (1982, see bibliography).

12 NAW: TUGX 2142 SK39.

13 NAW: TUGX 2102 SK 34-9,165, 209–223.

14 ASV: Coll. Relaz. busta 80 c.15ff.

15 L. V. Watrous (1982, Chapter 8, note 12).

16 Noiret (see bibliography), p. 497.

17 ASV: DC b.14 c.230.

18 Stavrinidhes (see bibliography), no. 370-2.

13

Boots, mules and roads

Now [Balaam] was riding upon his ass ... And the ass saw the angel of the
Lord standing in the way, and his sword drawn in his hand ... But the angel
of the Lord stood in a path of the vineyards, a wall being on this side, and a
wall on that side. And when the ass saw the angel of the Lord, she thrust
herself unto the wall, and crushed Balaam's foot against the wall.

Numbers, **24,** 23–7

Boots

Crete is a land of razor-edged limestone, spiny-broom and prickly-oak; its history is the history of boots. In Pashley's time leather amounted to one-sixth by value of the island's imports. In World War II any partisan taken off Crete had to leave his boots on the beach for someone else. A good pair of European climbing boots, in our experience, lasts three weeks; the visitor should instead buy the stout and comfortable Cretan boots on the Street of the Leathersellers in Khaniá (Ky). Beautiful black high-boots are part of the men's national costume, and shepherds of the old school wear them on ordinary occasions.

Pashley and Spratt remarked:

every Cretan peasant wears *boots* ... which cost him from 60 to 80 piastres;* and that 35 piastres will suffice for the shoes of his wife and family ...

Pashley, 1834

* Something like £120 or $180 in the money of 1993.

The Cretan shepherds have ... had from the earliest times a very necessary but singular-looking sole to their boots, as all wear boots in Crete, peasant as well as gentleman. The soles are formed of a riband of untanned hide, tightly folded and sewn together; and this is stitched in separate pieces to the heel and toe of the flat inner sole, so as to present to the rock, for its wear and tear, only the edges of this folded riband of hide ...

Spratt, 1851–56

In ancient times there was a special Cretan boot, also worn by hunters in Greece.[1] Galen, in the second century AD, describes it as a kind of shoe with thongs attached that were wound round the shins like a puttee.[2]

No ancient boots survive, for there are no waterlogged sites which preserve leather. Minoan art shows most people barefoot or in sandals, but sometimes they wear boots or puttees: for example, the booted girls in the famous bull-leaping fresco from Knossós. If

154

boots were worn for the ceremonial or sporting occasions shown in the frescoes, we can dimly infer their existence for everyday usage. The steer-roping scenes on the Vaphéio Cups, of Cretan make, show that the Late Minoan cowboy outfit included boots with curly toes.

Vehicles

There is a great difference between towns and countries designed for carts and those for saddle- and pack-animals. A hundred and fifty years ago there was probably not a single vehicle on Crete; but it was not always so.

From as early as Middle Minoan I we have a clay model of a four-wheeled wagon from Paláikastro (Si). Carts were probably restricted to the plains: towns and villages like Zákro (Si), Gourniá (H) and Myrtos (H) had narrow streets with steps, where they could not have been used. There is no evidence that Minoans rode: they travelled on foot or, if they could afford it, in litters.

Chariots are recorded in large numbers in Late Minoan Knossós archives, but it is unlikely that in rugged Crete they were used in battle. More likely they were the conveyance of upper-class civilians, like a brougham or a sulky. The wheels, stored separately from the chariot, had only four spokes; the felloes were probably made from a single piece of wood bent into a circle, as in Iron Age Britain.

The later history of vehicles is unknown. By analogy with other places, we conjecture that they were used in the plains in classical times, peaked in the Roman period and died out perhaps with the Arabs. It is unlikely that they ever got far into the mountains. The only known vehicles until modern times are in a view of Candia (Herákleion (T)) in 1590, with four-wheeled mule-carts.[3]

Ancient roads

Minoan palaces presumably had vehicle roads, and a network of tracks or paths must have connected even remote settlements throughout the island. Sir Arthur Evans was the first to find what he thought to be the main road south of Knossós (T), and many archaeologists have since claimed to identify Minoan road structures,[4] especially in east Crete.

'Minoan' roads are not-very-distinctive tracks, paved with small stones. Their identification, although we have no reason to doubt it, is not easily proved: they do not have the straightness which marks Roman roads. The terrain often constrains a road to follow a particular route, regardless of date. Roads connect (or seem to connect) Minoan sites, but many Minoan sites were used at other periods: is a road that makes for Knossós (T) related to Minoan or to Roman Knossós? Excavation may not be conclusive: Minoan potsherds embedded in a road do not make it a Minoan road.

Of classical and Roman roads even less is known. Air photographs, on which Roman roads stand out so clearly, have been little used in Cretan archaeology. In World War II aerial photographs of Akrotíri and near Monastiráki (H) we have seen roads that run across the landscape regardless of obstacles. It is not unlikely that Crete has Roman roads like those in England or France.

Pendlebury, who knew Crete better than anyone not a native, listed 'natural' routes all over the island and how long each took to walk. In Crete, however, unless one has the actual fabric of a road it is difficult to be quite sure where the routes went. It is easy (for a mountainous country) to make roads, and there are few places which cannot be reached in at least two ways.

Greece and Crete seldom have holloways, sunk paths formed by water erosion under the steady treading of men and beasts.

This is another piece of evidence to deny Crete's reputation as a land that has eroded within historic times.

Venetian roads

Throughout medieval and modern Crete, roads (for pedestrians and animals) figure countless times in bans, perambulations, descriptions of property, reports of crimes, etc. They appear in Venetian pictures, for instance in Monanni's view of Réthymnon (R) in 1631, in which roads, bordered by houses, converge from the countryside on the town gate.

What Venetian roads consisted of is difficult to ascertain. Pictures show them merely as strips across the landscape, with no indication of surface or boundaries. Nor have we found archives dealing with the maintenance of road surfaces and bridges, or with obstructions and encroachments on the highway.

Perambulations from the beginning of the Turkish period name roads as the most abundant boundary features. In property deeds (mainly in middle Crete), out of fifty-two fields and vineyards, nearly two-thirds are stated to adjoin at least one road.[5] Given the size of fields (p. 145), this implies that in cultivated areas there would have been a road at least every 600 m.

Medieval bridges would not have been uncommon, to judge by those that survive on relatively minor roads – there is a beautiful one between Ayios Ioánnes and Khordháki (Am) (Plate 3).

Mules and kalderímia

Crete is pervaded by the remains of thousands of kilometres of constructed mule-track. The term *kalderími* comes from Turkish *kalderım*, 'road'. They form a network connecting every village and hamlet, chapel, outlying field, castle, and many sheepfolds and *mitáta*: the network is denser than all but the densest road-networks of England. Four *kalderímia* penetrate the high White Mountains: one, from Anópolis (Sf), goes through the High Desert over two passes of 2,150 m; another, from Ay. Ioánnes (Sf), traverses the tremendous cliffs and screes of Mount Zaranoképhala. No less dramatic is the *kalderími* that zigzags 900 m straight up the mountain behind Kavoúsi (H).

The average *kalderími* is 4½ m wide, carefully paved with flat stones – often with a row of big stones along the middle. It has steps where necessary and is therefore not a vehicle road. These roads have carefully-designed zigzags on steep gradients and retaining walls and parapets where they traverse cliffs. At river crossings we find paved fords and sometimes culverts. A good example of *kalderími* construction is the one that zigzags down across the deep and narrow Arádhena Gorge (Sf) (Figure 13.1).

In Crete, roads do not have to have defined boundaries. *Kalderímia* become lanes, with a wall on either side, only where they pass between fields that are walled. In open terrain the less-used *kalderímia* may be discontinuous, constructed only on slopes and screes, leaving level stretches unpaved. A little-used *kalderími* gets blocked with spiny-broom and other unpleasant plants, causing later traffic to make a new path in parallel.

Most of the main *kalderímia* have been destroyed by being turned into motor roads, but stretches of very wide *kalderími* survive in the bottom of the Imbros Gorge (leading into Sphakiá) and on the sides of the Kavoúsi Gorge (leading into Siteía).

A land of *kalderímia* had to make locally, or to do without, any object too long or heavy for a mule – or rather, too heavy for half a mule, since a pack-saddle carries two loads which must balance. Millstones had to be transported in pieces; long timbers would be

13.1 Kalderími *road crossing the Arádhena Gorge (Sf). July 1987*

difficult. The cast-iron platen of an olive-press was often the heaviest inanimate object (90 kg) ever brought to a remote place such as Samariá (Sf).

When and how were the *kalderímia* made? It is often assumed that they were made in the Turkish period, but this seems to be based merely on the word for them being Turkish. The only real evidence is that some give access to Turkish castles of the 1860s, but that does not date the entire network. The Turks in the war of the 1820s contrived to take cavalry into the Askyphou Plain (though not out of it), which suggests that roads were better than they later became. We suspect that most *kalderímia* are Venetian roads, maintained and added to in the Turkish period; some

could be much older.

The Turks loved bridges, and a few Turkish bridges survive in Crete. At Ayia Rouméli there are two, marooned mysteriously in the gravel at the mouth of the Great Gorge; both are in Venetian style, although probably of early Turkish date. The Turkish style of high slender arch is rare in Crete; there is one at Koxaré (AV), and a splendid one over the Megapótamos above Préveli (AV), with an inscription recording that it was built by the monks in 1850.

The *kalderími* system probably began to decline in the late nineteenth century. By 1909 Trevor-Battye could report only that 'here and there are the remains of the paved roads of the Venetians', but he found the *kalderími* over the Arádhena Gorge (Sf) being repaired. We are told that certain *kalderímia* in the Akrotíri are as late as World War II.

Modern communications

In the revolt of 1867 it was almost impossible to take wheeled artillery along the chief road of Crete from Réthymnon (R) to Herákleion (T).[6] Shortly after, great plans were made for roads. Cretans were supposed to work nine days a year on roads or to pay a sum in lieu, and Vely Pasha hired a Mr Woodward as a road engineering consultant.[7] Several magnificent bridges, built then, are still in use. Above Myrtos (H) is a bridge of three great arches of accurately-cut marl blocks – numbered by the masons – dated 1884; a similar bridge dramatically spans a gorge on the way from Réthymnon to the Eastern Amári. These were evidently meant for vehicle roads, but the roads themselves were not completed before Crete became independent. Even in 1909 there were no carriage roads except within a few miles of the cities and Ierápetra (H).[8]

Road-building began again in the 1920s and was a source of

employment in the years of the Depression. By 1930 the adventurous could motor from Khaniá (Ky) to Ay. Nikólaos (Me). Roads of the 1930s have a distinctive character: rather narrow, solidly built with masonry or very good dry-stone retaining walls, nearly as good as those of the Turkish period. By the next interruption, World War II, tarred roads had reached most parts of Crete, including the south-west corner – but not quite to such important places as Anóyeia (My) or Khóra Sphakíon (Sf). The road failing to reach the latter was an important factor in the retreat after the Battle of Crete in 1941. (This road, above the Imbros Gorge (Sf), is almost unchanged today.) Efforts were apparently concentrated on new road-building, letting the *kalderímia* fall to ruin. Transport got worse to places still remote from roads; this may have influenced depopulation.

Crete acquired the telephone early; Trevor-Battye reports the making of a line to Kritsá (Me) in 1909, long before there was a carriage-road. By 1939 there was a telephone in almost every village. The early lines, on their imported chestnut poles (which have lasted sixty years), are still in use in remoter areas.

There were two railways. One had about 4 km of track extending west of Herákleion harbour; the other had some 8 km between Khaniá (Ky) and Soúdha harbour. Plans for a railway from Khaniá to Herákleion (T) were not resumed after World War II.

Road-building was resumed in the 1950s. Post-1955 roads tend to be wide, and dug rather than built, with only perfunctory attempts to hold up the sides. Many are now in disrepair: it is very easy to make roads in Crete and difficult to maintain them.

In the 1970s, under the regime of the Greek Colonels, the new main road was made from Khaniá (Ky) to Ay. Nikólaos (Me); it is direct and fast, and nearly killed one of the authors. The corresponding road through the south of Crete is still not finished at the time of writing; it passes through very unstable terrain, and provides some excellent illustrations of slumping (p. 19). The bridging of the Arádhena Gorge in 1987 brought a road to Ay. Ioánnes (Sf), the last remaining village in Crete which it would be practicable to reach.

In the last ten years the bulldozer has been busier than ever, making roads (of a sort) to even the smallest and most isolated field or sheepfold. For its size, Crete has more roads than England. As we have seen, this has been the first human activity to overcome the natural stability of the landscape, changing even the very geomorphology.

Notes

1 Hippokrates, Littré edition, IV p. 268.16.
2 *Notes on Joints*, **4**, XVIII/1.682–3.
3 Gerola, **3**, 13.
4 Y. Tzedhakis (1989), 'Les routes minoennes: rapport préliminaire – Défense da la circulation ou circulation de la défense', *BCH*, **113**, 43–75.
5 Stavrinidhes (see bibliography), vol. A, *passim*.
6 J. E. H. Skinner (1868), *Roughing it in Crete in 1867*, London, Bentley.
7 *Parliamentary Blue Book*, **73**, p. 1.
8 Trevor-Battye (see bibliography), p. 294.

14

Shepherding

*The cheese which is made here is bought up by the Venetians
and other Merchants, and transported to France, Italy, Zante,
etc. It is the best cheese that is made in any of the Southern
parts, and generally as good as our own Cheshire Cheeses, being
made as bigg.*

B. Randolph, 1687

It may be hard to imagine the hillsides of Crete not tinkling with sheep and goat bells or echoing with the mournful cry of a lost lamb or kid, but such was the case until the early Neolithic. Sheep and goats were introduced by the first settlers (Chapter 7), and Crete has never been the same.

Shepherding may bring to mind pastoral scenes of shepherds lying in the shade of a great oak watching their flocks frolic on rolling verdant hills, but the Cretan reality is more like the arduous, dangerous shepherding of the Bible. The blinding sun glares on grey and orange crags. A young shepherd flattens himself at the foot of a cliff, jealous of six inches of shade. The faint smell of sour milk is carried on the breeze. Dogs bark, shrill whistles and strange oaths pierce the air, and a couple of vultures circle overhead. However, shepherding undoubtedly has its romantic side. Long hours in the field, or stirring a cauldron of milk, are followed by conversational evenings over strong drink. The lonely shepherd has a holiday from the responsibilities of civilisation and society. (There are very few shepherdesses.) It is not only for love of money that a lad takes up crook and gun, saddles his mule, and tramps off into the High Desert (Chapter 17).

Seasonal movements

In Crete, as in much of Greece, people follow the growing season between winter and summer pastures. Summer pastures (*madháres*) are usually located in the mountains where herbs and grasses persist through the summer; winter pastures are on foothills, coastal plains and peninsulas. But the seasonal ***transhumance*** of flocks and people is often much more complicated. It may involve only the menfolk, or else whole households or entire villages. (Figure 14.1 shows some examples.)

Whole households or villages migrate in pursuit of other things besides herbage. Low hamlets or villages are sited at 200 m or less, and grow mainly olives. High hamlets and villages are at 700-1,000 m, where vines, apples, pears and other fruit thrive.

Grain can be grown at both elevations, but at different seasons.

Until recently high villages were considered the main or home settlement. A typical pair are Patsianós (120 m) and Kallikráti (750 m) (Sf). We were told that the main school had been at Kallikráti until the late 1970s because people spent more time there. Further west, Asphéndou (770 m) (Sf) is still the capital of the township of Vouvás (where the village is at 190 m), although few people now live there even in summer. Similar situations have been noted for the villages in the Lassíthi Plain.

This arrangement goes back at least to the mid-Turkish period. In 1834 Pashley noted that Patsianós was the winter village belonging to Kallikráti (Sf). However, nearly all the old churches are in low settlements, indicating that in the middle ages these were the main homesteads. Venetian lists do not discriminate between winter and summer settlements.

In high mountains there may be additional moves. In the Lassíthi, individual households would leave the plain and move in summer to farmsteads (metókhia) higher in the mountains. For example, families from Ay. Geórgios (L) have farmsteads in the satellite plain of Limniákaro. A metókhi consists of a stone-built dwelling, dairy and stores. Cheesemaking was the main activity, but there were also terraces and enclosures for vegetables, fruit and nut trees, and grain.[1]

Life in the mitáta

The secondary transhumance practised in the White Mountains is rather different. Women and children remain in the upland villages tending the summer crops. Only the shepherds move to the madháres at 1,400–1,950 m (Chapter 17).

A night listening to Cretan mantinádhes – songs chiefly of heroic deeds enacted in these mountains from the revolt of 1770 to World War II – leaves one with a romantic, almost magical impression of life in the madháres. In reality it seems a harsh and lonely existence. The remotest mitáto, Kolokythás in Anópolis (Sf), is about nine hours' march across the High Desert and down the other side from the upland village. Beginning in late May or June (whenever the snow melts), the menfolk in an extended family take turns tending the flocks for three to four weeks at a mitáto. Like a metókhi, this consists of stone buildings, pens and enclosures. It is devoted to cheesemaking, cultivation being limited (at most) to a few potatoes because of the short season. An average flock comprises 400 sheep and a few goats (which help with the herding), and is tended by two or three men. The milking season lasts 8–10 weeks. When herbage or water give out or when snow falls, at latest in October, the shepherds return with their flocks to their families and villages.

Graviéra is the emperor of Cretan sheep's cheeses. The best is made and matured in the corbelled cool of a high mitáto and stored in deep limestone fissures, some of which contain permanent snow. When enough mule-loads have accumulated it is taken to market. It is, rightly, not cheap. In 1989 we were told that a single cheese of 8½ kg fetched about 8,000 drachmas ($50, £30). Anthótyra, a soft cheese pressed in a small basket, is made from the residue after graviéra. (Féta is a goat's cheese made mainly from flocks permanently in the foothills.)

Milk for cheesemaking is simmered in a cauldron. The fuel is cypress-wood, brought up by mule – 6 kg for a day's boiling. Over the twenty-five or so mitáta now operating in Sphakiá, this adds up to 10 tons of wood a year, which is not negligible considering the slow growth. The ancient coppiced and pollarded cypresses that line the routes up to the high pastures are witnesses to this peculiar institution.

Far from being remote, the high pastures have been integrated into Cretan society and economics. Marriages between families on opposite sides of a massif were frequently arranged when the fathers met in the *madháres*.[2]

Grazing rights

In many places, shepherds own their pastures. In Sphakiá, every *mitáto* belongs to a family, and its lands are carefully defined by perambulation from peak to peak; the capacity of a *mitáto* is mysteriously measured as so many *oká*, a Turkish unit of weight. Pastures are also hired: shepherds from Psilorítis frequently rent winter pastures in the Asteroúsia, paying in milk and cheese (about 2 *oká* of cheese per *oká* of pastureland).

Boundaries are seldom marked on the ground; goats and their sheep followers inevitably stray; and goodwill does not always prevail between neighbours. Grazing disputes have led to bloody feuds since Roman times, if not before. A document of 1435 records a conflict between two Sphakian families over grazing rights in the Sphakianó Gorge; the bloodshed was (we hope) ended by a dynastic marriage and an agreement over the use of the disputed pasturage.[3] A feud can change transhumance customs. We know of several Sphakian families opting to rent distant summer pastures, rather than use their own, in order to avoid a particularly nasty vendetta.

The importance attached to high-mountain pastures is also demonstrated by township boundaries (Figure 14.2). The great mountains have been parcelled out, through centuries of argument and bloodshed, into strikingly unequal wedges ending at the

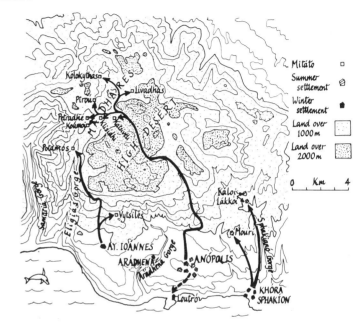

14.1 *Some transhumance connections in Sphakiá*

high summits. Lowland townships have more amorphous shapes. The dispute between Kritsá and Kroústas (Me) for the high Katharó Plain, although officially settled in favour of Kritsá, is still a sore point. Disputes over the Omalós were an everlasting anxiety of Venetian governors (p. 149).

History of shepherding

Archaeological survey in the *madháres* of Sphakiá has found traces of human activity from Final Neolithic and Early Minoan I

(3500-2400 BC).[4] Most of these early sites are located near modern *mitáta*, routes and springs, suggesting continuity over 5,000 years. There are gaps in the record, suggesting that the high mountains were abandoned at times – especially in the classical, Hellenistic, and Late Venetian periods – perhaps because of deteriorating climate. There is a similar pattern in the Lassíthi Plain.[5]

Today most flocks are kept for meat and milk, but in the past wool and goats' hair may have been more important. To determine what products were favoured depends on the sex and age of excavated animal bones. Animals kept for meat tend to be males, fattened and killed in their second year. If milk, cheese or yoghurt are of primary interest, male animals tend to be slaughtered between six months and a year. Females are kept on as reproducers and eventually lay their bones where archaeologists do not find them. When wool or hair is of prime importance, older animals are considerably more valuable than young ones. Castrated males produce plenty of wool, and can equal or outnumber females.

At Early Neolithic Knossós, meat seems to have been the primary product. During the Early Minoan period, animals were exploited for meat and wool. The palace economy of Late Minoan III seem to have emphasised wool. The word for cheese occurs in Linear B texts in mainland Greece, but not at Knossós (T) or Khaniá (Ky). However, brucellosis, a disease especially contracted from infected milk or cheese, was common in the Late Minoan III cemetery at Arménoi (R),[6] but it is hard to know how representative this picture is.

Sheep and goats are prominent in the records of Venetian Crete. Cheese was at times the second most important export. Market regulations refer also to meat, castrated mutton being the most expensive, lamb the cheapest.[7] Wool and skins are only occasion-

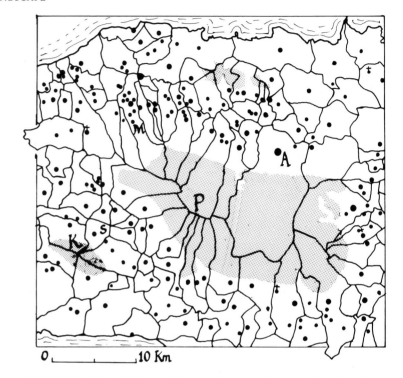

14.2 *Division of Mount Psilorítis (P) among the surrounding townships. Anóyeia (A) gets the lion's share. The same is repeated in miniature around Mounts Kédhros (K) and Sámitos (S). Land over 800 m is shaded*

ally mentioned; to judge by the parchment on which the records are written, the skins were of poor quality. There are many regulations about stray animals. Pasturage went on all over the island;

numbers of animals are not mentioned. By a regulation of 1349, one animal in twenty-five was supposed to wear a bell.[8] Those that fed on Psilorítis, we are told, had gold teeth from the herbs that they fed on, and some of the sheep had swivelling horns like an heraldic yale.[9]

In the Turkish period, cheese was difficult to export legally, and the amounts recorded vary.[10] In 1847 Raulin records 666,000 sheep and 239,000 goats, rather fewer than there are supposed to be now – but then they were taxed, now they are subsidised, and nobody but a shepherd really knows how many animals there are. They produced about 2,300 tons of cheese and 700 tons of wool a year. The principal areas for sheep were Sphakiá (where they still flourish) and Siteía (where they have declined). Goats were the chief wealth of Témenos outside Herákleion, which is hard to imagine today. The island also produced woollen cloth, the most highly regarded being the white cloth of Sphakiá and the dark brown of Lassíthi.[11]

In some areas at least, shepherding has declined from a peak in the nineteenth century. The 1881 census returns from Lassíthi record six shepherds for every ten cultivators, more than anywhere else except Sphakiá. By the 1960s there were only two dozen specialist shepherds left there.[12] The state of the vegetation in Siteía and in much of the phyllite-quartzite country of west Crete confirms a retreat of browsing (p. 118).

Sheep, goats, herders and the landscape

Shepherding has left marks on the landscape. A distinctive sign of browsing are the fantastic, gnome-like shapes acquired by trees and shrubs, especially prickly-oak. Giant old goat-pollards (Figure 6.6) are a feature of East Crete, especially along the road from Kritsá to the Katharó (Me).

Controlled burning to improve pasturage (p. 118), at low and middle altitudes, is now a more localised practice than it was earlier this century. In winter shepherds sometimes set fire to individual bushes, preferably *Genista acanthoclada*, to keep warm.

Shepherding is the indirect cause of many of the enclosure-walls, built to keep animals out of fields and especially vineyards.

Another clue to herding are random breaches in disused terrace walls, produced by sheep and goat-paths criss-crossing the slope.[13] This 'goated' appearance is often accompanied by field-houses turned into animal folds. It sometimes, though rarely in Crete, leads to gully erosion. Much of Crete went through a browsing phase in the 1960s, when agriculture declined and people emigrated; some of this land has now become woodland.

Recent changes

Secondary transhumance has been affected and partly eroded by roadmaking, part of the Ministry of Agriculture's programme to encourage herding on Crete. Roads are creeping towards even the remotest *mitáta*. Many herders rush back and forth daily in pick-ups – milk-cans swaying in the back – from *mitáto* or *metókhi* to the village. Processing and cheesemaking are becoming centralised at factories in upland villages, or even in Khaniá (Ky) or Herákleion (T). We cannot say whether this has resulted in a poorer and more uniform product.

Herding has been encouraged by European Community subsidy since 1985. At the time of writing this was from 5,000 to 7,750 drachmas (£15–23, $23–38) per animal per year.

Has government and European generosity produced the results expected? Since 1981 the official total of animals recorded for Crete has risen by about 60 per cent, but such numbers in general seem inflated, compared to what we observe on the ground. However, in Sphakiá, official numbers increased from 10,130 in 1983 to 14,480 in 1988; our own observations confirm this increase and perhaps more.

One might expect the subsidy to encourage overestimation of numbers. A long tradition of taxation per head, however, has left some shepherds so suspicious of officialdom that they still under-declare their animals. In spite of these efforts, shepherding is not prospering on Crete: it is the size of the flocks, rather than the number of shepherds, that seems to have increased. Not enough young men are taking up the profession.

Notes

1 H. Blitzer (1982), 'The nineteenth and early twentieth centuries', in Watrous (Chapter 8, note 12), pp. 30-35.
2 Information from T. and C. Athetakis in Anópolis (Sf).
3 A. P. Vourdoubakis (Α. Π. Βουρδουμβάκης) (1939), 'Δύο ἀνέκδοτα ἔγγραφα ἐκ Σφακιῶν', Ἐπετήρις Ἑταιρείας Κρητικῶν Σπουδῶν, **2**, 256–62 (we are grateful to Dr Simon Price for bringing this document to our attention).
4 L. Nixon, J. Moody, V. Niniou-Kindelis, S. Price and O. Rackham (1990), 'Archaeological survey in Sphakia, Crete', *Classical Views*, **34**, 213-20.
5 Watrous (1982, Chapter 8, note 12).
6 Jarman and Jarman (1968), in 'Knossos neolithic part II'; P. M. Warren and Y. Tzedhakis (1974), 'Debla: an Early Minoan settlement in west Crete', *BSA*, **69**, 299–341; M. R. Jarman (1972), 'The fauna', in Warren (1972, Chapter 7, note 32); Killen (1964, Chapter 11, note 8); McGeorge (1990, Chapter 8, note 22).
7 ASV: DC b.10, entry for 1360.
8 BNP: Ital. 2086 p. 501.
9 BNP Ital. 384 p. 3 [Barozzi].
10 Triantafyllidou-Baladié (1988, Chapter 7, note 36), p. 202.
11 Randolph (see bibliography), p. 85; Olivier (see bibliography); Raulin (1868, see bibliography), pp. 268, 263.
12 S. Grigor (1985), *The Village on the Plateau*, Studley, England.
13 Moody and Grove (1990, Chapter 12, note 1).

15
Buildings

When thou buildest a new house, then thou shalt make battlements for thy roof, that thou bring not blood upon thine house, if any man fall from thence.

Deuteronomy, **22**, 8

[Falling off flat roofs has long been a hazard in Crete.]

Crete is the only region of Greece where there still occur a large number of vernacular buildings of the 16th, 17th, and 18th centuries.

Kh. Valianos, 1987

Ever since the Neolithic, traditional flat-roofed houses reminiscent of the Bible, Ancient Egypt or Anatolia have been an un-European aspect of Cretan culture.

Books on Cretan houses deal with the structure and use of old-fashioned houses as they are today.[1] Chronological study – changes in the design of new houses, in existing houses, in the use of houses – has only just begun. Two reasons are often given for not attempting it. Crete (it is claimed) has such a history of war and earthquake that no house lasts for more than a century or so; or Cretan house-plans are too conservative and unchanging to be datable. These claims are contradictory (the shorter a house lasts the more opportunity there is to change it) and untrue. It is impossible to burn a stone-built Cretan house to the ground. Some of those we have studied were burnt forty years ago and abandoned, but are still standing to their full height and could still be repaired. We often find evidence of damage and repair. The argument from conservativeness needs to be proved: Cretan houses vary greatly, and it would be surprising if some of this variation did not arise from changing fashion.

There is no lack of material. Old houses in Crete are not cherished as in other countries, but disused and allowed to decay. This creates an immense conservation problem, but an immense opportunity for study. A ruined house is more instructive than one in use, as the construction and alterations are not hidden by modern restoration.

Ancient buildings

Unlike those of mainland Greece, the ancient cities of Crete did not collapse into piles of marble column-drums for the visitor to marvel at. Instead they are marked by rock-piles, pottery scatters and lime-kilns. Many of the stones have been reused in later buildings or burned into lime (see below). *Spolia* (ancient architectural fragments) are to be looked for in country chapels whose plaster has fallen off, and in villages and hamlets.

This is not to say that ancient buildings do not survive in the Cretan countryside – the trained eye can often discern an ancient foundation under a recent wall – but they are rarely prominent. The size of the stones is a clue. If they are too big for two people to carry, and are stacked two or more courses high, the wall is very likely to be ancient. Large dressed stones lying about in the countryside or built into terrace walls are also likely to be pre-medieval, especially if they are not aeolianite (p. 17).

Vegetation can be an indicator of ancient buildings, especially in the drier parts of Crete. Water-demanding trees and shrubs tend to grow on walls and rock-piles because the ground underneath retains moisture longer, since it is never exposed to the sun. The Frangokástello Plain provides an excellent example: almost every large clump of carob trees marks a Late Roman farm.

Not many *free-standing* walls over 1.5 m high will be older than Roman. Roman and Byzantine walls are often well preserved because they commonly used lime-mortar and cement: the stones stay stuck together, making it more difficult for following generations to rob and recycle them. Nevertheless, ancient brick was often 'mined' out of the walls, probably to be used as temper in the pink hydraulic plaster that lines cisterns. Ancient Phoenix (modern Loutró (Sf)) is a good place to observe this.

Medieval and later dwellings

Architecture, etiquette and materials
Writers often suppose that vernacular houses were the homes of 'peasants', simple artless shelters built personally by their owners using materials to hand, their design determined by the environment and the properties of the materials. This is a naïve interpretation. Even the humblest Cretan dwelling, and many a field-house, has hewn stone doorways and window openings, and imported planks, window-bars and iron fittings. These imply masons, sawyers, smiths and carriers. Building a house was ruled by etiquette, tradition and fashion, often in defiance of practicality and economy. Nearly every chapel has lime-mortared walls and a vault, which no middle-class house had.

Old-fashioned Cretan houses are of stone mortared with mud. Timber-framing is confined to cities, and mud-brick is rare. Lime is used for internal rendering and whitewash. Walls are often very carefully built in a distinctive style of rubble masonry, large squarish blocks alternating with areas of small flat stones set horizontally. This style of walling comes naturally in phyllite-quartzite country in west Crete, quartzite forming the square blocks and phyllite the flat stones. But it is also to be found in limestone areas, where the rock is unsuitable.

Among timbers, juniper, although small, is the favourite, then cypress; both are used well outside the areas where they grow. Next come chestnut and oak, then pine, then carob (despite its crookedness); walnut and olive are used at a pinch. Buildings in Sphakiá, where there is plenty of timber, are not radically different from those in woodless areas.

Roofs

Most Cretan houses have flat roofs. The roof is multi-layered, of load-bearing timbers (*joists*), connected by shorter pieces of wood, over which comes a layer of vine-prunings, oleander leaves, reeds, etc., surfaced with a layer of clay. The clay (which may be brought from a distance) is rolled every year with a stone roller – an ancient column-drum will do – to keep it (nominally) waterproof. The water runs down a plastered channel on the side of the house, often into a cistern underneath.

Here, and here only, the conservativeness theory is right. Roofs of this type have been normal in Crete since the earliest buildings: for example, clay with impressions of 'brushwood' (which in the photograph looks like reeds) was found in Neolithic Knossós.[2]

The summer visitor probably thinks of flat roofs as an example of vernacular architecture adapted to a dry climate. They are used, as in Biblical Jericho, for keeping organic produce away from the goats:

> But [Rahab] had brought [the spies] up to the roof of the house, and hid them with the stalks of flax, which she had laid in order upon the roof.
>
> *Joshua*, **2**, 6

But in winter Crete can be very wet indeed. The torrential rains of Askyphou (Sf), as wet as Wales, pour on to frail earthen roofs. The mind boggles at the thought of getting rid of a downpour on the acres of flat roofs of the Palace of Knossos. Mainland Greece, with a broadly similar climate, has an ancient (though not Bronze Age) tradition of tiled roofs: archaeological sites there are littered with tile-sherds. Flat roofs seem to have originated in a desert area, been taken to an unsuitable climate, and continued there, in defiance of practicality, for 6,000 years. This is partly why Cretans do not now cherish old houses. A modern concrete house, ugly and uncomfortable though it is, at least keeps the wet out until the concrete rots.

In Cretan tradition tiles are sacred, reserved for chapels. Tiled-roof houses are probably relatively recent. Often they are covered with machine-made interlocking tiles made by the firm of 'GUICHARD FRERES, MARSEILLE' in the 1910s, which replace older half-round tiles of a kind used in mainland Greece since Byzantine times.

The kamára-*house and its relatives*

The *kamára*-house (Figures 15.1, 15.2a) is a rectangle, typically 8 m by 5 m inside, divided lengthwise by a great arch (*kamára*). The joists span only half the width. The arch does not reach to the ends of the house, otherwise it would not be stable. Of the four 'quarters' formed by the abutments of the arch, one is usually walled off with a transverse arch, forming a walk-in fireplace for cooking. The other three are partitioned and form chambers for bedrooms or storage. In the bigger *kamára*-houses, the chambers are two-storeyed. Typically such a house has its long side to the street and its back to the slope; the door is in the middle of the street side, with a window high up on either side to light the upper chambers. An end-entry house, with the door in one of the quarters, is common on narrow sites.

This is often thought of as the typical Cretan house, although it occurs mainly in Sphakiá, Kydhonía, Apokórona, Réthymnon, and in far-east Crete. It occurs in summer and winter villages alike. It appears to be absent from wide areas in the middle and from the far west. It is also found on Rhodes.

15.1 *Ruined* kamára-*house, Imbros (Sf). April 1989*

A variant is the *kéntis*-house (Figure 15.2c), in which a great beam (not an arch) divides the roof from end to end. A forked post (*kéntis*) supports the structure one-third of the way along the beam. If no tree was long enough, two lengthwise beams may meet over the post. Usually it is heated by a central fire, which blackens the timbers with soot. Chambers may be situated in one end, or may be separate rooms. An intermediate between the *kamára* and *kéntis* types is what we call the pro-*kamára* house, with a beam along the length of the house, its span reduced by short walls projecting into the house from one or both ends (Figure 15.2b). These types seem to be an older pattern, persisting in places too remote for specialised masons, or in field-houses. The *kéntis*-house is common on Gávdhos (Se). In a very stylish form, it is the usual house-type of Kárpathos, and Dr Nikos Vernicos regards it as characteristic of the south-east Aegean.

Some other types
Cretan house-types are bewilderingly varied. In most of Sphakiá the *kamára*-type is normal, but not in the west: there is not one such house in the deserted village of Samariá (Sf). Instead there are two-storey houses: narrow, with no lengthwise arch or beam (so that all the joists span from side to side), floored with joists and boards, and roofed with the usual earthen construction. Usually there is a one-storeyed front part to the house, often spanned by a *kamára* and acting as a kind of large porch, with a kitchen and a built-up chimney in one corner (Figure 15.2d). The principal room is the upper one; occasionally it has a carved ceiling. It is reached by an outside stone staircase or across the porch roof. It has no fireplace.

Another Sphákiot house-type is long and narrow, up and down the slope, so that the front has two storeys and the back only one.

Each of these types of house may stand on its own. The *kamára*-house can be the home of a single person or a poor family, with space for storing barrels, harness, etc. But a house can also have extra rooms and outbuildings, and a walled courtyard with a gateway. A *kamára*-house can be extended by building on rooms at the ends, or by knocking two such houses end-to-end into one. Such alterations are often later undone by blocking the internal doorways. Many houses have stood through several phases of alteration (Figure 15.4).

Chronology

In a ruined house or deserted village it is possible to work out the order in which houses were altered or added to, and of roof-raisings, insertions of arches, conversions of two-storey to one-storey houses, fires, etc. (Figure 15.4). Layers of limewash can be counted and fashions in colour-wash noted. The increasing use of lime and the coming of cement and steel are useful dating features. Dates can also come from inscriptions and architectural details, especially in the Mesará.[3] A large house may have a dozen or more haphazardly-arranged rooms; careful study shows it to originate from a simple *kéntis* or pro-*kamára* original, to which other rooms, or whole houses, were added one by one over a long period.

Whether any house-type goes back beyond the Byzantine period we cannot say. The *kamára*-house has a distinctive groundplan, but we know no excavated examples of it. However, in Minoan Myrtos (H) and other places, piers projecting into rooms suggest something like the pro-*kamára* arrangement.

In Sphakiá, we are beginning to conclude, the oldest type may be a simple, one-storey, narrow rectangle. The pro-*kamára*, the two-storey downslope house and probably the *kéntis*-type seem also to be medieval. On present evidence, the *kamára*-house is a late-medieval development, probably originally urban; a few have Gothic arches inserted into an earlier pro-*kamára*. The two-storey kind with a front arch became fashionable in the seventeenth century. New *kamára*-houses were built up to about 1900.

Documents are of some help. Venetian artists depict most Cretan houses with flat roofs. Oddi's pictures of 1601 shows what look outwardly like *kamára*-houses.[4]

Deeds of sale from the mid-seventeenth century onwards mention houses of one or several rooms and of one or two storeys, both in cities and villages. Most houses had a court, and often kitchens, stables, wine-presses, privies and wells. Houses, then as now, were often ruined or partly ruined. Two-storey houses must have been usual in Sphakiá by 1771, when the Sphákiots promised the Turks not to live in them.[5] The round-arched doorway of cut stone, a relatively late feature, is depicted by Sieber in the house in Réthymnon (R) where he stayed in 1817.

We have so far not found any systematic difference between the houses of Christians and Muslims. However, we know of a house in Ay. Vasíleios district, once inhabited by 'Turks': an inward-looking house round a courtyard, its blank outer wall provided with musket-loopholes.

Field-houses

These are outlying houses, used during harvest or pruning-time – or in time of war. They can vary from huts or caves (Figure 3.4) to miniature dwellings, complete with chimneys. Usually, but not always, they lack arches and dressed stone. They often show many phases of building. It is often not possible to be sure whether a ruin was a field-house, a half-year-house, or a demoted dwelling-house.

Field-houses most often go with vineyards or gardens. Thryphtí (H) is a whole village of vineyard-houses. Field-houses in eastern Merabéllo are associated with cereals. Olives least often have them, since until recently most olive-groves were not far from villages or hamlets.

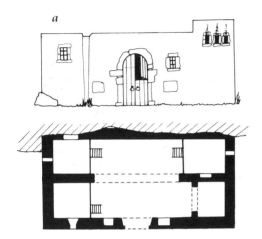

a

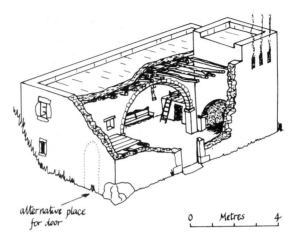

alternative place
for door

0   Metres   4

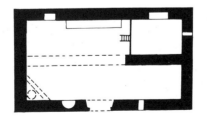

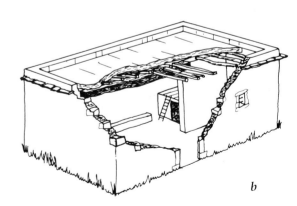

b

15.2 *House-types in elevations, plan and perspective. These are idealised, and omit most of the accretions which actual buildings generally have:*
(a) kamára-*house (b)* pro-kamára *house (c)* kéntis-*house (d) two-storey house with external* kamára *and chimney (these latter being a later addition).*

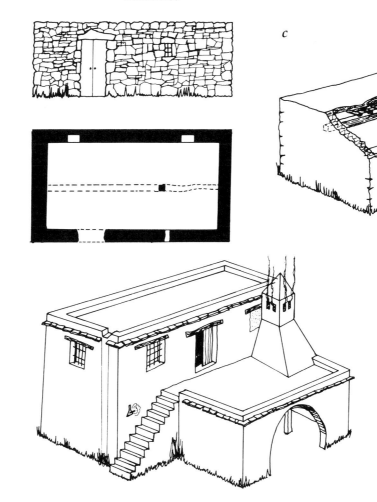

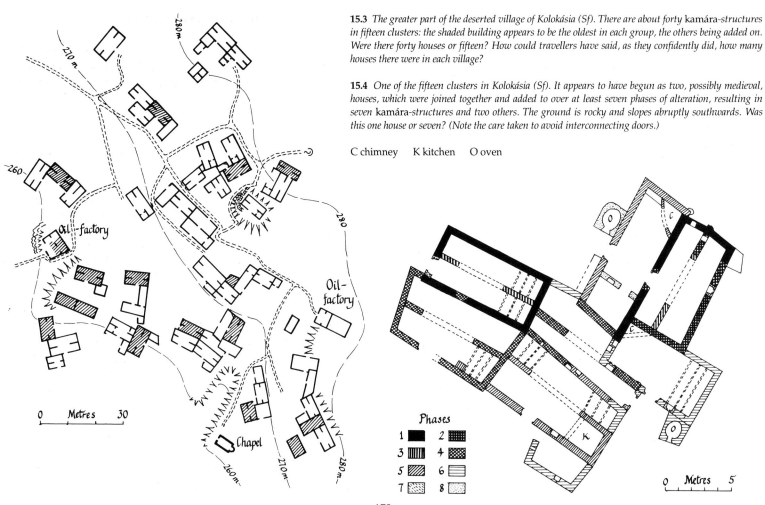

15.3 *The greater part of the deserted village of Kolokásia (Sf). There are about forty* kamára-*structures in fifteen clusters: the shaded building appears to be the oldest in each group, the others being added on. Were there forty houses or fifteen? How could travellers have said, as they confidently did, how many houses there were in each village?*

15.4 *One of the fifteen clusters in Kolokásia (Sf). It appears to have begun as two, possibly medieval, houses, which were joined together and added to over at least seven phases of alteration, resulting in seven* kamára-*structures and two others. The ground is rocky and slopes abruptly southwards. Was this one house or seven? (Note the care taken to avoid interconnecting doors.)*

C chimney   K kitchen   O oven

Oil-factory

-260-
-280m-
-210 m-
-280-
Oil-factory
Chapel
-260 m-
-210 m-
-280 m-

0 Metres 30

Phases
1 2
3 4
5 6
7 8

0 Metres 5

Manor-houses and villas

Upper-class country houses were conspicuous in Minoan Crete, but
have not been since. There were resident Creto-Venetian rural
nobility: for instance, Andrea Cornaro, in his will in 1611, enumer-
ates the furniture and library of his manor-house at Thrapsanó
(Pe).[6] However, they did not accumulate great wealth, or if they
did they did not invest it in Crete. Their Turkish successors faded
away in the eighteenth century, leaving Crete without a country
aristocracy.

Some modestly aristocratic houses survive in decay. Venetian
ones are in late-medieval or Renaissance style, with decorative
arches and windows; usually a narrow rectangle in plan, often
with outbuildings. They differ from vernacular houses in having
three storeys, stone vaults, staircases, and in the lavish use of cut
stone (often aeolianite brought from the coast). Venetian polite
architecture continues with little change into the early Turkish
period: characteristic of both are flared bases to the walls and
projecting courses in the form of roll-mouldings.

Gerola, the authority on Venetian architecture, listed about 110
such houses (Figure 15.5a). Many have disappeared, but there are
others that he missed. Some are in villages and hamlets, for example Kournás (Ap); others are out in the fields and appear to have
functioned as villas, upper-class country houses with their own
farms. They are not castles (Figure 15.5b), although some of them
are legendary through their adaptation as forts. In 1821 Ali
Alidhákis fought a desperate siege against the Sphakiots in his
villa at Embrósnero (Ap), which stands today exactly as he left it.[7]

The plain of Khaniá still has a few beautiful late-Venetian and
Veneto-Turkish villas in romantic high-walled gardens with
Baroque archways, a simpler version of the wonderful *kámpos* of
the island city of Chíos.

Specialised buildings

Disused houses tend to decline through wine-presses, olive-
crusheries, stores, stables, piggeries, to a final use as latrines. There
are also purpose-built oil-mills and the like, sometimes elaborate
buildings with several arches.

Mitáta

Shepherds in the *madháres* of the White Mountains and on Psilorítis
(Chapter 14) live in dry-stone 'huts'. These are usually round, with
roofs built as ***corbel-vaults***: successive courses of horizontal stones
overhang, one above the other, reducing the opening until it can be
closed by a great slab. Doors and windows have stone lintels. A
mitáto consists of a group of such huts, one being a workshop for
boiling cheese, the others for storing cheeses and for living quarters.

Mitáta are best built of platey limestone. The neatest are on
Psilorítis, but those of the White Mountains are triumphs of
drystone construction. Some are rectangular, with great transverse
arches up to 5m in span, and corbel-vaults between. The *mitáto* is
often thought of as the aboriginal Cretan house, and schemes have
been drawn up by which other house-types might have 'evolved'
from it. The parallel with Mycenaean corbel-vaults such as the
Tomb of 'Agamemnon', and similar but humbler tombs in Crete, is
irresistible: even the relieving-arch over the doorway is there.[8]

However, *mitáta* themselves are undatable, and the earliest
record is of the *mitáto*-like chapel on the summit of Psilorítis, visited
by Belon in *c.* 1550. The gap in time is slightly reduced by the
corbelled domes of a few ancient churches, such as the Archangel
Michael at Episkopí (Ki) (p. 180). Corbel-vaults have never been
usual for ordinary houses. The *mitáto* could have been invented

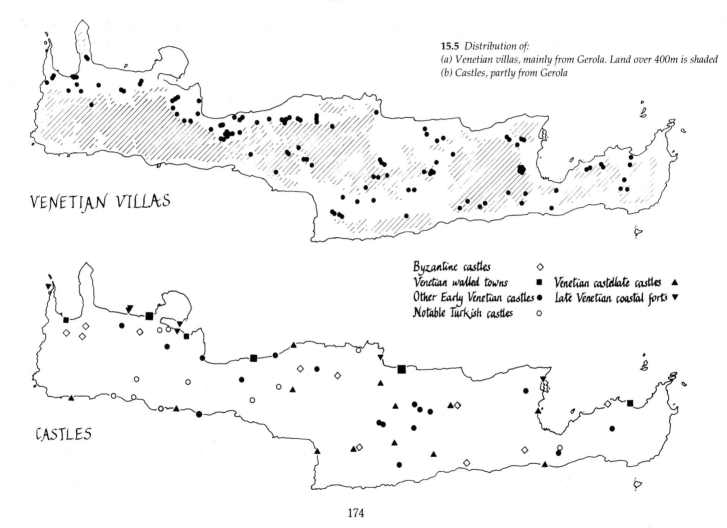

15.5 *Distribution of:*
(a) Venetian villas, mainly from Gerola. Land over 400m is shaded
(b) Castles, partly from Gerola

VENETIAN VILLAS

Byzantine castles ◇
Venetian walled towns ■ Venetian castellate castles ▲
Other Early Venetian castles ● Late Venetian coastal forts ▼
Notable Turkish castles ○

CASTLES

independently in a platey-limestone area where there was no timber to make a wooden roof or to hold up a conventional vault while the mortar set. Whether the inventor was inspired by an ancient *thólos*-tomb we do not know.

Mills

Crete has a high-technology kind of water-mill. A **leat** taps a stream and channels water horizontally along the valley side until it is about 6 m above the valley floor. At this point the mill is

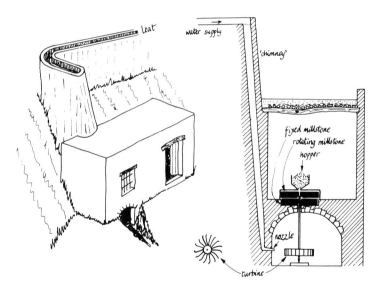

15.6 *Cretan water-mill and section showing how it works, the latter simplified after Valianos*

placed. The water falls down an almost vertical, chimney-like shaft with a sideways nozzle at the bottom. It squirts on to the curved wooden blades of a turbine, mounted on a vertical shaft beneath the mill (Figure 15.6). The top of the shaft projects through the mill floor and turns the upper of a pair of millstones, into which the grain is fed from a hopper.[9]

This kind of mill is known also from Cyprus. It makes very efficient use of steep, fast, and variable mountain streams.[10] The millstones are of lava from the island of Melos, or of hard conglomerate; they are composite stones, assembled from small pieces brought on muleback. Each mill has a crane for lifting and turning over the stones to dress the grooved surface. A mill rarely has a dwelling attached: it would have been used only for a few weeks at a time.

Mills are rarely still in use, although one can be seen grinding at Záros (Ka). There used to be hundreds if not thousands, even in east Crete where streams rarely flow. They belong to some of the most romantic landscapes: for example the eight mills below the gorge Hà (H), or Manouratómylo in verdant Amári, a double chimney-mill with a medieval bridge and snow-capped Psilorítis behind.

There are other types of water-mill. We have seen two overshot wheels of the usual European type. The fourteen chimney-mills in the Gorge of Samariá (Sf) are far too many to grind grain, and some were probably sawmills, serving the trade in cypress boards (pp. 132-3).

Windmills are mainly east Cretan (especially northern Merabéllo). They were not steerable, and worked only when the wind was in the right direction. They are built in rows across mountain passes which funnel the wind. The usual Cretan windmill has a long narrow D-shaped tower with its rounded end facing the wind. They apparently had cloth sails (like those that still work in the Cyclades) mounted on a slanting wind-shaft with gears to transmit the drive to the stones.

Both kinds of mill are probably medieval inventions: water-mills are mentioned by Buondelmonti in 1415. Early Turkish deeds mention several water-mills and the occasional windmill.

The Lassíthi windpumps are described on p. 43.

Castles (Figure 15.5b)

The Venetians organised Crete into nineteen castellates. For most of these a castle was established in the thirteenth century for collecting taxes. (There had been a number of Byzantine castles.) Castles were also to overawe a rebellious populace, and to deter or catch raiders from the sea. Mostly they were built, very reluctantly, by the government, which hated spending money on Crete. Some nobles built castles of their own, despairing of any other way of keeping out corsairs (Chapter 18).

Not much remains of the original Venetian castles; many of them were already ruinous by the seventeenth century. Perhaps the best-preserved, though still ruinous, is Sphakiá castle in Khóra Sphakíon.

Frangokástello (Sf), 'Castle of the Franks', was built in the mid-fourteenth century, after the castellate castles. The visitor should shut his eyes to bungalows and parked cars, and try to imagine the lonely magnificence in which it stood until the 1970s. It is a simple rectangle of high walls, with a square tower at each corner, and remains of internal buildings. Over the doorway are the Lion of St Mark and the arms of the noble Venetians concerned. It follows a standard pattern for castellate castles. Close examination shows that the biggest corner tower was built first, according to a standard pattern for smaller forts, entered by an upstairs doorway and a drawbridge. Only later was the quadrangle added. By Crusader standards, Frangokástello is not much of a castle. There are no outer defences, too few loopholes covering the bases of the walls, no gatehouse, and not even a proper wall-walk; the weaponry apparently consisted of fourteen archers.

In the sixteenth century the Venetians built other castles near the cities and on islets (p. 207). That on Spinalónga islet (Me), a well-preserved example of sixteenth-century military architecture, is famous for its twentieth-century history as a place of relegation for lepers (p. 98). (For coastguard posts (*vigle*) see p. 199.)

The Turks took the strategic qualities of Crete seriously. They filled the island with castles: perched on crags above the mouths of the Samariá and Trypití Gorges (Sf), dominating passes in the Kouloukoúnas Mountains and behind Réthymnon (R), overlooking mountain-plains or lowland basins. The castles form a well-thought-out network, capable of signalling to each other and connected by *kalderími* tracks. They are often marked by the place-name Goulé (p. 107). They are built of a distinctive type of masonry, rendered in yellow cement; the walls are pierced with musket loopholes about a metre apart (as at Frangokástello (Sf), which was adapted as a Turkish castle). The flat roof has a parapet with more loopholes and sometimes ports for guns. The bigger castles are often D-shaped, with round towers at the corners, giving extra fire to cover the approach (up zigzags or stairs) and to sweep the bases of the walls. The interior has a large barrack-room and a court, round which are the magazine, latrines and a cook-house with a chimney. There were flat earthen roofs like those of Cretan houses, presumably carried on internal posts.

Most of the Turkish castles appear to date from after the great revolt of 1866. This was the last period in Europe of castle-building in the medieval tradition, then 350 years out of date. We wonder why the Turks assumed that their enemies would not have artillery: even the smallest mountain gun, sending shells crashing through the earth roofs, would have made short work of almost any of the castles.

Some of the bigger castles diverge from the standard pattern and have several building phases: for example Koxaré (AV), whose great hall has two thick vaults inspired by the Venetian arsenals at Khaniá (Ky).

Turkish castles, though little more than a century old, belong to a world as remote from us as the Minoans. What was it like to serve in Samariá castle, in the heart of the mountains most dreadful to Turks? Who were the masons who built the castle? What did the soldiers (and their animals) eat? How did they get on with the villagers? Where did they spend their pay? Castles and garrisons undoubtedly influenced the economy. The two big castles in Askyphou (Sf) had at least 250 musket-loops and twenty gun-ports, implying at least 500 men. Although they may not have been fully manned all the time, this means an addition of one-third to one-half to the civilian population of the Plain.

Castles testify to the increase in woodland since they were built. Many are surrounded by prickly-oaks and cypresses, which would hardly have been allowed to remain when they would have covered an attacker.

Lime-kilns

Scattered in the landscape are round structures varying from 1.5 m to 5 m in diameter, whose insides are often blazingly white. These are lime-kilns, furnaces used to heat limestone, which decomposes into lime for making mortar, plaster, or whitewash. They have a stoke-hole on the windward side to create an up-draught to produce the very hot fire needed. They are usually built of undressed stone, although the jambs of the stoke-hole can be hammer-dressed. Complete lime-kilns, with floors and roofs, are rare today; there is one still operating in the traditional way near Mókhlos (Si).[11]

Lime-kilns need to be near sources of fuel and limestone, and near users of lime. One might think that in a limestone country almost any stone would do, but this is not so. Lime-burners like their rocks to be of a size handled by a single person. Screes, natural sources of such stones, are often inaccessible. The preferred raw material is collapsed walls and buildings; archaeologists have often remarked on the association between ancient settlements and later lime-kilns. Lime is heavy, nasty stuff, and was sometimes made on the spot – a chapel or castle may have its own kiln – or transported by boat. The latter may account for the frequent occurence of kilns in coastal archaeological sites. The sides or head of a ravine also seem to be common locations for limekilns, possibly for the up-draught.

To judge by their associated pottery, surviving lime-kilns are seldom earlier than Late Venetian. Many are much later: in Spratt's time houses were less often whitewashed than they are now. It is somewhat of a mystery how the Romans and Byzantines made the quantities of lime that they used, but small lime-kilns, for making plaster, are known from Minoan times.'[12]

Notes

1 E.g. D. Vasileiadis (*c.* 1980) (Δ. Βασιλειάδη) *τό κρητικὸ σπίτι*, Athens, Kollaros.

2 J. D. Evans (1964, Chapter 11, note 5), p. 146, Plate 59.1.

3 Kh. Valianos and S. Kokkoris (Χ. Βαλλιάνου καὶ Σ. Κόκκορη) (1987), *Κρητική παραδοσιακή Αρχιτεκτονική*, Vóroi, Μουσέιο Κρητικό Εθνολογίας.

4 BMV: Ital. VI.1(5061).

5 Stavrinidhes (see bibliography), vol. A, *passim*; Dhetorakis (see bibliography), p. 310f.

6 BMV: Ital. VII. 911(8392).

7 Pashley (see bibliography), II, 159.

8 P. M. Warren (1973), 'The mitata of Nidha and Early Minoan tholos tombs', *Athens Annals of Archaeology*, **6**, 449-56.

9 Kh. Valianos (Χ. Βαλλιάνου) et al. (1985), *Νερόμυλοι Δυτικής Μεσαράς Κρήτης: φυσικό οικοσύστημα καὶ υδάτικο δυναμικό*, Vóroi, Μουσέιο Κρητικό Εθνολογίας.

10 N. G. Calvert (1973), 'On water mills in central Crete', *Transactions of the Newcomen Society*, **45**, 217-21 (we are indebted to John Hunter for this reference).

11 We thank Phil Betancourt for this information.

12 P. M. Warren (1981), 'Stratigraphical Museum excavations, 1978-80, Part 1', *Archaeological Reports (Journal of Hellenic Studies supplement)* 1980-1, 73-92.

16

Sacred landscapes

*For this cause left I thee in Crete, that thou shouldest ... ordain elders
in every city, as I had appointed thee ... there are many unruly and
vain talkers and deceivers ... one of themselves, even a prophet of their
own, said, the Cretians are alway liars, evil beasts, slow bellies.*

Reputed Letter of St Paul to Titus, **1**, 5,10,12

Pre-Christian sacred landscapes

Prehistoric

The Minoans began the Cretan tradition, which continues to this
day, of worshipping in seemingly remote places. They had sanctuaries in their homes and towns, but their art also shows ritual cele-
brations on mountain-tops and in olive-groves. At least nineteen
sacred caves are known[1] and 25 peak sanctuaries; so far there is no
evidence for Minoan sacred springs.

Peak sanctuaries are in the eastern three-quarters of Crete; the
most famous is on Mount Yúktas (T).[2] They seem to us to be in
remote and inaccessible terrain, but in the Middle Bronze Age they
were an integral part of the settlement pattern. Each sanctuary
appears to have belonged to a unique political territory, and could
be reached within three hours' walk from the main settlement. In
addition, it was important that the sanctuary be visible from the
settlements it served. These requirements locate peak sanctuaries
on prominent ridges and hilltops rather than on the highest
summit of a massif, which is often not visible from the valley floor.
Sanctuaries vary in elevation from 215 m (Petsofás (Si)) to 1,168 m
(Kería (Ma)).[3]

Many Minoan signet rings and sealings show figures worshipping before individual trees. A stroll through an ancient olive-
grove allows one to imagine such a place. Sometimes the trees are
depicted within an enclosure-wall, known to Minoan scholars as a
Sacred Enclosure. The Káto Syme Sanctuary (V), found in 1972 on
the south slopes of the Lassithi Mountains, is the best excavated
example of such a shrine. Activity began in the Middle Bronze Age.
The site is not remarkable topographically, except that two gullies
come together; water could have been a determining factor.[4]

Classical, Hellenistic and Roman

Several of the gods of Greece are mentioned on Linear B tablets, by far the earliest evidence for them. In classical times, Crete was known for divinities who were variants of the ordinary gods of Olympus. Cretan Zeus was born on the island, brought up in the Cave of Mount Ida, and (some said) died there and was buried.[5] Britomartis and Diktynna were goddesses (or the same goddess?) vaguely like the orthodox Artemis. Cretan Herakles was different from his lion-rending namesake. We might think this was a survival of an independent theogony, but in Homer and Hesiod, the earliest poets, Cretan gods are less peculiar than in later writers.

Caves (unlike peaks) continued to be important sanctuaries in the Greek and Roman periods. The cult of Idaean Zeus, in the cave above the Nídha Plain, was famous throughout the Greek and Roman world; the cave has recently been re-excavated by Ioannis Sakellarakis.[6] The similar cave at Psykhró in the Lassithi Plain, whose sacred history goes back to the Neolithic, was much used at the same time, though ancient authors seem not to mention it. Arkoúdha cave on the Akrotíri was an important centre for the cult of Artemis.

The Sacred Enclosure at Káto Syme (V) probably continued without a break up to the Roman period. Between the eighth and fifth centuries BC the shrine, then dedicated to Hermes and Aphrodite, seems to have been connected to rites of passage for young men. Such rituals are noted by the ancient authors and mentioned in an inscription from Phaistos, according to which young men were supposed to serve Aphrodite Skotia during a two months' retreat before entering upon adulthood and marriage.[7] A possibly similar sanctuary may be located near the chapel of Ay.

Nikólaos in the Samariá Gorge (Sf). This site was first noted by I. Noukhakis, surveyed in 1987,[8] and recently test-trenched by Vanna Niniou-Kindelis. The finds include bronze bulls among other ritual artefacts.

Christian sacred landscapes

Roman and Early Byzantine Christianity

Crete is a land of ancient Christianity. The *Epistle to Titus* appears to say that St Paul visited the island about AD 60 and later installed St Titus as its first archbishop; although its authorship is doubtful, Crete was certainly converted early and completely.

In the Early Byzantine period, Crete had Christian basilicas worthy of the piety and wealth of this most prosperous period. Sanders listed nearly seventy, and we know several others. They were large buildings, on the scale of an English parish church, with a nave, aisles and an apse, adorned with marble columns, mosaic floors, and wall-paintings. They indicate a typical European parish organisation, in which every large village (or its equivalent in hamlets) has one church, big enough to hold most of the population every Sunday.

Almost every basilica has been demolished, reduced to a stump or a plinth. Their sacred function is continued by a small part of the great building, adapted into, or rebuilt as, a medieval chapel. At Ayia Rouméli (Sf) there is a chapel occupying the east end of a 'sawn-off basilica', whose mosaic floor is still exposed; this in turn had been made out of the remains of a supposed temple of Apollo. There are very few exceptions. Górtyn (Ka) is dominated by the shattered but upstanding Basilica of St Titus. At Episkopí (Ki) there is a most wonderful round church of St Michael the

Archangel, still in use, complete with mosaic floor and later wall-paintings.

What happened to the basilicas is not known. Some say they fell victim to Iconoclasts, others to Saracens – though there is no evidence that the Saracens broke the Muslim tradition of tolerance to Christianity, still less that they demolished great masonry buildings. Did the basilicas collapse in the earthquakes of the Early Byzantine Paroxysm (p. 15)?

Medieval churches
After the loss of the basilicas, the ecclesiastical landscape went in a direction peculiar to Crete and some other islands. We notice today the lack of large ancient parish churches. Most villages have a big central church, but it is rarely even 200 years old. There are chapels in profusion in villages and hamlets, out in the fields, scattered in wild lonely places: the chapel of the Holy Cross on the summit of Mount Ida, of St Paul among the wave-notches beneath the towering cliffs of Sphakiá, that on the Tigáni peninsula at the remote end of Gramboúsa, and thousands of others (Figure 16.1). Cretan chapels are tiny buildings of exquisite and miniature beauty. Some have aisles and little domes, but are seldom as big as a small English church; many are no bigger than an English church porch. Small though they are, many have several stages of addition and alteration. They rarely if ever had a tower; the bell, if any, hung in a tree or, rarely, in a little arched bell-cote.

Crete is famous for medieval wall-paintings in chapels. Gerola and Lassithiotakis catalogued 845 painted chapels (Figure 16.2).[9] Our observations indicate that they found about 85 per cent of all the painted chapels, and that at most one-third of the medieval chapels are painted. This makes at least 3,000 medieval chapels in Crete, roughly five per township. There are at least as many post-medieval ones.

Chapels can date from any period in the last thousand years. Wall-paintings are sometimes signed and dated, or can be dated by the artistic style; there are also graffiti. For example, a chapel of St Anne is perched at the head of the gorge Hà (H), with cliffs garlanded with endemic plants, a little garden and a spring, and its bell hanging in a great pine-tree. On the painted interior (one of several known to us not in the catalogue) a succession of Venetians have scratched their names:

1450 A di .8. auosto hic fuit p'b'r petrus buffo
1450, on 8 August, the Rev. Peter Toad was here.

Many passers-by, including some of the noblest names in Venice, left their marks, which suggests that the lonely track past the chapel was then a main road to Siteía. In some chapels the eyes of the painted figures have been picked out, either (some say) by Muslims who disapproved of complete pictures of the human form, or (others say) by Christians who thought that eyes of painted Saints had aphrodisiac virtues.

Graffiti give only the latest possible date for a painting, and paintings are often centuries later than the building. Gerola and Lassithiotakis show that datable wall-paintings are predominantly of the fourteenth century, but occasionally as early as the tenth; they cease rather suddenly in the early sixteenth. The most active period of chapel-building, being earlier than the paintings, was thus probably the thirteenth century. Other dates come from the Italianate custom of embedding fine, highly datable majolica or Turkish pots (*bacini*) in the walls.[10]

16.1 *Medieval chapel. Note the off-centre door, the five* bacini *above it, and the unsuitable concrete roof. Deserted village of Lophiá (AV), September 1989*

Cretan chapels follow, in miniature, the European sequence of architectural styles. Some of these can be roughly dated, as where a chapel in one style has been extended in another, or where chapels are depicted in Venetian manuscripts. Byzantine resembles Romanesque, with round arches and lofty proportions (Aikyrgiánnis between Alikianoú and Kouphós (Ky)). Cretan thirteenth-century High Gothic has pointed arches, dog's-tooth ornament, and deeply moulded doorways (Mikhális Arkhángelos in Monastiráki (Am)); later Gothic has flowing curves and ogee shapes (Ay. Demétrios in Komitádhes (Sf)). The Italian Renaissance

passed by rural Crete, but in the sixteenth century there appears a Cretan version of the Mannerist style (Arkádhi Monastery (R)). In the eighteenth century there follows a distinctively Turkish style, often again with Gothic arches (Kritsá (Me)). In the nineteenth century there appears a curious 'primitivist' style, peculiar to Crete and southern Greece, with rough carvings and classical pilasters that branch and bend (parish church of Vasilikí (H)). Next comes another Gothic revival, distinguished from original Gothic by the buildings being often large and covered with a hard smooth cement (Khrysoskalítissa Monastery (Ki)).

The distribution of medieval chapels is incompletely known and is biased by the painted ones. On present evidence, they are concentrated in the hills and bases of the mountains; they avoid high mountains, coastal plains, and fertile areas (Figure 16.2).

If painted chapels are a representative sample, the commonest dedications (in descending order) are to the Virgin Mary, St George, St John the Evangelist, Our Saviour and St Nicholas. The commonest remaining saints are those of the Roman Empire, like St Anthony the Hermit of Egypt, St Marina (an Anatolian martyr), St Constantine the first Christian Emperor and St Irene his mother. They mostly, like St Nicholas, came from the eastern half of the Roman Empire. Medieval chapels are thus dedicated to saints who would have been well known in Crete during its Early Byzantine prosperity.

Other dedications to saints of the first two centuries of Christianity are rare. Paul and Titus, founders of the Cretan Church, are particularly neglected. There are few saints (St Paraskevé is one) from nearer the time that the chapels were built. There are few saints with a Cretan connection: Crete produced its fair share of saints, such as the Holy Ten of Górtyn and the Four Martyrs of

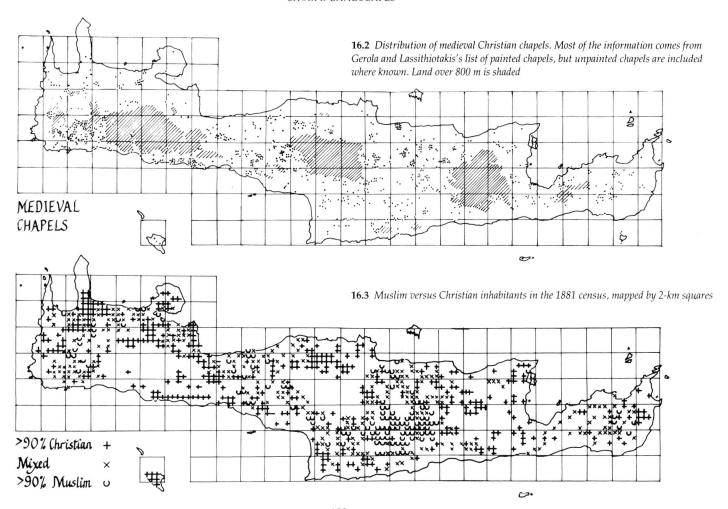

16.2 *Distribution of medieval Christian chapels. Most of the information comes from Gerola and Lassithiotakis's list of painted chapels, but unpainted chapels are included where known. Land over 800 m is shaded*

MEDIEVAL
CHAPELS

16.3 *Muslim versus Christian inhabitants in the 1881 census, mapped by 2-km squares*

>90% Christian +
Mixed ×
>90% Muslim ∪

183

Réthymnon (sometimes depicted in Cretan formal garb), but none achieved more than a local cult.

How were churches used? There are a few sizeable ones, for example the cathedral of St Myron at Ayios Myron (Ma), or the (shockingly dilapidated) Byzantine-Gothic transitional church of the Holy Apostles at Khóra Sphakíon. But few parishes can have had a building capable of holding all the local population. This is not a matter of poverty: rich places had more, not bigger, chapels than poor places. In the First Byzantine period the islanders changed, for some reason, from the usual European pattern of public worship.

What they did instead we can only conjecture. The answer may seem obvious: worship took the form of a *panegyri,* when everyone gathers (as they still do) on the saint's day of some lonely chapel. The Liturgy is celebrated with the congregation standing outside; lambs and fowls are slain, barrels broached, the passing traveller invited, and the night passes in joyous festivity. This is all very well for the summer feasts of Our Lady or St John Baptist, but it is hard to imagine it in the pouring rain for St Nicholas (6 December) or the biting wind for St Blaise (11 February). Nor would time allow a priest to get on his donkey and celebrate in several chapels on one Sunday.

The coming of Islam

At the Conquest, the Turks acted with strict Islamic propriety towards Christianity. They started by bringing back the Orthodox bishops banished by the Venetians. Christian monasteries flourished in the early Turkish period. Nevertheless, about one-quarter of the population converted to Islam. This puzzled contemporaries such as Tournefort, as it puzzles modern scholars. There was little worldly advantage in turning Muslim: in some respects, such as not doing military service, Christians were better off. Had the conversion been the other way it would unhesitatingly be ascribed to the eloquence of Christian missionaries. The most we can say is that there was a religious revival to the benefit of both Christianity and Islam.

All the cities were predominantly Muslim. In the countryside, whole villages and hamlets tended to convert together, although many were mixed (Figure 16.3).

What has Islam done to the ecclesiastical landscape? Outside the cities with their minarets, the visitor is unaware of its existence. We know of only a handful of rural mosques, or churches converted to mosques. Churches, dating from before the Turkish Conquest, are no less common in former Muslim than in Christian areas. This applies equally to *painted* churches, to which Muslims might have objected as breaking the Second Commandment. Sélinon, which was half Muslim, has probably more medieval churches for its area than anywhere in the world. It is not just that Muslims neglected to demolish churches: outside the Turkish castle at Koxaré (AV) is a ruined medieval chapel which was allowed to remain even though it interfered with the fire of the castle's guns.

Was the distinction between the two religions as sharp in practice as in theory? Did converts to Islam necessarily give up Christianity? There are eighteenth-century stories of crypto-Christians practising both religions.

The later history of churches

Size was not irrelevant to medieval chapels, for many of them show signs of being extended during the middle ages. During the sixteenth century there began a movement towards bigger churches.

This is illustrated at Spíli (AV) by a succession of churches on different sites, from the earliest, enlarged out of a medieval church, to the biggest in the twentieth century. (The belief that churches were not built in the Turkish period because the Turks forbade it is flatly contradicted by numerous datestones.)

Dr Simon Price draws our attention to a list of the clergy of Sphakiá in 1634.[11] This shows a nearly conventional parish arrangement, with each priest responsible for a main church and a number of dependent chapels. If this was typical of Crete, it could explain the centralised church-building of succeeding centuries. Bigger churches are not uncommon in the eighteenth century, and become increasingly abundant (with towers) in the nineteenth. This was in addition to further building of chapels. Thus developed the ecclesiastical landscape of today.

Monasteries

Cretan monasteries have a trick of being in extraordinary, wild, dangerous places: Khrysoskalítissa (Ki) (the Holy Monastery of Our Lady of the Golden Step) in the far south-west, Toploú (Si) in the far north-east, Kapsás (Si) in a crumbling and thirsty gorge of the south-eastern desert, Koudhoumá (Mo) beneath the tremendous cliffs of Mount Kóphinas in the Asteroúsia, Ayios Kharálambos (Sf) by the pirate-haunted Frangokástello coast (Figure 16.4). This may be by chance: the site may be determined by a shepherd finding a miraculous icon, which could happen anywhere. Or the choice may be deliberate: some monasteries grew out of the cells of hermits, who turned their backs on the world and the flesh, and sought out desert and magnificent spots in which to commune with God and wrestle with the devil.

The Orthodox Church knows nothing of the different monastic orders of the West. Monasteries are larger or smaller versions of the same plan: a courtyard around the abbey church, surrounded by the little two-storey houses of the monks, the refectory, store-houses, powder-magazine and library. Abbeys needed to take care of themselves, and have a high blank outer wall and often a tower for defence. There is often an outlying farm (*metókhi*), worked by the monks themselves, like the granges of abbeys in the West.

Monasticism in Crete goes back at least to the First Byzantine period, as shown by the monastery on Pseíra islet (Si).[12] Most medieval monasteries were small and impermanent: several villages are named Moní ('Monastery') or Monastiráki ('Little Monastery'), but no trace of a monastery survives. Some of the present monasteries claim to be of medieval foundation or have Gothic buildings, like the beautiful cave-church of Phaneroméni (H). Many later monasteries incorporate pre-existing medieval chapels, as at Toploú (Si), Ayios Kharálambos (Sf), and Arvi (V).

In the Late Venetian period Cretan monasticism burst into flower, producing the fine Mannerist architecture of Arkádhi (R) and Tzangaról (Ak). The Conquest hardly interrupted this prosperity: the Sultans understood and valued monks and made them independent of the local Turkish authorities. Monasteries gained a reputation as seats of learning. Late Venetian and early Turkish are indistinguishable in monastic architecture.

In the nineteenth century monks seized musket and scimitar and became leaders of revolt. Almost every monastery has tales of battle, siege and sack; every Greek knows of the blowing-up of the grand magazine of Arkádhi (R) in the revolt of 1866. However, one would hardly notice this by looking at the buildings. Monasteries had a knack of rising above disaster. The nineteenth century, even the dark years of the 1830s, is well represented in monastic architecture.

16.4 *Monasteries listed by Psilakis, with others known (now mostly deserted)*

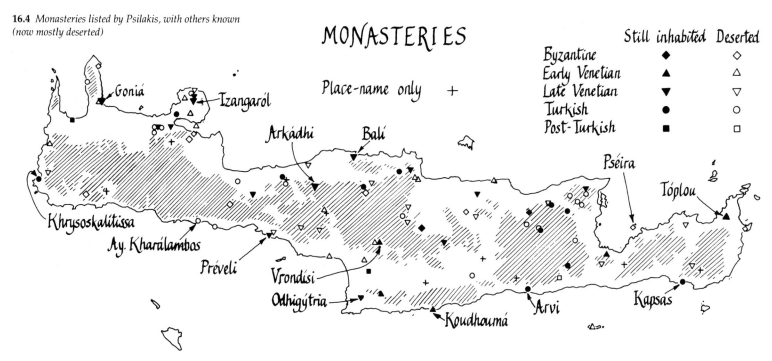

MONASTERIES

Place-name only +

	Still inhabited	Deserted
Byzantine	◆	◇
Early Venetian	▲	△
Late Venetian	▼	▽
Turkish	●	○
Post-Turkish	■	□

Gonia
Izangaról
Arkádhi
Balí
Pseíra
Tóplou
Khrysoskalítissa
Ay. Kharálambos
Préveli
Vrondísi
Odhigýtria
Koudhoumá
Arví
Kapsás

Monasteries did not perish by the sword of Islam, but by apathy in the twentieth century. Vocations have dwindled, estates were gradually confiscated, and granges are deserted. They are still holy and much-loved places, and their stout buildings resist decay; but their people are reduced to the Lord Abbot, one or two other monks, perhaps a venerable nun, and a number of cats. But nunneries have fared better than male monasteries, and better times may be on the way. The collapse of Communism in eastern Europe has brought renewed energy to Orthodox monasticism.

Monasteries probably had an effect on the development of the landscape – they remind us of the Cistercian tradition of farmer-monks – but this should not be exaggerated. Préveli was one of the greater abbeys; local tradition credits it with vast estates. At the height of its fortunes in 1864, however, it had less than a hundred hectares of farmland attached to the abbey, a few hundred hectares of farmland scattered through sixteen townships up to 42 km away, 14,500 olive-trees, and well under a thousand hectares of mountain grazing.[13] It may have been one of the biggest landowners in Crete, but it had perhaps one-twentieth of the endowment of a great abbey in medieval England.

The meaning of the ecclesiastical landscape

In Crete churches seldom become redundant. Nearly every chapel, even if shattered in some forgotten earthquake, is still sacred and has a little icon and a lamp in a hole in the wall. Chapels are solidly built and seldom destroyed except to build something else.

Why are chapels where they are? Often for private reasons: built in fulfilment of a vow, on the orders of an angel in a dream, in thanksgiving for rescue from shipwreck, etc. But many isolated chapels once had settlements round them. The chapel remains upstanding when all else has crumbled.

What does the distribution of medieval chapels mean (see Figure 16.2)? It does not correspond to village *versus* hamlet settlement, nor to the absence of coastal settlement due to danger from corsairs. It is evidently a matter of survival. If the difficult upland of Sélinon, Kíssamos and Amári is full of chapels today – costly painted chapels, too – it is hard to believe that there were never any in the rich lowlands of Khaniá, Apokórona or north-west Mylopótamos. The non-survival of chapels has nothing to do with Muslim iconoclasm. It appears to be Christian prosperity, especially in the nineteenth century, that swept them away in order to build something grander on the site. As in many countries, poverty has preserved antiquities.

Continuity of sacred places

It is difficult to confirm the continuity of sacred sites from one epoch to the next. Crete is not a good part of Greece to illustrate the once-popular theory that hilltops once sacred to Apollo are now dedicated to the Prophet Elias, or that St Demetrius is the successor to the goddess Demeter. Caves, hilltops and springs sometimes have both Christian and pre-Christian sacred associations. Some pagan sacred caves now contain chapels, e.g. Arkoúdha (Ak) and the cave of Ay. Sophiá in the Topólia Gorge (Ki). However, the majority of known Bronze Age sacred caves do not contain Christian remains.

Although middle-elevation peaks are dotted with chapels and Minoan shrines, it would be misleading to relate the locations of hilltop chapels to those of Minoan peak sanctuaries. No known peak sanctuary remained in use beyond Late Minoan III. Almost as many peak sanctuaries have telecommunication stations as have chapels! As Alan Peatfield points out, the topography, in relation to settlement sites, causes the same hilltops to be selected in different periods for different sacred or secular purposes.[14]

Notes

1 E. L. Tyree (1974), *Cretan Sacred Caves: archaeological evidence*, Ph.D. dissertation, Columbia, Univ. of Missouri. For a detailed account of Cretan prehistoric shrines see Rutkowski (bibliography).
2 A. Karetsou (1983), 'The peak sanctuary of Mt. Juktas', in R. Hägg and N. Marinatos (eds.), *Sanctuaries and Cults in the Aegean Bronze Age*, Stockholm, Svenska Institutet i Athen, pp. 137-53.
3 A. A. D. Peatfield (1983), 'The topography of Minoan peak sanctuaries', *BSA*, **78**, 273-80.

4 A. Lembessi and P. Muhly (1987), 'The Sanctuary of Hermes and Aphrodite at Syme, Crete', *National Geographic Research*, **3**, 102-13; A. Lembessi and P. Muhly (1990), 'Aspects of Minoan cult: sacred enclosures. The evidence from the Syme Sanctuary', *Archäologischer Anzeiger*, 315-36.

5 Callimachus, *Hymn to Zeus*.

6 Y. Sakellarakis and E. Sakellaraki (1981), 'Drama of death in a Minoan temple', *National Geographic Magazine*, **159**, 205-23; Y. Sakellarakis and E. Sakellaraki (1992), '2. Archanes-Anemospilio' in Myers et al. (see bibliography), pp. 51-3.

7 A. Lembessi and P. Muhly (1987, note 4); M. Guarducci (1935), in *Inscriptiones Creticae*, **4**, 270.

8 L. Nixon, J. Moody et al. (1988, 1989 see bibliography).

9 G. Gerola, translated and supplemented by K. E. Lassithiotakis (1961), *Τοπογράφιχος κατάλογος τῶν τοιχογραφμένων Ἐκκλησιῶν τῆς Κρῆτης*. Herákleion.

10 Dr Margarethe Hahn drew our attention to the importance of these pots.

11 M. K. Khaireti (Μ. Κ. Χαιρέτη) (1968), *Ἡ απογράφη τῶν ναῶν καὶ τῶν μονῶν τῆς περιοχῆς Χανιῶν τοῦ ἔτους 1627*, pp. 335-71.

12 C. Davaras, P. P. Betancourt and W. R. Farrand (1992), '38. Pseira', in Myers et al. (see bibliography), pp.262-67.

13 From an extent in the Abbey.

14 A. A. D. Peatfield (1983, note 3).

17

The high mountains

As for the Cypresses, they do not grow in forest country, as many have supposed: for they grow one here and another there, in various regions of the mountains … they always seek the south side, and have the property, that again after one has cut them at the base, the trunk always never fails to send up many shoots. The Cypresses in this place do not grow up in height, but play too much at growing in thickness. So one sees very broad cypress chests, made in the city of Candia [Herákleion (T)].

Pierre Belon on Mount Psilorítis, 1555

The highest trees

All round the White Mountains and Psilorítis, trees come to an abrupt end at an elevation of 1,650 m. The highest are cypress or prickly-oak. In the interior of the White Mountains, the limit rises and other species join in. The highest upstanding tree in Crete, at 1,810 m on Mount Avlimonára which towers above the Samariá Gorge (Sf), is a cypress; a few metres lower is an *ambelitsiá* (p. 71) and a maple, with pine a little lower still. Above the highest trees there is a narrow zone of a bushy juniper (*Juniperus oxycedrus*), one stunted individual of which reaches 2,050 m on Mount Orinó.

The last extraordinary cypresses before the tree-limit (Figure 17.1) are among the oldest trees in Europe: low, massive, spread-ing, often less than a metre high but with trunks more than a metre thick; with dead boughs, bleached from some long-past ice-storm, they cling to life on their remaining foliage. Annual rings show that some are well over a thousand years old; they could provide a record of good and bad years back to Roman times. They are the European equivalent of the famously long-lived bristle-cone pines of Arizona, but they are something more. These oldest cypresses are *coppice stools* (Figure 6.4), cut at intervals of several hundred years (is this the world's longest coppicing cycle?). Cypress wood weathers but does not rot, and stubs of four coppicings ago can still be discerned.

In the Alps, the tree-limit has been depressed by grazing: trees grow on cliffs up to 200 m above the last trees in accessible places. Not so on Crete. There are no higher trees on cliffs; the highest trees have been stretched to the ultimate possibility of tree growth. Only once in several hundred years does an exceptionally good season enable new trees to arise. The dieback indicates a slight retreat of the tree-limit during the lifetime of the present trees – they were frostbitten in the cold winter of 1992.

The tree-limit is very stable; there is no sign that it has been more than about 50 m higher. Why is it so low? In the Alps, far to the north, trees go 500 m higher than in Crete. Crete illustrates the principle that in small and isolated mountain ranges the limits of climate and vegetation are compressed, compared to the interiors

17.1 *Ancient coppiced cypress at the tree-limit. On route from Anópolis (Sf) to the High Desert, April 1989*

of great massifs. In the Southern Alps, the highest olives are at about 200 m and permanent snow at 2,900, a difference of 2,700 m. In Crete, the olive limit is 750 m; the snow-line, if the mountains were high enough, would be at about 2,600, a difference of only 1,850 m. The same principle operates on a smaller scale within the island: trees go higher in the interior of the White Mountains than on their edges or on the smaller massifs of Psilorítis and Lassíthi.

The low tree-limit in Crete may be influenced by other factors. The Alps have special alpine trees, which Crete lacks, apart from *ambelitsiá*. Prickly-oak, a typical tree of the warm Mediterranean, here goes almost up to the tree-limit. However, it is very likely that there exist ***ecotypes:*** that the prickly-oak and cypress of high altitudes are not the same as in the lowlands, but have evolved adaptations to a different climate. Moreover the high White Mountains are dry in summer, as well as cold; growth, particularly of seedlings, may be hindered as much by drought as by cold.

The high-mountain madháres

Above the trees in the northern half of the high White Mountains there is a rocky, rounded landscape, undramatic, without gorges or big cliffs, thinly and rather evenly vegetated. Its special feature are hundreds of sinkholes (Figure 3.9). The biggest, Livádhas, 'Meadow' – presumably an ironic name – counts as a small mountain-plain. Others, down to a metre or two across, form chains along the bottoms of dry valleys.

These *madháres* are pastures (Chapter 14) with special buildings (p. 173). The corresponding landscape on Psilorítis covers the whole upper part of the mountain, although the main grazing areas are lower.

The *madháres* of the White Mountains are largely confined to platey limestone, often interbedded with shales and phyllites. This bedrock, more water-retentive than crystalline limestones, supports a vegetation dense enough to pasture up to 5,000 sheep and goats.

The principal plant of rocky slopes is the endemic *malótyra* (*Sideritis cretica*), a sage-like perennial with white woolly leaves and yellow flowers, which is gathered and sold as 'mountain tea'. *Daphne oleoides,* another undershrub, forms little thickets with sweet-scented flowers and orange berries. Tournefort describes *petramygdháli (Prunus prostrata)* thus:

> a sort of Plumb-Tree, which all these Rocks are embellish'd with, and which flourishes in proportion to the melting of the Snow: its stalks are not more than half a foot in length; the Branches are very bushy, loaded with Flowers of a flesh-colour; its Fruit is hardly bigger than a white [currant].

There are three hedgehog-plants (p. 112), from three different families: *kounágatho* (*Astragalus angustifolius*), *galatoatsivídha* (*Verbascum spinosum*), here at the top of its vast altitudinal range, and *Satureja spinosa*. Among endemic herbs are a hound's-tongue (*Cynoglossum sphacioticum*) and the aroid *dhrakodhé* (*Arum idaeum*).

Sinkholes and plains with silty soils are more vegetated, and are covered with spiny thickets of *loutsiá* (*Berberis cretica*), a non-endemic. Little patches of turf are full of endemics, such as *Chionodoxa cretica* and the flat-plants *piperóriza* (*Pimpinella depressa*) and *Hypericum kelleri* – this last peculiar to the White Mountains.

The larger sinkholes show signs of past cultivation. Until the 1950s they were used for growing potatoes. They display enclo-sure walls, lynchets and *Berberis* hedges between the fields. The Katsivéli basin, at 1,940 m, is the highest evidence of cultivation in Crete. Abandoned fields have the endemic thistle *Cirsium morinifolium,* one of the few tall plants in the *madháres*.

It is a puzzle that sheep and goats flourish as they do on this vegetation. Plant cover is sparse, growth slow, and much of the vegetation is poisonous (like *Daphne* and *dhrakodhé*), unpalatable (like *malótyra*), or spiny to a degree which deters even flock-goats. Grasses are sparse and very bitten-down; they consist of *Poa timoleontis* and an apparently undescribed *Sesleria. Prunus prostrata* provides much of the browse. Among other edible plants are a little dandelion and its relatives *Lactuca alpestris,* with only four ray-florets, and *Crepis sibthorpiana.* Late in the season animals stomach the tips of *malótyra* and *loutsiá*.

The *madháres* of Mount Ida are similar in general appearance, but many of the plants are different. *Phlomis lanata* and *Euphorbia acanthothamnos* range to a higher elevation than in the west. *Polygonum idaeum,* flattest of flat-plants, grows in the sinkholes (Fig. 6.3). In the screes is the gorgeous *Corydalis rutifolia,* which is rarer in west Crete.

The *madháres* are not a cultural landscape to the same degree as most other parts of Crete, but they have no less of an archaeological record (Chapter 14). Shepherds keep about as many animals as the vegetation will stand. If grazing were to be discontinued, we conjecture that plant cover, especially grasses, would somewhat increase. However, comparison with cliffs indicates that the character of the vegetation would not radically change. Cliffs in the high White Mountains are not vegetated differently from the rest of the landscape as they are at lower elevations. The rare, non-endemic grass *Bromus tomentellus* and maybe the endemic *Draba cretica* are the only distinctive cliff plants. It is quite likely that in pre-settlement times native mammals browsed the high slopes no less than they are browsed today.

The High Desert

In the southern, higher half of the high White Mountains there is the most extraordinary landscape that even Crete can show (Plate 9). Rows of conical peaks, all looking much alike and all sloping at an angle of 32°, sweep down into dry valleys, each of which is a chain of invertedly-conical sinkholes. The colours are salmon-pink and black: pink limestone mountains and black limestone sink-holes, with white and red between. This beautiful, sinister land-scape is full of rugged detail: abrupt little cliffs, jagged depressions, sudden headlong shafts with ice at the bottom, and crevasse-like fissures. The 32° slopes are of rock, thinly and treacherously covered with scree. The most sinister place of all, the Pavliá depres-sion, is a wide expanse of black limestone, impassably criss-crossed by fissures. Northern hemisphere comparisons fail: a colleague who has seen the ice-free terrain around McMurdo Sound assures us that here is the Cretan equivalent of Antarctica.[1]

At first sight this place is utterly barren. In reality, like most deserts, it is full of curious, specialised plants, of which the most wonderful is *blávi* (*Anchusa cespitosa*), a long-lived woody flat-plant covered with green tongue-like leaves, studded with flowers of blue (Plate 10). Nearly half the flora of the High Desert occurs nowhere else, proving that the desert, or something like it, has been in existence for at least most of the Pleistocene. It is a counter-exam-ple to those who claim that all landscapes are forever changing.

What makes the desert is the crystalline limestone rock, which is porous and impure; it crumbles into scree and breaks down in-to sand and silt. The finer fraction erodes away leaving the sand behind; there is nothing to retain water. Snowfall is probably enor-mous. The snow melts and the melt-water disappears into screes, fissures and sinkholes. Although the desert in general is higher than the *madhátres*, the boundary is determined by the edge of the better-vegetated platey limestone. Psilorítis (and probably the Lassíthi Mountains) have different limestones at this height, and no desert.

This is a real arctic-alpine periglacial landscape, formed by frost and solution which are still active. On gently-sloping or level summits there are **stripes and polygons**, formed by cycles of freezing and thawing in a slurry of stones and mud; the alternating expansions and contractions separate the coarse and fine material into a regular pattern. The 32° slopes, called Richter slopes, are also made by frost. This particular angle is the slope at which scree lies. A thin layer of scree protects the underlying rock from frost action. Any hollow gets filled with scree; any projection above the 32° slope is exposed and shattered by frost. Excess scree trickles into the dolines and dissolves, leaving sand.[2]

Plant life is chiefly on rock outcrops. The chief woody species, *petramygdháli*, flattens itself against the rocks. Among hedgehog-plants, *Astragalus angustifolius* makes its way up here, and is joined by the sea-lavender relative *Acantholimon androsaceum*, its intensely spiny cushions covered in pink blossom. Endemic dwarf herbs shelter in crevices and among the hedgehog-plants and shrublets, such as *Centranthus sieberi* (a dwarf red valerian with showy pink flowers) and *Scutellaria hirta*.

On compact earth there is a distinctive set of tiny plants, for example *Euphorbia herniariifolia*, and the flattened dandelion-like *Crepis fraasi*. Small patches of the *Berberis–Astragalus* plant commu-nity, indicating slightly more water, line the edges of the sandy bottoms of depressions, and occasionally grow nearly up to the top of Mount Pákhnes. On the very top the chickweed-like *Arenaria fragillima* is the highest plant in west Crete.

A few species are adapted to life in screes, such as the little pea *Cicer incisum* and the dwarf endemic bladder-campion *Silene variegata. Senecio fruticulosus*, another endemic, is a close relative of the Oxford Ragwort introduced to English cities.

Hares find the sparse vegetation. On the highest peaks we have found quantities of scarlet ladybirds (ladybugs) under the stones, and have wondered what these carnivorous insects can live on.

In the High Desert the cultural landscape seems at last to have reached its limits. Men seldom come here, except to cross from Anópolis (Sf) to the *madháres*. On the Mount of the Holy Ghost (Ayion Pnévma) there is a ruined chapel, the only one in the high White Mountains. The only other structures are groups of 'hut-circles', evidently temporary bivouacs, on some of the peaks.

Although there is almost nothing to eat or drink in the High Desert, stray goats and sheep (and *agrímia*) make their way up here. They lie on the snow in high summer; their parallel tracks, like faint terraces, cover the screes.

High mountains and Cretan civilisation

Mount Ida was one of the first parts of Crete to be widely known to the outside world. Belon climbed it three times in the 1550s, and countless travellers after him. The *madháres* and High Desert were little known to outsiders until the twentieth century; it was not even known for certain which was the highest peak. They were first explored by botanists attracted by the endemic plants.

To Cretans the high mountains have always been a well-known part of the island's culture. The place-names are no less ancient and mysterious than those of the rest of Crete. High mountains are revered as a place of solitude and, on occasions, the last stronghold of the eagles of freedom. Although the average Cretan probably never sets foot in them, it is the sight of the mountains that has brought courage in the dark days of the past.

Notes

1 We are indebted to Dr John Shaw for much of our understanding of the High Desert.
2 J. P. Bakker and J. W. N. Le Heux (1952), 'A remarkable new geomorphological law', *Proceedings, Koninklijke Nederlandse Akademie van Wetenschappen*, **55B**, 399-410; M. J. Selby (1971), 'Slopes and their development in an ice-free, arid area of Antarctica', *Geografisker Annaler*, **53A**, 235-45.

18
Coasts and the sea

Many villages are totally destroyed and uninhabited, which are these, namely: Lithineas, Grea, Mancassea, Caredhi, Sacano, Lomnoni, Sacro, Vlighu, Adharavastu, Clisidhi, Anatoli, Sanctus Georgius, Sacro, and all the coastal monasteries. ... and many others sacked ... out of which more than three hundred prisoners are still in the hands of the enemy ... many people from that district, refusing to stay in obvious danger of the enemy, have left these parts ... all that district is in confusion and flight, and besides a great part of those who remain have had to sell their beasts and all that they have, to ransom their prisoners from Turkey. The gentry of the district, seeing the ruin of their tenantry, have done all they could and more to preserve them, and some of them have built castles and towers at great expense, hoping by these works to give their people a chance to stay ...

Petition of Cretans to the Venetian Senate, 1471

Owing to the stringencies of the present time it is not possible to begin anything new in the matter.

Reply of the Senate [1]

[These places are all in far-east Crete.]

The coasts of Crete are wild and terrible. Walls of cliff, razor-edged beachrock ledges, or surf-pounded beaches can be deadly in sudden storms even in summer. The north coast, more populous and seemingly more hospitable than the south, has peninsulas which make it a dangerous lee shore in the prevailing northerly winds, especially to early ships which could not sail close to the wind. The south coast is more straightforward, but is liable to squalls off the mountains.[2]

Crete lacks good harbours. Except on the islet of Dhía (Pe) and at Spinalónga (Me), there are no good natural inlets sheltered from all winds. Soúdha Bay is too big to be a good harbour for sailing ships: with its narrow entrance and no tide to help, it is difficult to get out of in foul winds; it was not much used until the coming of steamships.

Things were not always quite so bad. In antiquity and in the middle ages there was a definite sailing season from March to October, so maybe the weather was then more reliable. Some harbours, like the Minoan one at Mókhlos (Si) or the Hellenistic one at Phalásarna (Ki), have been lost to sea-level changes. But we doubt whether Crete has ever been a good island for legitimate seafaring. Whatever may be said for Bronze Age seafaring,[3] for most of its history Crete was not much of a shipowning island. Most of its trade was carried in ships from elsewhere.

The obstacles did not deter pirate raiders, who could land on a beach, sack a village, and be off before the weather changed. Crete is an inward-looking island. The wise mariner gave it a wide berth; the wise landsman avoided the sea, the bringer of enemies.

Sea-level changes

The coastline of Crete did not look to the Minoans as it does to us. It is a classic place for changes in the relative levels of land and sea. There are two causes: *eustatic* changes in the absolute amount of water in the sea, and *tectonic* changes due to movements of the earth's crust (Chapter 3). Eustatic changes are gradual and the same everywhere, but tectonism produces sudden, local changes.

During glaciations, sea-level was lowered around Crete. Sand blown up from the exposed sea-bed was cemented to form aeolianite sandstone (p. 17). One of the most instructive deposits can be found in a collapsed sea-cave at Kakó Plaï on the north-east coast of the Akrotíri. Four aeolianite strata are separated by three strata of colluvium washed down the slope. This sequence proba-

bly reflects fluctuations in climate and sea level related to successive glaciations.

When the sea-level stays constant it eats into cliffs to produce what is commonly, if inaccurately, known as a *wave-notch*, which can be up to 3 m deep. Raulin in 1847 was the first to appreciate that the series of sea-notches at Soúyia (Se) marked former, higher, levels of the sea. Varying gradually in height, notches occur above water only round the western third of Crete (Figure 18.1), which proves that they record tectonic, not eustatic, changes. The best sequences, with up to seven successive notches, are preserved at Khrysoskalítissa and Phalásarna (Ki); these have been radiocarbon dated from splash-zone organisms which encrusted the notches when they were wet. The highest notch, 7.9 m above present sea-level, is the most recent (*c.* AD 400); the lowest, about 6.3 m above sea-level, is the oldest (*c.* 2800 BC). The notches appear to represent successive submergences of the west end of Crete, about 30 cm for each jolt, since 2800 BC. After the last notch there was a great jerk upwards, attributed to the Early Byzantine Paroxysm (p. 15).[4]

The ups-and-downs of west Crete are shown also in the aeolianite quarries at Stavrós on the Akrotíri. The quarries are partly submerged and filled with quarry debris cemented into beach-rock; but sea-notches are cut into the quarry faces. At the time of the original quarrying (which cannot be older than the Bronze Age) the land was higher than it is now, but then there was a period when it was lower than today.

The earth movement that lifted up west Crete tilted east Crete downwards. This change may have been as great as that in the west, but is less appreciated because the notches are now under water.

Wildlife of the sea and shore

Even in this polluted age, the sea around Crete is alive with edible fishes and invertebrate creatures waiting to be caught. The legendary, incomparable *skáros (Scarus cretensis)*, the only non-tropical species of parrot-fish, has been the favourite fish since Roman times.

Sea-urchins *(Paracentrotus lividus,* etc.), flapjack lobster *(Scyllarides latus)*, spiny lobster *(Palinurus elephas)*, octopus *(Octopus vulgaris)* and moray eel *(Muraena helena)* live on rocky sea-bottoms and are culinary treats. Shrimps, prawns, squid *(Ommatostrephes sagittus)* and cuttlefish *(Sepiola rondeleti)* live in open water. The small fish

18.1 *Sea-notches marking former higher relative states of the sea. West of Loutró (Sf), July 1987*

that live along the rocky shores include red mullet *(Mullus barbatus)*, scorpion-fish *(Scorpaena scrofa)*, stargazer *(Uranoscopus scaber)*, gilthead *(Sparus aurata)*, and many others – each with its Greek name. In deeper water are swordfish *(Xiphias gladius)* and tunny (tuna-fish, *Thynnus thynnus)*.

Marine fauna figure prominently in Minoan art. Dolphins decorated the walls of the 'Queen's Megaron' at Knossós (T); octopus, cuttlefish, flying fish, crabs and shark vertebrae are common motifs on Minoan pottery, jewellery and sealstones. Actual remains are rare. Shark vertebrae are known from Middle Minoan III at Kommós (Py) and Gourniá (H), and occur sporadically in Archaic, Classical and Roman contexts at Olous (Me) and Kommós.[5]

Marine molluscs formed a minor part of Minoan and Graeco-Roman diet. Limpets *(Patella* spp.), attached to rocks in the splash zone, were especially popular. The winkle *Monodonta turbinata* has been used for food and as a decorative shell since the Neolithic.[6]

'Tyrian' or Imperial Purple comes from *Murex brandaris*, a creature of moderately deep water. Its shells occur sporadically at many archaeological sites on Crete, and could be due to people using it for decoration or food (it tastes of snails). Crushed remains in industrial quantities (it takes 12,000 creatures to make enough dye to colour the trim of a single garment[7]) have been found only in Middle and Late Minoan levels at Paláikastro (Si), Mállia (Pe), and on Kouphonísi (Si). These three sites apparently monopolised the production of purple on Crete in the Bronze Age, pre-dating the better-known purple industry of Tyre by about 100 years.

Fish-bones do not survive easily in archaeological contexts. How widely sea-fish were eaten would depend on access to the sea and the perils of piracy. Fish were sold in Candia market in the fourteenth century AD; the boats were kept at a place called

Dermata.[8] Fishing-boats are occasionally shown in Monanni's pictures of 1631. A Late Venetian picture of Réthymnon (R) shows men fishing with a net and fish-traps from the town beach; Plaka's view of Goniá monastery (Ki) in 1745 depicts an angler standing where an angler often stands today.[9] Crete also consumed (and still does) stockfish, salt cod brought from northern Europe.

Because most of the coast is steep and lacks tides, rock-pools are rare. One of the few good locations is the extreme south-west corner near Khrysoskalítissa (Ki). The conglomerate has been hollowed by wave action, resulting in pool after pool teeming with small fish, bright pink algae, crabs and the like, and extraordinary seaweeds such as the living bag *Codium bursa*.

Sand-dunes are scattered round Crete, especially on the Pyrgiótissa coast, at the south-west corner of the island, and on the southern islets. They have a rich flora, including two special trees, sea-juniper (p. 63) and tamarisk. In spring the dunes are pink with the blossoms of the little *Silene colorata*, followed by the yellow flowers of the white-leaved *Medicago marina* and *Otanthus maritimus*. The famous sea-lily, *Pancratium maritimum*, is a dune plant. On some dunes there are the spiny, pale-green, sheep-sized tussocks of *Centaurea spinosa*. Plants of other coastal localities, such as cliffs and aeolianite, include the Cretan palm (p. 65), the recently-discovered *Silene greuteri*, and the yellow poppy *Glaucium flavum*. The fleshy umbellifer *Crithmum maritimum*, one of the two plants known in England as samphire, is gathered from the rocks and eaten as *glystrídha*.[10]

Sea-wolves

The ecology of Crete was for millennia distorted by piracy. The classical Greeks believed that Minos, king of Knossós, acquired a navy in order to suppress pirates.[11] Piracy was the *casus belli* for the Roman and Turkish conquests.

Cretans themselves had a reputation as pirates and slavers. Already in Homer, Odysseus *incognito* could pass himself off as a respectable Cretan buccaneer.[12] It may be no accident that the seventh century BC Law Code of Górtyn has much to say about slaves and ransoms, for example:

> If anyone, bound by necessity, should get a man gone away to a strange place set free from a foreign city at his own request, he shall be in the power of the one who ransomed him until he pay what is due.
>
> *(column VI)*

In Hellenistic times the harbours of Crete may have been largely used as pirate bases and for disposal of booty.[13]

Crete has experienced more of the other side of Mediterranean piracy. Much of the good land lies on coastal plains. In the Roman and Byzantine periods, when pirates were efficiently executed, these plains were thickly populated. At other times they have been risky places, to which people came trembling from inland villages to plough, sow and harvest; for long periods they were abandoned. This pattern goes back into prehistory, with the contrast between the populous coastlands of the Minoan Palace Period and their desertion at the end of the Bronze Age.[14]

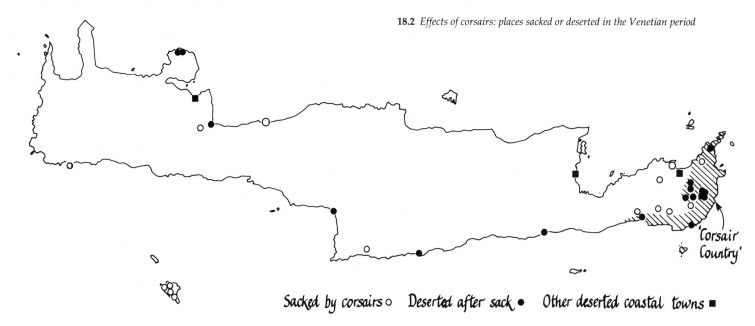

18.2 *Effects of corsairs: places sacked or deserted in the Venetian period*

Sacked by corsairs ○   Deserted after sack ●   Other deserted coastal towns ■

Corsairs

In the Venetian period piracy was no amateurish affair of tipsy buccaneers flying the Jolly Roger. It attracted investment and personnel like any other branch of the shipping business. Muslim corsairs operated, at first from Turkey, later from North Africa; their Christian brethren included the Knights Hospitallers at Malta. Each side was perpetually at war with the infidel, even when Venice and the Sultan were supposed to be at peace. Their objective was booty and prisoners: not so much slaves (trouble-some and unrewarding) as persons for whom ransoms could be arranged. Corsairs earned their dividends by taking infidel ships, but undertook forays on land when it was safe to do so.[15] By the time Muslim corsairs reached Crete, they would be running short of provisions (especially water) and might need to land before going on to the shipping lanes around Kárpathos.[16]

The corsair problem was partly created by the Fourth Crusade in 1204, which broke Byzantine naval power. The earliest medieval documents record a few settlements in remote, exposed coastal localities, like Erimópolis (Si) and Myrtos (H). From the fourteenth century onwards documents speak of organising shipping in convoys for protection, and then report increasing attacks on land. The far-east of Crete, close to shipping lanes and remote from Venetian garrisons, was hardest hit – particularly in the great raid of 1471. Many villages, some of them 15 km inland, disappear from the lists of inhabited places (Figure 18.2). Only the monks of Our Lady of the Cape (Toploú (Si)) built high walls and defied the corsairs – although even they were sacked by the Knights Hospitallers in a moment of absent-mindedness.

By the sixteenth century, almost the only permanent settlements on the coast of Crete were the cities and castled towns. Even these were not safe: Réthymnon (R) was sacked by Khair-ed-Din of the Red Beard in 1538, and again in 1567 and 1571. For a hundred years *Provveditori* and *Rettori* listed the abandoned coastal plains, and shook their heads over the number of measures of wheat not being grown. Nothing short of Turkish conquest could solve the problem.

We hear of coastguard defence in the form of *vigle*, look-out posts to which local people were assigned on guard duty; they were supposed to burn fires at night to show that they were at their posts. Nearly 2,000 men were supposed to watch the sea every night in summer. Occasionally this worked: one night in 1556, corsairs ventured 4 km into the Asteroúsia Mountains to sack Andiskári (Ka), but the men of Pigaidhákia (Ka) grabbed weapons, intercepted their getaway and recovered the prisoners.[17] A seventeenth-century file of letters deals with hundreds of *vigle*, which could be on mountain-tops well inland.[18] *Vigle* are little round stone structures on hilltops, which often sit on ancient sites and puzzle archaeologists.

Suppression of piracy was one of the functions for which the Venetians maintained galleys in Crete. The great vaulted arsenals at Khaniá (Ky) are each big enough to house one galley. They were built in the late sixteenth century; eleven of the original nineteen survive, two being in ruins. In the middle ages the 'triremes', like those of antiquity, were propelled by hired rowers; they got pay rises in 1422 and 1471.[19] Later the Venetians avoided this expense by using *angarie,* labour services. This was an unpopular task: the conscripted men rowed alongside convicts, and the galleys spent much of their time on distant duties which brought little benefit to Crete. Galleys, each rowed by 168 men[20] besides soldiers and crew, were a drain on the manpower of Crete.

The Turkish conquest brought relief. As subjects of the Grand Turk, Cretans were no longer supposed to be attacked by Muslim corsairs who were Ottoman subjects too. Nor did they have to spend months at the oar. Christian corsairs could prey on Turks and Muslim Cretans; but they found that to plunder Christians, even Orthodox, led to trouble with the Holy Inquisition. Corsairs scourged the Mediterranean until 1820, but they no longer devastated Crete.

The corsair landscape

Settlement returned slowly to the abandoned land: people did not quickly break a bitterly-learned habit. Even in 1868 they were reluctant to cultivate the Frangokástello Plain because it was too exposed to attack from the sea.[21] A few coastal villages, such as Myrtos (H) with its grid of streets, were founded (or re-founded) in the late nineteenth century, but coastal settlement was not well established until the 1930s after a break of some 400 years.

In far-east Crete there is a landscape of colonisation, roughly contemporary with the colonisation of eastern North America. In the early Turkish period people began to drift back, re-founding villages mostly where there had been villages centuries before; the names were still remembered, and the churches, which the corsairs could not carry away, were reused. To live in the arid far-east-Cretan environment was not an art that could be re-learnt in one or two human generations. By the end of the nineteenth century, the area achieved a spell of prosperity; but since then, cultivation has retreated again to places, like Ano Zákro (Si), that have good springs. High, arid, shelterless, waterless villages like Karydhi and Xerolímni (Si) are sliding towards desertion.

Far-east Crete today is remarkable for the scarcity of terracing: what terraces exist are mostly very degraded and could easily date from before the abandonment. Probably in a colonial landscape labour was at a premium, and the population never outran the land that could be cultivated on the flat.

Shipping and harbours

Harbours for small ships were numerous in ancient Crete. Among Bronze Age harbours, Amnisos (Pe) (the port of Bronze Age Knossós) and Mókhlos (Si) are well known. There is Bronze Age material around most of the later harbours, for instance Khersónisos (Pe) and Loutró (Sf).

Almost every classical and Hellenistic city-state had access to a harbour; some were shared.[22] The *Stadiasmós*, an undated description of Aegean coasts, has a number of terms for different kinds of harbour and anchorage. Ancient harbours can be difficult to recognise because they have been submerged or uplifted through tectonic movements. A famous example is the uplifted harbour at Phalásarna (Ki) on the west coast, where a recent re-investigation indicates that this harbour went out of use long before the uplift; it may have been artificially blocked to deny it to pirates.[23]

In the middle ages, by far the most important ports were Candia and Canea (Herákleion (T) and Khaniá (Ky)). Candia had an artifical harbour, which has always given trouble: for example, in 1395 a galley was built expressly to carry stones for repairing the mole. The port of Canea, although protected by a natural reef of rock, needed frequent attention. In 1396 an engineer was appointed to the two ports at a salary of 450 *hyperpera* a year (six times the pay of a common rower). The Venetians probably found this arrangement convenient for preventing smuggling, and did not encourage the building of other harbours.

Although Herákleion and its predecessor Amnisos did not have good harbours, the sites have a unique advantage which goes far to explain why the chief town of the island should always have been near here; it may help to explain the otherwise nondescript location of Knossós (T). The four harbours on the nearby islet of Dhía (Pe) are better than any in Crete; a ship approaching the north coast could make for these harbours and wait for a favourable wind to land at Candia or Amnisos.

The Sphakiots had their own shipping (p. 134), which operated out of the inadequate and inaccessible harbour at Loutró. In the seventeenth and eighteenth centuries they got as far in the shipowning business as any Cretans have done. Spratt in the 1850s found a small shipowning Muslim community living in the castle on Spinalónga Island (Me); they traded as far as England. The general improvement in communications within Crete, beginning about this time, involved the sea as well as roads. Improvements in rigging and ship design, as well as the disappearance of piracy, made coastal traffic safer and more efficient. Many little harbours can still be identified by decayed nineteenth-century warehouses, where coasting caiques used to pick up sacks of carobs or set down planks or millstones.

Notes

1 Noiret (see bibliography), p. 7 520.

2 See J. H. Pryor (1988), *Geography, Technology, and War: Studies in the Maritime History of the Mediterranean 649–1571*, Cambridge, Cambridge University Press.

3 R. Hägg and N. Marinatos (eds.) (1984), *The Minoan Thalassocracy: Myth and Reality*, Stockholm, Swedish Institute in Athens.

4 Y. and J. Thommeret et al. (1981), 'Late Holocene shoreline changes and seismo-tectonic displacements in western Crete', *Zeitschrift für Geomorphologie*, **NF Suppl**. 40, 127- 49.

5 D. S. Reese (1984), 'Shark and ray remains in Aegean and Cypriote archaeology,' *Opuscula Atheniensia*, **15**, 188-192.

6 D. S. Reese (1984), 'Topshell rings in the Aegean Bronze Age', *BSA*, **79**, 237-8.

7 D. S. Reese (1987), 'Palaikastro shells and Bronze Age purple dye production in the Mediterranean basin', *BSA*, **82**, 201-6.

8 ASV: DC b.14bis c.64v; Vidulich (see bibliography), p. 51.

9 A. Nenedhakis (A. Νενεδάκης) (1983), *Ρέθεμνος: τριάντα αιώνες πολιτεία*, Athens, pp. 17, 24–5.

10 For coastal vegetation in general see: G. Gehu et al. (1987), 'Données sur la végétation littorale de la Crète', *Ecologia Mediterranea*, **13**, 93-105.

11 Thucydides, *History*, I.iv.

12 *Odyssey*, XIV.202ff.

13 On early piracy see R.F. Willetts (1965), *Ancient Crete: A Social History*, London, Routledge, ch. XI; P. Brulé (1978), *La Piraterie Crétoise Hellénistique*, Paris, Centre de Recherches d'Histoire Ancienne, Besançon, vol. **27**.

14 Moody (1992, Chapter 8, note 4).

15 P. Èarle (1970), *Corsairs of Malta and Barbary*, London, Sidgwick & Jackson.

16 Pryor (1988, note 2).

17 ASV: Provv. Terra e Mar b. 728, letter from Rector of Candia 10 Aug. 1556.

18 MCV: Cicogna 2712.

19 Noiret (see bibliography), pp. 294, 512.

20 ASV: DC b.82 (*relazione* of Benetto Dolfin).

21 J. F. H. Skinner (1968, Chapter 13, note 6), p. 197.

22 V. Niniou-Kindeli (Β. Νινιού-Κινδελή) (1990), 'Στοιχεία για την οδική σύνδεση της Λισσού με την Υρτακίνα και την Έλυρου', *Πεπράγμενα του ΣΤ' Διεθνούς Κρητολογικού Συνέδριου*, Α2, 49-58.

23 F. Frost and E. Hadjidaki (1990), 'Excavations at the harbor at Phalasarna in Crete: the 1988 season', *Hesperia*, **59**, 513-27.

19

Islets

… they sailed close by Crete. But not long after there arose … a tempestuous wind, called Euroclydon. And when the ship was caught, and could not bear up into the wind, we let her drive. And running under a certain island, which is called Clauda, we had much work to come by the boat …

Acts of the Apostles, **28**, 13-16
[one of the few ancient references to Gávdhos]

22 June 1318. Publicly proclaimed by Richard, herald, that nobody dare to go to the island of Cuffonisia, [property] of the nobleman Nicholas Pantaleon Pataruli, to cut wood or take little animals or do anything new or damaging … on pain of 25 hyperpera, *without permission of the said Nicholas Pantaleon.*

Kouphonísi in the *Book of Bans* [1]

Crete has about thirty-four offshore islets (Figure 19.2). We have visited six and have gathered varying information about the rest. Only Gávdhos (Se) still has a permanent population, cultivating terraces and growing, grinding and baking their own grain (Figure 19.1). Anyone sympathetic to the old-fashioned Cretan way of life will find it a wonderful and enlightening place. Getting to Gávdhos, and especially leaving it, can be an adventure: we remind the visitor of what happened to St Paul in those waters, as quoted above. Gaidharonísi (H), ('Donkey Island' – you may call it Khrysí ('Golden'), if you think it rude to mention donkeys) is the most accessible: boats go from Ierápetra in summer. It is grimly hot and rocky, with ravenous seabirds and curious little woods of 'cedars' (sea-juniper). The Dhionysiádhes, three white ghosts that shimmer on the horizon from Siteía, must be among Europe's least known islands.

Mókhlos (Si), an important Minoan and Roman site, has only recently become an island by rising relative sea-level. On many of the islets the sea-level has risen since Roman times, but on Gávdhos (Se) and Ay. Theódhoroi (Ky) it has fallen.

19.1 *Old-fashioned cultivation: Vatsianá, Gávdhos. May 1989*

Environment

These, like most small Greek islands, are more arid-looking than the mainland, despite being usually less browsed in recent years. The coasts of Crete are drier than the interior, and this effect extends out to sea. Gávdhos (Se) is an exception: it rises to 350 m, and its south-west side is a wall of cliff which evidently attracts rain and mist. The islets are very windy: wind blows away the soil and raises great sand-dunes, especially on Kouphonísi (Si).

The islets are varied in shape, from pancakes to pinnacles, and diverse geologically. Kouphonísi is an island of marl, conglomerate and sand-dunes. Pseíra is a tilted outlier of platey limestone and sandstone, with tremendous cliffs. Gaidharonísi (H) is partly igneous, apparently the outpouring of an underwater volcano.

Gávdhos has a core of hard limestone and metamorphics, thickly overlaid with marls and sandstones. It is much more erodible than Crete, full of active gullies, with one gigantic badland. At the southern tip Gávdhos runs out into a spine pierced by the Kamarélles, 'Little Arches', three great sea-caves – a fittingly dramatic end to Europe.

The islets are short of water: Gávdhos has small springs but relies mainly on cisterns. Otherwise the only sources are shallow, brackish wells on beaches.

Flora

The islets are unlike Crete in their flora. The remoter ones have been cut off for at least hundreds of thousands of years; few Cretan endemics reached them. *Verbascum spinosum*, one of the commonest plants of Sphakiá, is unknown on Gávdhos. *Ebenus cretica* is very common in south-east Crete, but not known from Kouphonísi or Gaidharonísi, which ought to be excellent habitats. As far as we know, the islets have developed few endemics of their own: Kouphonísi has a peculiar form of *Anthyllis hermanniae*, big dense spiny tussocks with yellow flowers.

Several African plants reach the islets but not Crete itself. An example is the desert undershrub *Periploca angustifolia*, common on Gávdhos and Gaidharonísi. The legume *Astragalus peregrinus* reaches Kouphonísi. *Androcymbium rechingeri* gets to Elaphonísi (Ki), but not, apparently, the hundred metres or so further to mainland Crete.[2]

Many other plants are missing from the islets. Gaidharonísi, Gávdhos and Kouphonísi have no cypress, no oak, and are blessedly free of spiny-broom and Jerusalem sage. However, one of the

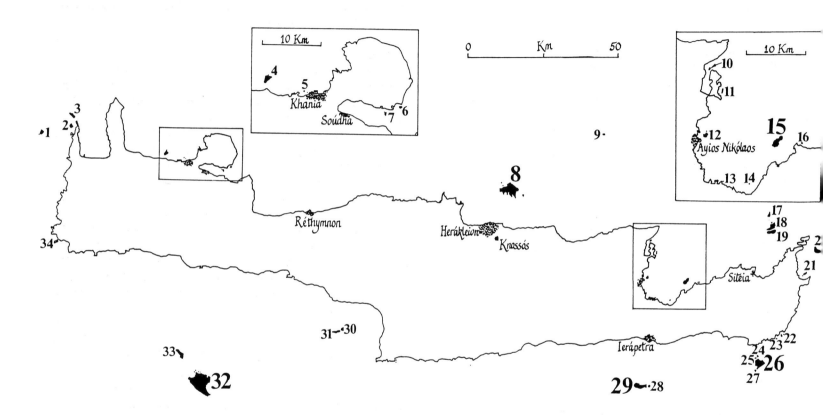

19.2 *Islets around Crete*

Number on map		Area sq km	Altitude m	
1	Pondikonísi (Mouse I.)	0.3	164	
2	Imeri (Tame) Gramboúsa	0.7	124	castle
3	Agria (Wild) Gramboúsa	0.7	103	
4	Turlurú, Ay. Theódhoroi	0.8	156	2 castles; *agrími*; cave
5	Lazarétta	0.02	low	old quarantine station for Khaniá port
6	Maráthi, Pálaia Soúdha	0.09	low	
7	Soúdha	0.12	low	castle
8	Dhía	12	268	*agrími*; Neolithic; Minoan
9	Avgó	unknown	low	
10	Spinalónga Island	0.08	c. 30	castle; modern leper settlement
11	Kolokytha	0.12	low	
12	Ay. Pándes	0.35	c. 50	*agrími*
13	Vryonísi	0.01	c. 25	cliff inscription; Byzantine fort or monastery?
14	Kónidha	0.02	low	
15	Pseíra	1.4	204	Minoan town; Byzantine monastery
16	Mókhlos	0.07	c. 50	Minoan & Roman site (but then not an island)
	Dhionysiádhes:			
17	Paximádha (Rusk)	0.3	133	
18	Dhragonádha	3.2	128	
19	Gianisádha	2.0	147	
20	Elassa	1.8	72	
21	Grándes	0.24	42	
22	Kavállous	0.013	59	
23	Koúmita	0.03	11	
24	Strongyló (Round Island)	0.13	19	
25	Laphonísi, Makroúlo	0.06	7	
26	Koúphonisi	4.2	86	Minoan, Roman town
27	Trákhylos	0.10	43	
28	Mikronísi	0.13	16	
29	Gaidharonísi (Donkey I.)	5.1	27	Minoan & Roman
30	Little Paximádhi (Rusk)	0.6	166	
31	Great Paximádhi	1.1	252	
32	Gávdhos	29.8	345	copious Minoan & Roman
33	Gavdhópoula	2.6	133	
34	Elaphonísi (Hart Island)	0.5	low	

commonest undershrubs on Gávdhos is *Globularia alypum*, absent from the adjacent part of Crete.

Vegetation

Most of the islets are barren-looking. The three on which *agrímia* have been put (p. 47) are extremely browsed: Dhía (Pe) has nothing more than phrygana and the occasional lentisk shrub; on Ay. Theódhoroi (Ky) the extremely distasteful woody *Euphorbia dendroides* is prominent. Most of the others are now little browsed, and this shows in their vegetation. Vryonísi (Me), separated by a narrow (but deep) strait, has abundant *Atriplex halimus*, a very palatable undershrub rare on the mainland opposite. Kouphonísi (Si) has hardly a tree except a few big tamarisks buried in the dunes, but it has a remarkable set of big undershrubs, including sheep-sized tussocks of a special form of *Anthyllis hermanniae* and some of the largest *Atriplex halimus* in Crete; steppe is abundant and varied.

Three are more vegetated. Pseíra has maquis of lentisk, the common coastal shrub. Gaidharonísi (H) is more than half low tangles of land-juniper, lentisk and sea-juniper. The woods are relatively stable; some of the sea-junipers are more than 200 years old.

Gávdhos is dramatically wooded, more than half tree-covered. Sea-juniper, here also called 'cedar', is more extensive than anywhere in Crete; the woods have a bizarre appearance because the trees die back from time to time, looking (in Xan Fielding's words) 'like pagan prophets struck dead while uttering a blasphemy, each limb a pointed curse'.[3] There are also land-juniper, lentisk and Cretan pine; woods of the latter are often bent almost horizontal by the wind. All these woods have sprung up in the last 120 years. Before this the island was virtually treeless. In the 1850s it had 'no trees or shrubs, except a few karoubs in the valleys, and a sort of stunted juniper growing amidst the blown sands upon the northern shore'.[4] There are, however, a few older sea-junipers scattered among fields.

The cultural landscape

Gávdhos has been intensively cultivated; about 80 per cent of the island is terraced under the trees. The remaining little fields grow old-fashioned varieties of wheat and barley. Livestock are down to about 1,000 goats; vines are confined to one spot; olives are restricted to sheltered places; and the island is noted for beekeeping. In an area of about 35 sq. km there are at least seventeen hamlets, mostly with -*aná* names, about five of which are still inhabited. The houses are austere and old-fashioned, mostly of the *kéntis* type with big sea-juniper timbers; the *kamára* has yet to find acceptance in Gávdhos.

Gaidharonísi and Kouphonísi were cultivated until about the 1950s by people coming from the mainland. Only rabbits browse them today.

Prehistory and ancient history

Apart from Gávdhos, none of the islets has been inhabited for 1,500 years, except by lighthousemen and the occasional hermit. At most they have been visited by herders or cultivators from the mainland. This lack of recent settlement is in contrast to the sometimes extraordinary richness of the Minoan and Roman past. Gávdhos and Dhía were even inhabited in the Neolithic.

On Pseíra there was a Minoan town, excavated by Richard Seager and recently again by Philip Betancourt.[5] It ran to fine buildings, fine pottery and wall-paintings. The island was highly cultivated, with terraces of massive construction (p. 143). Gávdhos, Gaidharonísi, Kouphonísi, and possibly Dhía also had important Minoan communities, still to be investigated in detail.

In the second century BC the island of Claudos [Gávdhos] tithed all its products by land and sea, excluding flocks, vegetables, and harbour-dues, to the temple of Pythian Apollo in Górtyn.[6]

Kouphonísi has the remains of a considerable Roman town, with brickwork, mosaics, huge cisterns and even a theatre. The remains of a great marble statue on a stepped pyramidal base still crown the summit of the island. Gávdhos is full of less well-defined Roman remains. Much of the island is densely strewn with Roman sherds, left behind by the soil blowing away. It is the only island significantly mentioned by Roman writers, who say that it had a temple of Aphrodite and later its own bishop. Gaidharonísi also has a Roman village, with field-systems, tombs and probably a sawn-off basilica; it may previously have had a Hellenistic settlement. Two Roman sites are reported from Dhía.[7] Even little Vryonísi (Me) has an inscription carved into a cliff.

Pseíra came back into use in Early Byzantine times, when there was a short-lived monastery. There may be a similar one on Vryonísi.

Venetian

The islets lapsed into obscurity. Except for Gávdhos, they seem never to have been re-settled – although Tame Gramboúsa, Turlurú (Ay. Theódhoroi), Gaidharonísi and Kouphonísi have medieval chapels.

The *Book of Bans* in the fourteenth century has entries for Kouphonísi and 'Standia' (Dhía). Kouphonísi was private property and trespassers were warned off it. A large fine on poachers suggests that it may have been a rabbit-warren. Kouphonísi, Gaidharonísi and some other islets have rabbits today, which are not wild on mainland Crete. The rabbit is a west Mediterranean animal, introduced at an unknown date to various small Aegean islands such as Délos, presumably (as on similar islets in medieval England) for meat and fur. Dhía was state property: in 1360 the grazing was advertised to the public at so much per animal, and poaching was prohibited under penalty of only 2 *hyperpera.*

Buondelmonti in 1415 visited (and confused) Gaidharonísi and Kouphonísi. It was probably on Kouphonísi that he noticed

> multitudes of birds wandering like infants pissing in the night, which are busy feeding their chicks, white like pigeons, under unbreakable grasses for making ropes.

The island still has the tough grass *Lygeum spartum,* and its cliffs still resound to the cries of gulls and shearwaters. Gaidharonísi was

> flat and formerly beautiful with monks. It produces trees of varnish and a multitude of *hebanus.*

The varnish-trees could be lentisk, which produces a resin, but *hebanus* is a puzzle – was it sea-juniper? Remains of outbuildings around the chapel today suggest a monastery.

All we know about medieval Gávdhos is that it had at least three chapels. By 1622 it was permanently inhabited by a few poor Sphákiots, but others came over from Sphakiá to cultivate it. Then there was a nasty incident. The great English corsair Sanson descended with seven Tunisian ships, presumably to occupy Gávdhos as a base. He caught about 200 Sphakiots on the island, sacked their houses and churches, stole their animals, ruined their crops, took some of them prisoner, and ran the others to earth in caves. The Venetian authorities sent militia under Monanni (the topographer) to dislodge the pirates, which was done after a four-sided quarrel involving the arrest of a French and a Knights Hospitaller captain. Monanni sent in a lengthy report accompanied by a beautiful aerial view of the islet, which was treeless except for a few cliffs and dunes and small patches elsewhere.[8] Many of the present place-names are recognisable; the huge gully at the north-west corner already existed.

Later history

After the Turkish conquest, Gávdhos exchanged Muslim corsairs for Christian, with whom, maybe, the inhabitants got on a little better. The traveller Pococke in 1745 reported that 'the Maltese corsairs supply themselves there.' The island prospered, reaching a peak in the nineteenth century. Raulin in 1845 was told that there were 1,500 inhabitants – a figure which he, like ourselves, found incredibly large. In 1881 the population is given as 417. There are a few ambitious houses from this period.

Four islets – Tame Gramboúsa, Turlurú (Ay. Theódhoroi), Soúdha (Ky), and Spinalónga (Me) – have Late Venetian castles. Turlurú was the scene of a great battle at the Conquest. The other three were kept at the surrender and remained in Venetian hands until 1715: one wonders how it felt to be a Venetian governor relegated to these outposts. Spinalónga became a Muslim town, and after the Muslims were expelled, a place of relegation for all the lepers in Crete. Soúdha Island is one of two Cretan castles still in military use – a decayed castle of the North Atlantic Treaty Organisation.

In the early twentieth century Gávdhos and Kouphonísi acquired magnificent lighthouses (the one on Kouphonísi built of blocks robbed from the Roman pyramid), but both were blown up by the British in World War II and never reinstated.

During the twentieth century Gávdhos has declined. The fields fell out of use: the shelly sand, if not constantly disturbed, forms a strong crust which discourages further ploughing. From a state of 80 per cent cultivation and 20 per cent pasture it has become 60 per cent woodland and 4 per cent cultivation. After World War II it had a penal settlement; exile there was more fearful than prison.[9] Many of the people today have emigrated to a Gávdhiot colony in the town of Palaiókhora (Se), but come back for the summer. Remoteness has so far protected Gávdhos from the usual kind of development, which would have destroyed a traditional way of life that its remaining inhabitants value.

Conclusions

The islets are a puzzle. The contrast between the desolate present and the consistently rich Minoan and Roman past could not be stronger. What drove so many people to live, and live at times comfortably, on these specks of land? Not ordinary agriculture. Some of the islands were a little bigger when relative sea-level was lower; their environment may have been better; but no conceivable change of environment would make them more attractive than mainland Crete. Their folk were evidently doing something special. What was it?

An essential for settlement on small islands is freedom from pirate raids. Only Gávdhos, the biggest, seems to have come (by a hair's breadth) through the corsair period. Were the islanders pirates themselves? This has been proposed for Kouphonísi, but can hardly apply to all the islands. A lower sea-level than now could have given Gaidharonísi a harbour and a better water-supply.

We conjecture that there was some special crop or practice associated with each island – for example, sponge-diving, or growing *hebanus* (whatever that was) or extracting Imperial Purple from the murexes whose shells abundantly litter Kouphonísi.

Notes
1 Vidulich (see bibliography), no. 194.
2 W. Greuter (1967), 'Contributiones floristicae austro-aegaeae 10-12', *Candollea*, **22**, 233-53.
3 X. Fielding (1953), *The Stronghold*, London, Secker & Warburg.
4 Spratt (see bibliography), II. 154, confirmed by Raulin (1868, see bibliography), p. 930.
5 P. P. Betancourt and C. Davaras (1988), 'Excavations at Pseira, 1985 and 1986', *Hesperia*, **57**, 207-26; Davaras et al. (1992, Chapter 16, note 12).
6 Willetts (1965, Chapter 18, note 13); *Inscriptiones Creticae*, **4**, 184.
7 Sanders (see bibliography), p. 146.
8 ASV: DC: Lettere dei Rettori di Candia, busta 10; CD: Rettori di Candia F.10/1.
9 X. Fielding (1953, note 3).

20

Conservation and the future

*our government of Crete has written ... on the subject of filth ... thrown out
of our city of Candida [Herákleion (T)], which over time and time has grown
into great mountains called* Copreas *[dunghills], so that unless something is
done our city will in a short time be uninhabitable, both because of the space
taken up by these many and great* copreae, *and because of the stink and
corruption and uncleanness of the air ... Agreed ... the said* copreae *or filth
shall be completely taken away and carried out of the city ... and in the place
where there are* copreae *of private persons, when they are carried away, some
structure or house shall be built, or such a fence shall be made that no more
filth shall be thrown there ...*
  For 72 – against 1 – abstentions 2.

Decree of the Venetian Senate, 1407 [1]

The impact of civilised mankind on islands has generally been disastrous. There are many dreadful examples, such as St Helena, where the indigenous ecosystem collapsed within decades. Pigs and rats replaced native animals; felled woods did not sprout; aggressive and commonplace exotics displaced native plants; unstable soils washed into the sea.

Crete was not so fragile. Disaster stopped at the destruction of the indigenous mammals. Exotic creatures did not overrun the island; it retained its indigenous plants and its soils. This was probably because Crete, unlike many islands, had had large animals, so that the flora had already adapted to cope with browsing. Crete was not volcanic; any fragile soils had already been lost in Pleistocene erosions.

Successive Cretan civilisations learned to live with their environment and with the native (and long-introduced) plants and animals. They created one of the most beautiful and harmonious landscapes in the world,[2] and avoided the sudden boom-and-bust cycles reported from other Mediterranean mountain countries.[3] But for centuries, travellers from France, Britain and mainland Greece, finding Crete different from their homelands, have pronounced it a 'degraded land' and have presumed to tell Cretans how they ought to run their country. This is a gross misunderstanding. On the contrary, traditional Crete has much to tell the rest of the world about living in harmony with the landscape.

Over the last twenty years, however, this harmony has broken down. This fact is instantly impressed on visitors arriving at Herákleion Airport. But elsewhere the outsider should not rush to judgement. Much of the harmony still remains; the rest of the world can still learn from aspects of Cretan land management. Some practices, which appear to most outsiders to be destructive, are traditional and normal. For example, we do not endorse the blame heaped upon shepherds and goatherds and their flocks; grazing and occupational burning are essential to maintain the Cretan landscape. The recent increase of trees and grazing-sensitive plants is sufficient evidence that they are not, in general, carried to excess.

We are concerned to identify those changes which are real, and are not part of the normal dynamics of the landscape – particularly those which extend the commonplace at the expense of what is rare or beautiful or has meaning, or which de-Cretanise Crete and make it the same as everywhere else. It is not the changes as such which we take exception to, but the tendency to carry them to extremes. Olives, roads and irrigation are all good in themselves, but they have spread to such a degree that we doubt whether those who are responsible know when to stop.

Tourism

In the middle ages, Crete was a stopping-place on the pilgrim route to Jerusalem. In the nineteenth century, Khaniá (Ky) had a modest tourist trade from people going to the Suez Canal (and also, we are told, from Egyptian holidaymakers). It is less obvious why Crete (rather than, say, Sardinia) should have had such a huge attraction for tourists from the 1970s onwards. It is a uniquely glamorous island, but the majority of tourists ignore the glamour and remain on an unexciting and tideless beach.

We need not dwell on the uglification of Crete by hundreds of hotels, in a foreign style of architecture, neither beautiful nor functional, which makes no concession to its surroundings. Some of the more recent architecture is better, but hotels still appear at random, often in the most inappropriate situations. The only even partly successful constraints on their building are archaeological and military regulations. Hotels bring trouble with sewage and rubbish – one way to get rid of rubbish is to throw it into the sea and let the next resort deal with it. Some have walled sea-fronts, which destroy (by marine erosion) the very beach on which their livelihood depends. Hotels are not even very efficient in promoting the prosperity of Crete, for much of the income generated goes to foreign operators. Tourism tends to move on when fashion changes, leaving dereliction behind.

So far, hotels have spoilt about one-eighth of the coast of Crete – but they could be built tomorrow almost anywhere on the remainder. By the mercy of Providence, most of the densely built-up coasts are in the least distinctive parts of the island.

Recently a number of hotels have begun to take the initiative in coming to terms with their environment. A conference was held on the subject at Réthymnon (R) in 1992. Hoteliers are coming to appreciate that holidaymakers do not enjoy surroundings which they would not tolerate at home. One hotel began the battle to save the Aposelémi Delta, a first-class site for aquatic birds, knowing that many visitors are birdwatchers.

One of the few definite successes in conservation is due to the Sea Turtle Protection Society of Greece. It might be thought that turtle-beaches and hotels are utterly incompatible, but this turns out not to be so. On the island of Zákynthos turtles have become a matter of local pride, and visitors take an intense interest in caring for them. There are signs that this is happening at Réthymnon also.

Farming

The great changes in Cretan husbandry in the last sixty years have brought prosperity to farmers with suitable land, and have put many others out of business. A few crops have been intensified at the expense of a diversity of crops. Crete produces excellent oranges, which have grown here for centuries. But now all the warm valley bottoms of north-west Crete, once a mixture of culti-vation, are filled with orange-groves, in which there is little wildlife but a few ordinary tropical weeds. The economics are dubious. In each of the last four seasons much of the crop has been thrown into ravines or fed to sheep.

Greater still is the increase in olives, which comes on top of previous increases. It is hard to oppose the ancient craft of olive-cultivation, but when most Cretan valleys are a sea of olives from cliff to cliff the point has been reached when enough is enough. (Many other Mediterranean valleys are a sea of olives too.) Whether it will be possible to gather or to sell all these olives remains to be seen, but other evils follow. The invention of plastic pipes has brought the idea that the irrigation of olives is a necessity rather than a bonus. The search for water has dried up rivers and springs. At the time of writing it is proposed to destroy the Sphakoúriac Gorge (Am) – one of very few phyllite gorges – by a dam, and most other non-limestone valleys are at risk. Olive processing produces nasty residues, which pollute the remaining river water. All this is for a subsidised monoculture unlikely to last long.

Plastic greenhouses are a not-so-new technology: one of us remembers the first ones, tunnels supported on bent reeds, in the Ierápetra Plain in 1968. They have a bad reputation, especially among those who work in them, for the over-use of toxic chemicals. Often they grow crops which are better grown elsewhere. They are ugly, especially as (like all greenhouses) they are derelict for much of their lives. (In 1988 about one-third of those in the Myrtos (H) area were in ruins.) The plastic ends by blowing about Crete until it reaches the sea. However, the idea is not intrinsically bad; some of the greenhouses are being replaced by more permanent structures.

The bulldozer

Crete has for centuries been very well supplied with roads, and it is extremely easy to bulldoze new roads. The English or American visitor will be astounded at the density of roads, which reach almost every place however remote or insigificant. There is even a hare-brained – though well advanced – scheme for a road from Anópolis (Sf) to Thérisso (Ky) over the High Desert, and rumours of others intersecting the gorges on the south coast. It is evidently still not thought that enough is enough, or that there are certain landscapes which intrinsically ought not to have roads. Standards of roadmaking are not what they were: lack of construction is made up for by extra width.

The bulldozer is also the principal instrument of cultivation. When the level ground was used up, big terraces were carved out of the hillsides to grow more olives, or – surprisingly often – to grow nothing. The idea got about that stone walls were unnecessary. Although the amount of bulldozed terracing (or re-terracing) has a long way to go before it catches up with the abandonment of old terraces, a large area of maquis has been bulldozed in the phyllite-quartzite hills of Kydhonía in the last few years to grow even more olives.

Why Cretans love the bulldozer is not clear (the Peloponnese and Sardinia get by with far less roadmaking and terracing). Its effects are ugly and destroy the archaeology; roads often undermine ancient chapels. Terracing and roadmaking are not quite so destructive of vegetation: existing trees are nearly always spared and abandoned areas grow over again. However, they promote erosion on a much larger scale than anything else. It is unfortunate that such destructive methods should be used for projects unlikely to be of permanent value.

Dereliction

Anyone upholding Cretan values will be distressed at the decline and depopulation of the mountains. Houses are abandoned, the local factory closes, the school closes, the coffee-house struggles on for a few aged customers, but when they die there are no successors. This usually happens in hamlet country, and every time something special to Crete is lost. Another group of Cretans has given up their fierce independence and taken to town- or village-dwelling like the rest of Europe.

Things may not be as bad as they seem. A move to Herákleion (T) or even Athens does not necessarily mean giving up the mountain home. The decline in population follows a period of unreasonably high population fifty years ago. To some extent it is counterbalanced by the tendency of fewer people to live in a house: a settlement may lose one-third of its population yet stay the same size. Something like this has happened at least twice before in Cretan history.

Nevertheless, dereliction does result in the disappearance of the beautiful and distinctive terraced cultivation and gardening. The land becomes wooded, which may not be a bad thing except that most of the distinctive plants of Crete are not adapted to shade. However, all too often Crete follows the inexorable Mediterranean sequence of abandonment leading to pinewoods leading to terrible wildfires.

What can be done to induce people to stay in the mountains? In our view, there is a need to encourage inland tourism – not building hotels, but providing modest accommodation in existing houses for people who enjoy mountains. If this works in the modest, rainy mountains of England, why not in the glorious mountains of Crete? This is controversial; some people claim that inland development would escalate out of control as it has done along the coast. But it seems unlikely that the mountains will attract a mass market. If only 1 per cent of the tourists prefer the mountains to the coast, this could make all the difference to the survival of mountain communities.

There seems to us to be a real need for a good telephone system.

Buildings

We have mentioned the obtrusiveness of hotels, but new (and not-so-new) houses are almost as bad. Cretan architecture has been stuck in the 1930s for the last forty years. At the same time the tens of thousands of derelict vernacular buildings are not appreciated. Renovating these is expensive and difficult; there are few craftsmen who know how to do it.

The design of new churches is better than of houses or hotels, and some have magnificent new Cretan wall-paintings inside. This cannot be said of restorations of old chapels. Modern cement and old masonry do not mix. Love of concrete results in incongruous additions, and walls are cemented over as though to hide the existence of the historic building. (Surprisingly many of the medieval paintings listed by Gerola eighty years ago are no longer visible.) The decent wooden door is replaced by a hideous glass and metal one which lasts a few years, rusts and breaks, and is then replaced by another. Tiled roofs – often the original tiles, which have served well for seven centuries – are replaced by concrete slabs which overload the structure and rot in the Cretan climate; many 'restorations' have not lasted thirty years. We except the excellent work done by the Byzantine archaeological authorities (and occasional individuals or communities), but they can cope with only a few painted chapels, and apparently have no power to cause the rest to be left alone.

Wildlife

Endemic and rare plants are not at the forefront of Cretan conservation problems. It is difficult to generalise among hundreds of species, and we do not wish to prejudice anything that our colleagues in the University of Crete may find, but we have very seldom found evidence that even rare plants have declined. Cliff species are out of harm's way where they have grown for centuries, and those of the high mountains are in an environment which has not much changed. Some coastal species, such as *Centaurea spinosa*, have been encroached on by tourism, although the Cretan palm survives remarkably well. Of the 180 or so Cretan endemic or near-endemic plants, only five appear in the *International Red Data Book* as Endangered or Vulnerable; one has become endangered as a result of an attempt at conserving the *agrími* (p. 47).

We can point to a few potential troubles. A small area of Mount Psilorítis has been bulldozed in an attempt to introduce skiing, and we hear of a hare-brained plan to irrigate the Nídha Plain, which would destroy most of the unique *Polygonum idaeum* community. Rare plants of non-limestone cliffs – the *Osmunda* and *Woodwardia* community – are threatened by dams and road-widening.

Birds fare surprisingly well for a land with an armed populace. We have not recently encountered the practice of feasting on miscellaneous small birds. We are told, however, that birds of prey have decreased. As throughout Greece, wetlands (badly needed by migrating birds, as well as being a plant habitat) fare worst of all. The three principal *álmyroi* are seriously threatened: those at Georgioúpolis (Ap) and Ay. Nikólaos (Me) by tourist development, that west of Herákleion (T) by industry and farming.

Conclusions

The list of conservation problems is not endless. Air pollution is confined to very small areas: the excellent lichens are a witness to the non-acidity of Cretan rain. Crete has been spared invasion by aggressive exotic plants, which has ruined the vegetation of other hot countries. It has also been spared modern forestry: eucalypts are treated as they should be, as magnificent street trees, not (as in Portugal or Sardinia) infesting the landscape as a useless and fire-promoting forestry tree.

Many of the world's conservation problems are caused by outsiders with grand ideas who break up some modest but adequate existing economy. That is seldom the case here. We can complain when the World Bank finances an unnecessary dam in a tropical forest, or the European Community spends its taxpayers' money on subsidising unnecessary olives. It is difficult to know what to say when a Cretan puts his hard-earned savings into a hotel designed as best he can. Even the worst restoration of a chapel is a genuine expression of piety which nations like England could do worse than follow.

We doubt whether legislation is an effective way to promote conservation. Nobody, not even the Turk, has ever succeeded in reducing Crete to discipline and order. What about money? Crete draws large subsidies from the European Community, but hitherto there has been little interest in whether the roads, irrigations, etc., being subsidised are really beneficial – or even whether the money is spent on what it was granted for. Accountability might restrain hare-brained schemes.

We believe that the stimulus to conservation must come through education in Crete, as it has in our own countries. The Cretan character, which is a mixture of 'sentimentality, pride and egoism' (as a Cretan friend described it), could work in favour of conservation, instead of against it. Many older Cretans recognise and are proud of the features that define their landscape and civilisation; but often these have not been communicated to the middle generation. We are gratified to find the beginnings of an interest among young Cretans in landscape and vernacular building.

For some readers this will seem a defeatist conclusion: they will wonder how much of Crete will be left by the time education takes effect. However, the Cretan landscape is more resilient than outsiders appreciate, and there are still great areas left intact. Only ten years have passed since Crete could claim to be the most beautiful island in the world.

Notes
1 Noiret, (see bibliography), p. 175.
2 O. Rackham (Ο. Ράχχαμ) (1992), "Η διατήρη τῆς φύσης σέ πολιτικό τοπίο: τό ἱστορικόν πλαίσιον καὶ ἡ περίπτωση τῆς Κρήτης', *Γία νὰ Ζῆση ἡ Δημιουργία τοῦ Θεοῦ*, Constantinople, Ecumenical Patriarchate, pp. 107-14.
3 J. R. McNeill, (1992, Chapter 3, note 10).

Bibliography

General works relating to Crete and traveller's accounts (marked *),
referred to in the text and notes by the author's surname.

Allbaugh, L. G. (1953), *Crete: A Case Study of an Underdeveloped Area*, Princeton, Princeton University Press.

*Belon, C. (1555), *Les observations de plusieurs singularitez & choses memorables*, Paris, Gilles Corrozet.

Boschini, M. (1651), *Il regno tutto di Candia delineato …*, Venice, reprinted 1979, S. Giov. in Persiceto, Editrice Menior.

Bozinaki-Didonis, (1985), *Greek Traditional Architecture: Crete*, trans. P. Raup, Athens, Melissa.

*Buondelmonti, C. [travels 1415], *Descriptio Insule Crete et Liber Insularum, Cap. XI: Creta*, ed. M.-A. van Spitael, (1981) Herakleion, Σύλλογος πολιτικής Αναπτύξεος Ηρακλείου.

Curuni, S. A. and L. Donati (1987), *Creta Bizantina*, Rome, La Sapienza.

Dhetorakis, Th. (Θεόχαρη Δετοράκη) (1990), *Ιστορία τῆς Κρήτης*, Herákleion.

Evans, A. (1921 and later), *The Palace of Minos at Knossos*, New York, Macmillan.

*Gerola, G. (1905, 1908, 1917, 1932), *Monumenti veneti dell'isola di Creta*, Venice, R. Istituto Veneto di Scienze, Lettere ed Arti.

Lax, E. and T. F. Strasser (1992), 'Early Holocene extinctions on Crete; the search for the cause', *Journal of Mediterranean Archaeology*, **5**, 203-24.

*Lear, E. (1864), numerous sketches, some of which are reproduced in R. Fowler (1984), *Edward Lear: the Cretan journal*, Athens, Denise Harvey.

Myers, V. V. and E. E. and G. Cadogan (1992), *The Aerial Atlas of Ancient Crete*, London, Thames & Hudson.

Noiret, H. (1892), *Documents inédits pour servir à l'Histoire de la Domination Vénitienne en Crète de 1380 à 1485*, Paris, Thorin.

Nixon, L., J. Moody and O. Rackham (1988), 'Archaeological survey in Sphakia, Crete', *Classical Views* **32**, 7: 201-15.

Nixon, L., J. Moody, O. Rackham and S. F. R. Price (1989), 'Archaeological survey in Sphakia, Crete', *Classical Views* **33**, 8: 159-73.

*Olivier, G. A. (An 9 [1801]) [travels 1793] *Voyage dans l'Empire Othoman*, Paris, Agasse.

*Pashley, R. (1837) [travels 1834], *Travels in Crete*, London, Murray.

*Pendlebury, J. D. S. (1939), *The Archaeology of Crete*, London, Methuen.

*Pococke, R. (1745), *A Description of the East, and some Other Countries*, London, Bowyer.

Psilakis, N. (1988), *Monasteries of Crete*, trans. J. Latham, Athens, Bank of Crete.

Rackham, O. (1972), 'The vegetation of the Myrtos region' and 'Charcoal and plaster impressions' in P. M. Warren, *Myrtos: an Early Bronze Age settlement in Crete*, London, Thames & Hudson, 283–304.

Rackham, O. (1982), 'Land-use and the native vegetation of Greece' in M. Bell and S. Limbrey (eds.), *Archaeological Aspects of Woodland Ecology*, British Archaeological Reports International Series, **146**, 177–98.

Rackham, O. (1983), 'Observations on the historical ecology of Boeotia', *BSA*, **78**, 291–351.

Rackham, O. (1990), 'Ancient landscapes', in O. Murray and S. Price (eds.), *The Greek City from Homer to Alexander*, Oxford, pp. 85–111.

*Raulin, V. (1858, 1860 [travels 1845]), 'Description physique de l'île de Crète', *Bulletin de la Société Linnéenne de Bordeaux*, **22**: 109-213, 307-426, 491-584; **23**: 1-50, 70-157, 321-444.

*Raulin, V. (1868), *Déscription physique de l'Ile de Crète*, Paris, Bertrand.

Rechinger, K. H. (1943), *Flora Aegaea*, Vienna, Springer [supplemented by *Neue Beiträge zur Flora von Kreta*, Vienna, 1943].

Rutkowski, B. (1986), *The Cult Places of the Aegean*, New Haven, Yale University Press.

Sanders, I. F. (1982), *Roman Crete*, Warminster, Aris & Phillips.

Sfikas, G. (1987), *Wild Flowers of Crete*, Athens, Efstathiadis.

*Sieber, F. W. (1823), *Travels in the Island of Crete in the Year 1817*, London, Phillips.

*Sonnini, C. S. (An IX [1801]) [travels 1777-8], *Voyage en Grèce et en Turquie, fait par ordre de Louis XVI ...*, Paris, Buisson.

Stavrinidhes, D. S. (1984-87), *Μεταφράσεις Τούρκικον έγγραφων αφορώντων εἰς τήν ἱστορίαν Κρῆτης*, 5 vols, Herakleion, Vikelaia.

Thiriet, F. (1978), *Duca di Candia: ducali e lettere ricevute (1358-1360, 1401-1405)*, Venice, Comitato per le Pubblicazione delle Fonti relative alle Storia di Vénezia.

*Tournefort, P. de (1717 [travels 1700]), *Rélation d'un voyage au Levant, fait par ordre du Roy*, Lyon, Anisson et Posuel; [English translation, *A Voyage into the Levant*, London, Midwinter and others, 1741].

*Trevor-Battye, A. (1913) [travels 1909], *Camping in Crete*, London, Witherby.

Tsougarakis, D. (1988), *Byzantine Crete from the 5th Century to the Venetian Conquest*, Athens, Basilopoulos.

Turland, N. J., L. Chilton and J. R. Press (1993), *Flora of the Cretan Area*, London, HMSO.

Vidulich, P.R. (1965), *Duca di Candia Bandi 1313–1329*, Venice, Comitato per le Pubblicazione ... Venezia.

Warren, P.M., (1975), *The Aegean Civilizations from Ancient Crete to Mycenae*, Oxford, Phaidon.

Wells, B. (ed.) (1992), *Agriculture in Ancient Greece*, Stockholm, Svenska Institutet i Athen.

Index and Glossary

Main references are given in bold. Cross-references are in italic. Place-names in Crete are followed by the abbreviated name of the district:

Ak	Akrotíri
Am	Amári
Ap	Apokórona
AV	Ayios Vasíleios
H	Ierápetra
Ka	Kainoúrgi
Ki	Kíssamos
Ky	Kydhonía
L	Lassíthi
Ma	Malevyzi
Me	Merabéllo
Mo	Monofátsi
My	Mylopótamos
Pe	Pedhiádha
Py	Pyrgiótissa
R	Réthymnon
Se	Sélinon
Sf	Sphakiá
Si	Siteía
T	Témenos
V	Viánno

'History' includes prehistory   n: reference to an end-note   pn: place-name   •: endemic plant